FOREIGN TRADE
AND
INVESTMENT

FOREIGN TRADE
AND
INVESTMENT

A LEGAL GUIDE

THOMAS F. CLASEN

FOLEY & LARDNER • MILWAUKEE, WISCONSIN

Callaghan

CALLAGHAN & COMPANY
3201 Old Glenview Road, Wilmette, Illinois 60091

Library of Congress Cataloging-in-Publication Data

Clasen, Thomas F.
  Foreign trade and investment.

  Includes index.
  1. Foreign trade regulation—United States.
  2. Investments, American—Law and legislation.
I. Title.
KF1976.C58   1987   343.73'087   87-27754
ISBN 0-8366-0017-7 (pbk.)347.30387

Dedicated with gratitude and affection
to my parents
Milard and Catherine Clasen

PREFACE

A few years ago, when I began teaching a seminar on international business transactions at the University of Wisconsin School of Law, I was surprised at the lack of a concise textbook which could be used to train future lawyers in the practical issues presented by this increasingly important subject. While there are a number of excellent treatises on various topics encompassed within this general subject, as well as a few multi-volume works which cover the area in great detail, none of these is designed to provide the nonspecialist with a practical overview of the most common legal issues involved in international business.

This book is intended as an attempt to fill this gap in the literature. It contains few new insights into the area; it will not advance the scholarship. It will, I hope, provide the practicing attorney as well as the law student with a general understanding of the fundamental questions raised by international business transactions, supply some practical solutions and lead him or her to sources to learn more.

This book does not cover tax issues in any detail. International taxation, perhaps like all taxation, has reached a level of complexity that makes it impossible to treat concisely while still providing enough information so as to be useful to the reader. Thus, while a general familiarity with the tax issues presented by the topics covered in this book is essential, this can best be gained from specialized works on international taxation, such as Tillinghast's Tax Aspects of International Transactions, Postlewaite's International Corporate Taxation and Rhoades & Langer's Income Taxation of Foreign Related Transactions.

I would like to acknowledge with gratitude my colleagues at

Preface

Foley & Lardner who have added to my understanding of this area, especially Ralf R. Boer, Edwin P. Wiley, Michael S. Nolan, John W. Brahm, David S. Lott, Jamshed J. Patel and Helen E. Hartnell. I also want to thank my secretaries, Kathy Maddaugh, Olga Lopez and Loretta Greco, for typing and assembling the manuscript. And finally, I am grateful to my wife, Mary Pat, for her support and encouragement, and to my sons, Peter and Christopher, for their patience while I worked on this project.

July, 1987   *Thomas F. Clasen*
                                           Milwaukee, Wisconsin

CONTENTS

Contents

Contents

Contents

Contents

Contents

Contents

Contents

Contents

APPENDIXES

Contents

PART I

PRELIMINARY CONSIDERATIONS

CHAPTER 1

THE NATURE AND SCOPE OF INTERNATIONAL BUSINESS TRANSACTIONS

§ 1:01.   Definitions.

Probably as a result of overuse, the term "international business" has taken on various meanings. To some, it carries the connotation of professionals and executives flying around the world, wheeling and dealing in a half dozen different languages. To others it is synonymous with economic imperialism and is identified with the large multinational corporations with power and resources that exceed those of many poor countries combined. To still others, it is a neutral term that encompasses any business activities conducted within foreign countries, with foreign persons or involving foreign products.

In the strict sense, very few transactions are "international," since that term suggests activities of or relating to nations themselves. Perhaps a better term is "transnational," since the vast majority of transactions that normally are thought of as "international" are actually between two private companies doing business "across" their respective borders. One should also use care in equating "international business" with "foreign business," since the latter suggests that the activity takes place abroad, when in fact many such transactions are effected without leaving the country.

While this book will not clarify matters by employing more precise terms for the vast array of activities that it will address, it can at least define the term. "International business" is here meant any type of commercial activity that crosses national boundaries. The term therefore encompasses the movement of goods (importing and exporting), technology and industrial property (licensing), capital (foreign investment), and personnel (immigration) across borders. International business also encompasses technical services, such as banking and insurance, and while these are of increasing significance, particularly to U.S. companies, their special nature permits only limited treatment in this text.

§ 1:02. Growth and Development of International Business.

Those who were born after World War II probably cannot fully appreciate the enormous growth and development of international business in its historical context. Prior to 1945, international business was a mere fraction of today's level and, except for mining and agricultural industries, was largely confined to the relatively simple import and export transactions.[1]

Both because and as a result of the tremendous growth in international business during the last forty years, the tools and procedures have developed significantly. Advances in technology have brought us faster and more efficient ways of moving goods and personnel, as well as worldwide communication networks.

[1] See generally M. Casson, The Growth of International Business (1983).

Multilateral agreements, such as the General Agreement on Tariffs and Trade (GATT), have gradually reduced many of the barriers and inequities of international trade, while the acceptance of international regimes, such as Publication 400 of the International Chamber of Commerce respecting documentary credits, have reduced uncertainty. The availability of credit to finance foreign trade and investment and of insurance to minimize the risks has also contributed to the expansion of international business activities. Finally, as their experience with such transactions increased, company personnel working in the area, as well as their business and legal advisers, have become more creative in overcoming many of the traditional obstacles presented by doing business abroad. The result has been that a well-advised manufacturer in Chicago has little more difficulty buying parts from Taiwan than from Peoria, and faces only slightly more problems creating a new plant in Switzerland than in New Jersey.

The extraordinary growth in foreign investment also contributed to the birth of the modern "multinational enterprise." These giant companies, such as General Motors, Nestle, Shell and Siemens, control subsidiaries in dozens of countries. In certain instances, the organization of a local company was necessary, either from a commercial or legal standpoint, in order to enter a local market. At other times, the local company takes advantage of lower labor, energy or other production costs to produce a product that is more competitive in world markets. As these companies are combined with finance and insurance subsidiaries and various holding companies, the corporation as a whole increases its flexibility in responding to changing market conditions around the world, while at the same time enhancing internal management of credit, foreign exchange and taxes.

§ 1:03. Present Status of International Business.

As a result of this dramatic growth and development, international business has become a significant part of the total business activities presently being conducted. As late as 1970, imports into the United States totaled only $40 billion; by 1980 they had climbed to $240 billion, and in 1986 were in excess of $375 billion. In the last ten years, imports rose from 4% to nearly 25% of total sales in the United States. Total exports as a percentage of trade has also increased dramatically in many countries.

Perhaps nowhere is the importance of international commerce better exemplified than in Japan. Japan's trading companies, such as Mitsubishi and Mitsui, combine tremendous resources in manufacturing, transportation, finance, insurance and marketing with remarkable efficiency to buy and sell products and services worldwide. Four of the largest five companies outside the United States are Japanese.[2] Japanese commercial and investment banks and insurance companies are also world leaders. When it is considered that Japan essentially accomplished all this since 1945, the case is even more impressive. At the same time, it is illustrative of what progress can be made.

The United States, while the traditional leader in foreign investment, has lagged behind in international trade. United States exports in 1984 represented only 7.6% of its gross national product, compared to 16.2% for Japan and more than 30% for most of Europe.[3] In 1986, the United States experienced a record balance of payments deficit of $175 billion compared with $125 billion in 1985 and only $55 billion in 1980. The result was renewed calls for protectionist legislation and the introduction of numerous bills in Congress.

While there are many reasons why U.S. companies have not kept pace with their Japanese and European counterparts, one reason is that many U.S. companies, particularly small and medium-sized companies, have no knowledge of or experience with international business transactions, and are afraid of engaging in business abroad. Traditionally, these small and medium-sized companies have avoided considering foreign markets, or

[2] "Special Report: Spotlight on International Business," Forbes (July 28, 1986).

[3] International Trade Statistics, International Monetary Fund (1984).

have done so only when local markets are depressed. As a result, these companies move only limited resources into the development of foreign markets and, before their efforts have an opportunity to produce orders, the resources are moved back to domestic sales as the U.S. market recovers. Companies which do not engage in international trade, the most basic of international business transactions, are not likely to pursue international licensing or foreign investment, which are more complex.

Thus, many U.S. companies, despite having products that would readily compete abroad, do not engage in any form of international business. This lack of participation, since it is largely founded on inexperience, presents a tremendous opportunity, as well as a challenge, to the legal advisers to these companies.

CHAPTER 2

BASIC FORMS OF INTERNATIONAL BUSINESS TRANSACTIONS

§ 2:01. In General.

While modern international business transactions take a wide variety of forms, they can generally be grouped into four general areas: import and export transactions, international licensing, foreign investment, and banking and other services. The first three are traditional categories and are presented in this book in some detail. Their order of presentation also corresponds to their level of complexity and the frequency with which they are encountered. The last category, banking and other services, is relatively new, but is believed to warrant its own treatment both because of its special problems and emerging importance.

§ 2:02. Import and Export Transactions.

In general, the simplest of international business transactions, and the one that almost any company is likely to encounter, is the import transaction. An import transaction involves any of the variety of means under which a local company acquires goods that enter the country from abroad. In its most basic form, the importer may have ordered components or new materials from abroad, either through a local representative of the foreign seller or directly from the foreign company. Where a local representative is involved, the representative may assume responsibility for receiving payment, converting the currency, if necessary, to that of the seller, transferring the currency to the seller, contracting appropriate transportation and insurance, obtaining any necessary export permits or paying export taxes in the foreign jurisdiction, clearing the merchandise through U.S. customs, and insuring prompt delivery to the U.S. buyer. If no representative is involved, or if it does not assume all of these responsibilities, they must be allocated between the local buyer and the foreign seller. In certain cases, specialists such as customs brokers and freight forwarders can be utilized to perform many of these details.

The export transaction is, of course, nothing more than an import transaction viewed from the perspective of the seller. However, because the exporter must often compete with local suppliers of the same type of product, it is more common for the exporter to assume more of the various responsibilities described above, so that it can quote its product on an equal basis. In addition, unless the exporter can effectively sell its products on a prepaid basis where it has received payment prior to the product leaving its plant, the exporter is much more concerned with the various means of insuring prompt and complete payment. This involves certain procedures which are not always understood by companies engaged solely in importing.

Because of these differences, it is useful to separate the treatment of imports and exports. Part II on imports and import regulation is generally confined to U.S. tariff laws and regulations, and sets forth the process and procedures for bringing goods through

U.S. customs. That Part also deals with the various forms of import relief, mechanisms designed to protect U.S. industry from unfair or unduly injurious imports. Part III on exports, in turn, deals with the legal issues concerning the export sales contract, export documentation, payment procedures, insurance and transportation, and certain other issues. Part IV covers an additional topic of importance in the context of export transactions: the use of foreign agents and distributors.

§ 2:03. Licensing and Technology Transfers.

For a number of reasons, a U.S. manufacturer may be unable to sell its U.S. manufactured product abroad, even though the product itself may be of higher quality and competitively priced. Often the reasons are economic: perhaps the bulk or weight of the products would add unreasonable transportation costs. The reasons could also be legal: tariff or nontariff barriers may effectively prohibit imports of that product. While the U.S. company could establish a local subsidiary to manufacture the product, this usually requires a substantial financial commitment.

If the product involves a technology or know-how that is protected by patent, copyright or trade secret, one alternative is to make the technology available to a local manufacturer in exchange for royalties. This type of transaction normally takes the form of a license, under which the licensee is granted prescribed rights to use the technology in a particular geographical area under limited conditions and for a definite period of time. In return, the licensee may agree to pay the licensor a lump sum as well as continuing royalties based on production or sales. Licenses of this type often include obligations on the part of the licensor to provide training and technical assistance to the licensee's personnel. They may also grant rights to use the licensor's trademarks.

Licensing and technology transfers thus present an important opportunity for the owner of valuable technology to exploit such asset while avoiding the problems associated with export sales or direct foreign investment. Nevertheless, licensing is not without its own risks. Chief among these is that the licensee may become a competitor of the licensor once the technology is disclosed to it. Collecting royalties on the licensee's full production is also often troublesome. While local laws, particularly in developing countries, limit some of the licensor's options, these and various other problems associated with licensing can be minimized by a carefully drafted license agreement. Part V will discuss these risks and their corresponding treatment in the license agreement. That Part will also cover local laws governing licensing and the protection of intellectual property abroad.

§ 2:04. Direct Foreign Investment.

Direct foreign investment[1] encompasses those transactions under which a company creates its own establishment abroad. It thus includes a foreign branch, foreign subsidiary or foreign joint venture. A branch can be distinguished from a subsidiary in that the former is a mere extension of the same corporate entity, such as another office, while the latter has a separate corporate identity, often created under the laws of the local jurisdiction. A joint venture is normally organized as a local corporation or similar entity in which two or more unrelated companies participate as shareholders or partners. Each of these types of foreign establishments can be used to perform a variety of functions, ranging from simple sales and marketing activities on behalf of foreign manufacturers to assembly or full-scale manufacturing.

Frequently, the decision to enter a foreign country through direct investment represents the natural evolution of a company's

---

[1] Foreign investment has traditionally been classified as either direct investment or portfolio investment. Direct investment usually conotes ownership or control by one person of at least 10% of the voting securities of an incorporated enterprise or an equivalent interest in an unincorporated business enterprises. See 15 CFR §801.67(j). Portfolio investment usually encompasses a smaller interest which is not intended to allow the investor to control or actively participate in the investment.

activities there. Perhaps the market has been sufficiently developed through exports so as to sustain local production. In other cases, a local establishment may be necessary to penetrate a local market. Many times, however, the reasons are legal: perhaps imports of a particular product are effectively excluded as a result of tariff or nontariff barriers so that local production is required.

Legal issues also typically govern the decision to enter jurisdictions in the form of a branch, a wholly-owned subsidiary or a joint venture. In general, foreign branches are inadvisable since they typically subject the entire company to the jurisdiction and procedural requirements of the local country. While a subsidiary is often the most desirable form, local laws forbidding 100% foreign ownership or offering tax or other incentives to locally controlled companies may require or encourage using a joint venture. Joint ventures may also be an appealing form of direct investment from a commercial point of view, allowing the foreign and local companies to combine their strengths (e.g., the foreign company's technology and the local company's marketing network) and at the same time share the initial capital commitments and risk of losses.

Because direct foreign investment necessarily subjects the foreign investor to the laws and procedures of the local country, the role of the lawyer in advising and protecting his or her client's interests is considerably more complicated. As suggested above, one must consider the legal consequences of doing business in the country as well as the appropriate vehicle for doing so. These issues, which primarily concern questions of local law, are discussed in Part VI. Since the structure and problems presented by joint ventures are of a special nature, they are discussed separately in Part VII. Finally, Part VIII reviews foreign investment in the United States, an area of equal importance to attorneys working on international business transactions generally.

§ 2:05. Banking and Other Services.

While the service industries have not traditionally been included in texts on international business transactions, they represent an increasingly important sector in international business, particularly for the United States. As a result of this significant growth, the United States has for several years argued for a new international regime covering the services industries under the auspices of GATT with the objective of forcing other GATT members to open their economies to foreign services. In the fall of 1986, the members of GATT opened a new round of trade negotiations in Uruguay, and agreed to include such a regime on the agenda.

Perhaps the most important of these services is commercial banking.[2] Four of the largest twenty U.S. multinationals are banks. Citicorp, Chase, and other large banks have branches or subsidiaries in dozens of countries. They not only engage in traditional banking services such as lending and deposit taking, but also provide global services in foreign currency management, trade finance, interest payments, collections, capital formation, etc. Large international banks have also become an important source of economic, financial and other information essential to international business managers. They also provide consulting and advisory services particularly important to newcomers in a foreign market.

In addition to commercial banking, the insurance, investment banking, and accounting industries are active overseas. Like the commercial banks, many of these organizations initially followed their industrial clients abroad to provide them with local services. As their local expertise grew, however, they began to branch into local markets wherever regulation allowed. Insurance, investment banking, and accounting firms now employ thousands of experts worldwide, providing a uniform and coordinated effort to problems in their specific areas of expertise. These service industries, as well as information processing, telecommunications and others, will significantly increase their international activities with the reduction of existing national barriers.

[2] See generally N. Deak & N. Celusak, International Banking (1984); G. Penn, Practice and Law of International Banking (1985); W. Baughn & D. Mandich (eds.), The International Banking Handbook (1983).

Preliminary Considerations

The provision of these types of services abroad often presents novel legal issues. Certain areas, such as banking and finance, are frequently well-developed under local law. In such cases, the U.S. lawyer must become familiar with local law and practices, and attempt to gain as much protection as possible for his or her client's interests. In other cases, such as in the information processing and telecommunication industries, there may be a complete lack of applicable law, requiring the lawyers to apply analogous principles or to structure the transaction so as to insure the applicability of U.S. or other foreign law. In most cases, uncertainties will necessitate the thorough analysis of the transactions and development of extensive agreements to cover the various issues. As usual, local lawyers must be consulted to deal with the regulatory and administrative law applicable to certain service industries.

CHAPTER 3

SPECIAL PROBLEMS

§ 3:01. In General.

International business transactions present a number of special problems for legal advisers. Among these are language barriers, subtle but important cultural dissimilarities, and differences in law and business practices.

§ 3:02. Language and Cultural Barriers.

Language differences should present far less of a problem for U.S. business persons than for their counterparts in non-English speaking countries. English has, of course, become almost universally accepted as the language of international business transactions. In practice, however, language differences still present certain obstacles in transacting business with native speakers of other languages. Even assuming that the deal will be negotiated and documented in English, translations are often required in

17

order for it to be approved at higher levels within the foreign party's company or for registration with the local government authorities. Moreover, problems often occur in negotiations or, even worse, afterward, when the parties do not attach the same meaning to a certain term or phrase. The bilingual negotiator is thus much better equipped to achieve a true meeting of the minds in a given agreement. If this is impossible, it is useful, and often necessary, to spend additional time discussing what is meant by a particular clause or saying the same thing in more than one way.

The wide acceptance of English as the language in foreign transactions has also acerbated the cultural barriers between U.S. businesspersons and their foreign counterparts. The failure of many U.S. negotiators to learn and appreciate dealing in a foreign language often desensitizes them to the subtle but often important cultural gaps between them and their counterparts across the table. In many places, this insensitivity has resulted in a stereotype of the U.S. businessperson as pompous, abrupt, calculating and untrusting. While these images usually break down as the relationship with the foreigner advances, they often present unnecessary problems in the early stages.

Entire books have been written,[1] and various seminars and workshops are available, to instruct U.S. personnel on these cultural dissimilarities. As one's experience with foreigners grows, one will be better suited to deal with these barriers.

§ 3:03. Foreign and International Law.

Unfamiliarity with foreign law presents another obstacle to lawyers involved in international business transactions. Arguably, the differences between state laws with which U.S. lawyers regularly deal should render them well-equipped to handle foreign law. In most cases, however, U.S. lawyers have little knowledge or even

---

[1] A humorous and yet insightful example is the Parker Pen Company's, Do's and Taboos Around the World (1985).

appreciation for the significant differences that exist between their own legal system and that of a foreign jurisdiction.

In general, there are two great families of law in western civilization: civil law and common law. Civil law took hold in Europe, and from there spread to Latin America and parts of Africa and Asia (including Japan). Civil law, supplemented by Islamic law, also prevails in the Middle East, other than in Libya and Iraq, where common law has been more influential, and the Arabian peninsula, where religious principles predominate. The legal system of the Scandanavian countries and to a large extent, the USSR, China and other socialist countries, are also identified with civil law. Common law was developed in England, and from there spread to other parts of the British Empire, including the United States, Canada, Australia, New Zealand, Ireland, and the West Indies. Common law also forms the basis for the legal systems of India, Pakistan, Burma, Malaysia, Singapore, and the former British Colonies in Africa and Oceana. Both civil and common-law countries, however, have adopted only those aspects of these legal traditions which were found most useful. They have also incorporated their own religious, curtural and philosophical traditions into their legal systems, resulting in unique bodies of law in most countries.

Traditional civil law has been contrasted with common law by reference to the former's reliance on codes rather than judge-made law, and the role of judicial precedent. On closer examination, these distinctions break down. Large quantities of Anglo-American law are now contained in statutes and codes, while European courts have developed significant legal principles which are now part of local civil law. In theory, common-law courts are bound by precedent while their civil law counterparts are free to consider anew any legal question before them. In practice, however, U.S. courts have developed techniques which often allow them to avoid following an apparent precedent. Civil courts, on the other hand, have demonstrated a trend toward following precedent as an effort to save time and provide more uniformity in the application of law.

One important distinction between common law and civil law

lies in the manner in which new law is developed. In common-law countries, which were originally characterized by a strong, centralized judiciary, judges assumed a major role in the development of law by adjudicating particular factual situations. In civil law countries, where a strong judiciary was viewed as aristocratic, the universities assumed a greater role in enunciating new legal principles. Law professors and other recognized scholars thus became the principal source of law and legal theory, both in the development of codes and in their application in the courts. Civil law has thus tended to be more systematic and comprehensive, while common law may be more pragmatic.

The Islamic world has struggled to assimilate the rules established by the shariah (Islamic jurisprudence) with modern international commerce.[2] The shariah encompasses much more than western law; it establishes basic principles of ethics and morality according to which believers are to guide their lives. The shariah is also believed to be divinely inspired and therefore immutable. Perhaps for these reasons, many countries found Islamic law unresponsive to modern legal problems. Turkey, Egypt, Syria and many other countries began to develop new civil codes and judiciaries, based mainly on Western systems but incorporating as much as possible from the shariah. This trend has continued among the progressive Islamic countries, though in the Arabian penninsula and now Iran, the shariah predominates. The continued adherence to traditional Islamic law has led to some contortious legal principles, particularly in the area of banking and finance where lenders must comply with the ban on usury.[3]

While Eastern Europe, the USSR, and China generally follow a civil law tradition, the role played by the state in social and economic planning tends to overshadow any resemblance to western legal principles, at least in the area of international commerce. Trading, to the extent it is permitted, is conducted with the state,

[2] See generally N. Coulson, Commercial Law in the Gulf States: The Islamic Legal Tradition (1984).

[3] See, e.g., T. Abdus-Shahid, "Interest, Usury and the Islamic Development Bank: Alternative, Non-Interest Financing," 16 Law & Pol'y Int'l Bus 1095 (1984).

typically through one or more foreign trade corporations. These trade corporations are typically independent legal entities authorized to enter into contracts, to hold property, and to sue and be sued. It is obviously incumbent on the foreign party to determine the status of the trading corporation, both to avoid problems arising out of principles of sovereign immunity and to determine the authority and law governing the entity.

In the case of international business transactions, foreign law and local law are usually much more important than international law. In certain cases, however, international treaties and conventions as well as accepted international customs and practices may have an impact on the law applicable to a given transaction. Where the parties are unable to agree on the application of a particular body of national law to govern a contract, they may agree to subject themselves to a United Nations code or to lex mercatoria, the international law merchant. Even where an agreement is reached to have a transaction governed by a specific body of national law, the courts of another jurisdiction may choose to ignore such choice of law where it is inconsistent with international law or local public policy.[4]

While materials on international law are reasonably well-developed and usually quite accessible, researching foreign law is one of the chief obstacles to providing effective counsel in an international business transaction. Primary sources are obviously the most important. Laws and regulations of many foreign countries are published in an official gazette to which the Library of Congress and certain regional libraries subscribe. Several services, including Commercial Laws of the World and Tax Laws of the World (Foreign Tax Law Association), International Tax Treaties of the World (Oceana), and Tax Treaties (CCH) publish translations of special laws. Regional and national services such as the Common Market Reporter (CCH), certain OAS publications and tax reporters on selected countries are also available. International Legal Materials (American Society of International Law) also publishes important new foreign legislation.

---

[4] See §29:02 on choice of law in international commercial agreements.

There are also numerous digests and secondary sources available on foreign law. Mathew Bender and others have published extensive treaties on the legal aspects of doing business in particular countries. These are particularly helpful when they contain the primary sources of law as well. Other treatises and digests cover specialized areas such as intellectual property, antitrust, licensing and franchising and taxation. The Martindale-Hubbel directory includes a digest of the laws of several foreign jurisdictions. The U.S. Department of Commerce and the State Department also publish periodicals that address local law in foreign jurisdictions and make their personnel available by phone to discuss particular problems. The U.S. Chamber of Commerce in many foreign countries also frequently translate and publish local laws of significance to their members. Investing, Licensing and Trading Conditions Abroad (Business International Corp.) provides current information on many countries. Newsletters, international law journals' financial newspapers and other periodicals are also helpful in researching foreign law and business conditions.[5]

[5] See generally Kavass, International Business Transactions: A Guide to Research Sources (1983); see also W. Slomanson, "International Business Transactions: A Selected Bibliography," 17 Law & Pol'y Int'l Bus 721 (1985).

CHAPTER 4

DRAMATIS PERSONAE

§ 4:01. In General.

Engaging in international business transactions frequently requires dealing with a number of individuals and organizations, some of which are not encountered in pure domestic transactions. Apart from the parties themselves, various governmental or international agencies and authorities may be involved. The U.S. lawyer is also typically required to work with the other party's local counsel, and frequently must select, supervise, and work with his or her own local counsel.

§ 4:02. The Parties.

Lawyers who spend a considerable amount of time in the international area will probably find that their clients are considerably

23

more heterogenous than those of their colleagues doing corporate, tax or labor work. While a significant amount of international transactions are effected by large companies where the lawyer may be working with an experienced Vice President in charge of international sales and the regional and country manager, in many other cases, the lawyer may be working with the president of a smaller company who personally assumes responsibility for its occasional foreign contracts. Although the duty to protect his or her client's interest is obviously the same in each case, the lawyer's functions will obviously vary depending upon the client's experience. The wide variety of companies who may be parties to the transaction, as well as the various types of transactions themselves, also make this area more challenging.

It is not uncommon for the lawyer to be asked to assemble some background information on the foreign party, or to suggest ways in which such information can be assembled. Among the standard sources are Dun & Bradstreet reports, bank references, commercial directors, and online data banks. The international departments of major banks may also have some information, or may obtain the same from their foreign correspondents. The commercial sections of U.S. embassies assemble information on local companies, some of which is published in the World Trade Directory by the U.S. Department of Commerce. Local chapters of the International Chamber of Commerce may also provide helpful information.

The foreign party to the transaction may also have a quite different legal status from its U.S. counterpart. This is perhaps best exemplified by transactions in China and the Eastern Block, where contracts are negotiated and entered into with governmental authorities who conduct all foreign transactions. In many countries, the banking, utility, transportation, mining, and other industries are operated by government-owned companies. Since governments often have different objectives in their business dealings and since they represent the only parties with which to deal, the negotiations and the resulting agreement may be substantially different than those with a private company. As discussed in the previous chapter, the authority of the entity to enter in the arrangement and its enforceability also present special issues when governments or their instrumentality are parties.

§ 4:03.   United States Government.

The United States Government also plays a significant role in international business transactions, not only by developing and implementing international ecomonic policy, but also by regulating certain international transactions and by assisting persons engaged in international business. While many agencies or authorities have some responsibilities in this area, the most important are the Department of Commerce, the Department of the Treasury, the International Trade Commission, and the Office of the U.S. Trade Representative.

In 1977, the Commerce Department assumed a number of regulatory and export assistance functions formerly administered by other agencies. Its regulatory functions include the administration of the export licensing and anti-boycott regulations, the anti-dumping and countervailing laws and various other foreign trade laws and regulations. Its export assistance activities include the supervision of the Foreign Commercial Service (the commercial attachés located in U.S. embassies throughout the world who provide information on the local business climate and opportunities) and the U.S. Commercial Service (approximately 50 trade specialists located in Washington who also provide information on country conditions and procedures). Commerce also assembles and publishes import and export statistics and other trade and investment information, and promotes U.S. exports through trade fairs, training programs and seminars.

The Department of the Treasury's activities in international transactions are now mostly confined to the U.S. Customs Service and the Internal Revenue Service. The Customs Service is principally responsible for the classification and valuation of imported merchandise, and the assessment and collection of import duties. In this connection, Customs is also responsible for the administration of certain special tariff-related statutes, such as the Generalized System of Preference and the Caribbean Basin Initiative, as well as the implementation of special duties and quotas. The Internal Revenue Service, of course, administers the Internal Revenue Code, which affects the structure of many international business transactions.

The International Trade Commission (ITC) primarily performs investigatory and research functions related to international trade. It conducts inquiries with respect to specific industries, analyzing domestic and foreign production, import levels, and other factors in order to determine the impact of U.S. tariff laws and regulations and to assess the tariff treatment of such goods in other countries. Its publications, including these specific industry or product reports, are thus quite useful. The ITC also investigates certain aspects of alleged unfair trade practices under the antidumping, countervailing and similar statutes and recommends to the President any remedies it deems appropriate.

The Office of the U.S. Trade Representative (USTR) is the President's chief spokesman in matters of foreign trade. The U.S. Trade Representative, who chairs a Trade Policy Committee comprised of representatives of various governmental agencies concerned with trade, is principally responsible for developing trade and direct investment policy in the U.S. and abroad. The USTR also represents the United States in bilateral and multilateral trade negotiations, such as those under the GATT, the Organization for Economic Cooperation and Development (OECD), and the U.N. Commission on Trade and Development (UNCTAD).

The USTR also serves as ex-officio member of the board of the Export Import Bank of the United States (Eximbank) and the Overseas Private Investment Corporation (OPIC), two other important governmental bodies. Eximbank was organized in 1934 as a wholly-owned government corporation whose purpose is to finance U.S. exports. As discussed in Part III, Eximbank utilizes a number of financial programs, including export credit guarantees, direct credit and credit guarantees for buyers, and refinancing and discount programs. Through its affiliate, the Foreign Credit Insurance Association (FCIA), it also provides export insurance for commercial and political risks associated with export trade. OPIC was founded in 1971 to facilitate U.S. controlled investment in developing countries. Its primary functions include providing investment insurance against political risks of nonconvertability of currency, expropriations and political upheaval, and financing investment feasibility studies as well as actual investments. OPIC also sponsors missions to developing countries and conducts other activities designed to encourage investment in underdeveloped areas.

§ 4:04. Foreign Governments.

A third player in the typical international business transaction is the foreign government. Like the U.S. government, foreign governments are involved both in the regulation of various transactions and in providing assistance, particularly through tax and other incentives, to encourage specific transactions.

From the regulatory perspective, one is likely to encounter many of the same types of laws and regulations that are utilized in the United States. These include a tariff code and related regulations governing imports, an income tax code, and the various corporate, commercial, labor, immigration and administrative laws that would affect a foreign company doing business locally. In many countries, however, a number of other laws may also have to be considered in planning a particular transaction. Several countries, particularly in the Third World, have specific laws regulating foreign direct investment and licensing of foreign technology or industrial property rights. These countries may also have much more extensive laws governing imports and exports, possibly requiring special permits. Even in developed countries, one must often deal with perhaps novel regulatory measures, such as the value added tax, special workers' rights and laws protecting agents and distributors upon termination.

On the other hand, many countries also provide assistance in connection with international business transactions. This often takes the form of tax holidays for direct investment either within the country generally or within underdeveloped regions, exemptions from import duties on machinery and equipment used for export production, subsidized financing for constructing and equipping facilities, and exemptions from restrictive or costly labor or other laws. These incentives are usually designed to encourage export production or import substitution in accordance with local economic policy. Their applicability may be conditioned on compliance with minimum local content requirements in the case of products, or majority local ownership and control in the case of direct foreign investment.

§ 4:05. International Organizations.

Various international organizations also regulate and facilitate international business transactions affecting member countries. The General Agreement on Tariffs and Trade was originally intended as a set of provisional rules governing international trade that would ultimately be superseded by the Charter of the International Trade Organization (ITO). After the ITO failed to materialize, the GATT became the principal vehicle for reducing tariffs and other trade barriers between its more than 100 members, as well as standardizing the various rules and procedures governing valuation of imports, government procurement policies, export subsidiaries, and relief against unfair trade practices. This regulatory framework forms the basis of the laws regulating international trade among member countries.

The guiding principal of the GATT was the undertaking by member countries to accord any "advantage, favor, privilege or immunity" granted to one country with respect to its imports to every other member (the so-called "most favored nation treatment"). Notwithstanding this general principal however, the GATT also allows groups of countries to combine in the creation of customs unions or free trade zones. The most important of these groups, the European Economic Community (EEC), was formed in 1958 under the Treaty of Rome. That Treaty, however, goes far beyond the creation of a customs union, extending to antitrust and measures against unfair competition, the elimination of restriction on the movement of persons, services and capital, and providing for cooperation in agriculture, transportation, social services, and other areas. Thus, lawyers involved in transactions with an EEC member must consult not only the law of the country itself but also the Treaty and the resolutions and case law adopted pursuant thereto. The treaties establishing the Andean Common Market (ANCOM), the Latin American Free Trade Association (LAFTA) and other international organizations provide similar sources of law that must be considered in appropriate cases.

In addition to these regulatory aspects, international banks and other organizations play a role in facilitating international transactions. The largest of these, the International Bank for Reconstruction and Development (World Bank) is principally engaged in funding development projects in the Third World. One of the Bank's affiliates, the International Finance Corporation (IFC), is designed to encourage private enterprise in developing countries by direct equity investment (which is often subsequently sold to a private investor) and by loans. Regional banks, such as the Inter-American Development Bank, the African Development Bank and the Asian Development Bank, are additional sources of financing in their respective geographical areas.

The International Chamber of Commerce (ICC) is another organization which is active in advancing international business transactions. The ICC performs various functions, including promotion of standard terms in conducting international trade (Incoterms) and procedures for documentary credits (Uniform Customs and Practices for Documentary Credits), maintenance of rules and a forum for dispute resolution through arbitration, and coordination with local chambers of commerce in sharing important economic information. The United Nations also plays a role in this area by developing statistical information, promoting international law (U.N. convention on contracts for the international sales of goods), and assisting in dispute resolution.

§ 4:06. The Lawyers.

A transaction between a U.S. company and a foreign company might typically include the U.S. lawyer, his or her foreign counterpart, and a second foreign lawyer selected to assist the U.S. company. In many cases, the U.S. lawyer will perform a role quite different from the lawyer representing the other side. To a much greater extent than in many other countries, U.S. clients are accustomed to utilizing lawyers in business transactions. After a basic agreement has been reached (and sometimes before), the U.S. client will frequently expect the lawyer to assume responsibility for negotiating the details and preparing all the documentation, ready for execution.

Foreign lawyers who are representing local clients are often given much less responsibility. They frequently do not participate in the negotiations at all, and are asked only to review the documentation once prepared. While this usually presents certain advantages for the U.S. party, including the opportunity to present the first draft of the documentation, it can also be delicate. A representative from a U.S. company who allows his or her lawyer to assume too much responsibility during the negotiations may be perceived as rude, untrusting or weak. Thus, U.S. lawyers in this context must be particularly sensitive to the other side, and must often encourage their clients to assume a more active role while the deal is being negotiated.

A second factor of which U.S. lawyers should be mindful in dealing with their foreign counterparts relates to the amount of documentation. In general, U.S. lawyers utilize much longer forms of agreements and other documents than those to which foreign lawyers, or their clients, are accustomed. Many U.S. lawyers assume that this is because U.S. law is more developed, and that more is better. It then leads to a fight to have the transaction governed by U.S. law. In fact, the reason may have more to do with the underdevelopment of U.S. law: the civil law described above fills in many of the gaps that must be handled contractually in the United States and other common-law jurisdictions, making many contractual provisions unnecessary. United States lawyers should carefully consider whether their clients' interests would be better served under U.S. or local law. In either case, they should also be sensitive to the difficulty they will encounter when they deliver long documents.

Finally, certain comments should be made with respect to selecting and working with local counsel.[1] First, one should note that as is true in the United States, only a small percentage of foreign lawyers have the necessary experience to handle complex international transactions. In some countries, lawyers are not trained in tax or certain other areas and the best advisers in such matters are accountants or other persons outside the legal profession. Foreign law firms are generally considerably smaller than their U.S. counterparts, and one may have to assemble a team of attorneys from various firms to handle a variety of transactions in a given country. Finally, in certain circumstances the local attorney's relationship with a particular governmental agency or authority may be more important than his or her legal acuity.

All of these reasons make the selection of foreign counsel from directories such as Martindale-Hubbel and The International Law List quite unsatisfactory. Much more useful are the recommendations of other lawyers or businesspersons who have worked with foreign lawyers on similar transactions. Law firms who engage in a considerable amount of international work typically maintain files or indices on foreign lawyers. The local U.S. Embassy or Chamber of Commerce may also be able to recommend local counsel. In any case, the local attorneys should be interviewed at their offices, if possible, to determine the level of their experience on the specific transactions and to insure that their physical resources (offices, personnel, word processing, and telecommunication equipment, etc.) is sufficient.

Finally, once local counsel is selected they should be made aware of the lines of communication with respect to the transaction. It is often more efficient, and usually desirable from the

---

[1] See Murphy, "A Guide to Foreign Law Source Materials and Foreign Counsel," 19 Int'l Law 39, 45 (1985); see also R. Hillman, "Providing Effective Legal Representation in International Business Transactions," 19 Int'l Law 3, 18 (1985).

client's perspective, for the foreign counsel to report only to the U.S. attorney who is responsible for the transaction as a whole. This is particularly true in multinational transactions which may require the coordination of lawyers in several different countries. The experienced U.S. lawyer is also in a better position to anticipate the needs of local counsel, and to overcome some of the communication barriers that can occur when legal problems are presented in lay terms in a different language. If the client prefers to deal with local counsel directly, as may be more expeditious for repeated transactions or after a rapport has been established, it is often desirable for the U.S. lawyer to receive copies of correspondence and documentation to monitor the progress and to participate as necessary.

PART I—SUGGESTIONS FOR FURTHER READING

Books

Korth, C., International Business (1985).

Levasseau, A., & Dahl, E., (eds.), Multinational Corporation: Investments, Technology, Tax, Labor & Securities (1986).

Lew, J., & Stanbrook, C., International Trade Law and Practice (1983).

Malawer, Federal Regulation of International Business: An Annotated Sourcebook of Legislation, Regulations and Treaties (1981).

Parry, A., EEC Law (2nd ed. 1984).

Walter, I., & Murry, T., (eds.), Handbook of International Business (1982).

Wood, Law and Practice of International Finance (1987).

Articles

Navarro, "A Bibliography of Latin American Law: Primary and Secondary Materials."

Note, "Undertaking Effective Research in International Law," 17 Int'l Law 381 (1983).

Slomanson, "International Business Transactions: A Selected Bibliography," 17 Law & Pol'y Int'l Bus 721 (1985).

PART II

IMPORTS
AND IMPORT
REGULATION

CHAPTER 5

IMPORTING GOODS FROM ABROAD

---

§ 5:01.   In General.

As discussed in Part I, importing probably represents the least complex of all international business transactions, and the most likely to be encountered by even small U.S. businesses. For the experienced importer, the legal issues presented by the typical import transaction are so routine that lawyers are only seldom involved. Lawyers can be of considerable assistance, however, in the initial planning and structuring of import transactions, where special exemptions or reductions from customs duties are available, or where the transactions are among affiliates presenting special tax considerations. In order to participate effectively, the lawyer must understand some of the preliminary issues faced by his or her client.

§ 5:02. Factors Influencing Decision To Import.

Numerous factors influence a business's decision to import a particular product rather than to manufacture or purchase it locally. The most basic of these relate to availability and cost. A significant portion of the imports into the United States consist of goods that are simply not available locally at any cost. This includes certain agricultural products such as coffee, cocoa, bananas and certain oil seeds and fibers, various minerals such as chromium and bauxite, and certain specialty items such as French and German wines and oriental carpets and ceramics. The only issue facing a company that desires to market these goods in the United States is whether to import these goods itself or to buy them from some other company who imports them.

The second basic reason for importing is, of course, price. Imports of a given product may simply be cheaper than those manufactured within the United States. In many instances, where the importer is dealing at arms' length with independent foreign manufacturers or distributors, the price will be easy to determine. Preferably, the exporter is willing to quote a duty paid price in U.S. dollars to a U.S. port. If not, the importer will need to determine the elements that are not included in the price, such as export duties, transportation, insurance, import duties, etc., to determine its actual cost. Where the goods are manufactured by affiliates, the price issue becomes more complicated, raising internal accounting questions that are often based on tax considerations.

Even where the importer determines that the price of a foreign product, together with transportation and related costs, favor importing, it must consider several other factors before proceeding. Some of these depend on the nature of the importer. A chain of retail department stores, for example, must consider how to organize its buying activities. It may, for instance, send its U.S. personnel abroad from time to time, rely on an independent purchasing agent permanently located abroad, or establish its own foreign buying office. A manufacturer who has elected to source certain of its products abroad faces other issues. It must often prepare and forward specifications to the foreign source and deal with the risk of disclosure of its proprietary information.

Many of these considerations, however, are common to most importers. These include (i) how to locate an interested foreign source, (ii) whether the foreign source can be relied upon to produce adequate supplies without delays, (iii) how to insure the quality and conformity of the merchandise with specifications or samples, (iv) how to structure payment so as to best protect the importer's interests, (v) what U.S. laws or regulations, such as special marking requirements or quotas, may impact on the manufacture or importation of the goods into the United States, (vi) whether the transaction can be handled through the U.S. company's purchase orders (and are they adequate for international transactions) or through a customized purchase agreement, and (vii) what is the process for getting the goods into the United States. These and other issues faced by the importer will be considered in the balance of this Part.

§ 5:03. Locating Foreign Supplier.

For many import transactions, the problem of locating a foreign source never arises. Foreign manufacturers often have representatives or distributors in the United States who call on potential purchasers, advertise in trade publications, take part in trade shows or otherwise make themselves known in the industry. These local agents and distributors will also typically assume most of the responsibility associated with importing, so that working with them is tantamount to working with a domestic supplier. Even foreign manufacturers who are not represented domestically are often well known in the industry, since they frequently supply goods to competitors or compete locally themselves.

In some cases, however, the U.S. manufacturer who is exploring the possibility of sourcing certain products abroad may have to take steps to locate the potential supplier itself. This may occur not only where foreign suppliers have not yet participated in a given domestic market, but also where participating foreign suppliers are unwilling, or unable because of other contractual commitments, to accept certain obligations demanded by the U.S. importer. In other cases, the U.S. importer may simply prefer to locate and deal directly with a new foreign supplier in order to obtain improved quality or to reduce costs by undertaking the tasks associated with importing the goods itself.

Some of the sources available for locating a foreign supplier are well known. These include certain directories, such as Marconi's International Register, Dun & Bradstreet's Principal International Business, and Moody's International. Local chambers of commerce or other trade associations often publish lists of manufacturers seeking export opportunities. These organizations will also typically provide assistance in response to individual inquiries. International trade shows often attract potential foreign suppliers. Certain public and private organizations also sponsor trade missions to specific countries or regions for foreign companies seeking local suppliers. The U.S. Department of Commerce publishes statistics on imports of given products from particular countries that are helpful in determining sources. These include Market Share Report's Commodity Series, Export Statistics Profiles, and International Market Research Surveys. It also publishes the World Traders Data Reports and certain other periodic materials which may be helpful in locating foreign suppliers. Certain online data bases, such as Foreign Traders Index and International Trade Information Service may also be helpful.

Once a list of potential foreign suppliers has been developed, the U.S. company may proceed as it would with a domestic supplier, by checking their background and reputation, obtaining samples, and requesting price quotations. Certain additional measures are often necessary, however, as a result of the international nature of the transaction. First, if at all possible, a representative from the U.S. firm should visit the potential supplier's facility to personally assess the ability of the supplier to produce the product. While this is often dispensed with due to the costs of foreign travel, it can typically be combined with the negotiation or execution of the purchase agreement and is often an essential compliment to information provided from references and other sources. Second, if proprietary technology or know-how is provided to the proposed foreign supplier in order to obtain samples, it should be done under a comprehensive nondisclosure agreement. Inquiry should also be made to insure that such agreements are enforceable locally, and that the provisionary transfer of technology is in compliance with U.S. and local law. Finally, care must be taken in determining which elements are included in the price quotations and which are for the account of the importer. If anything other than a "duty paid" price is quoted, the importer must determine what additional costs it must bear.

§ 5:04. Foreign Source Manufacturing.

To a large extent, the dramatic increase in imports into the United States in recent years is the result of an increased effort on the part of U.S. companies to manufacture merchandise abroad. This practice, known as foreign source manufacturing or "offshore sourcing" has expanded in recent years as the disparity in manufacturing costs in the U.S. and many Third World countries has increased. Offshore sourcing has also increased as a result of lower import tariffs and greater efficiencies in international transportation and communication. While some argue that the trend toward foreign source manufacturing, if unchecked, will ultimately hurt the U.S. economy by retarding productivity and investment, many U.S. companies have found it to be the only means of competing with their foreign counterparts.

The legal aspects of foreign source manufacturing depend on whether or not the foreign manufacturer is affiliated with the U.S. company. In the case of a foreign affiliate, such as a subsidiary in a large multinational corporation, there may be no need for a detailed manufacturing or supply agreement to govern the manufacture and sale of the goods. At the same time, it is generally desirable for tax and other purposes to formalize the buying and selling arrangements, to set forth the terms under which any technology is being provided to the foreign affiliate, and to provide for any other obligations by the parties. Special attention should be given to prices to be charged by the foreign affiliate which will impact customs duties and income taxes.

Where merchandise is to be manufactured by a non-affiliated foreign company, the terms of the manufacturing or supply agreement are more important. In many cases, the goods would be manufactured according to the U.S. company's specifications and standards. In addition to requiring the manufacturer to provide specific warranties that these specifications and standards will be met, the agreement should provide that the manufacturer supply the U.S. company with pre-production and production samples of the goods for approval. Any technology or other proprietary information (including specifications) should be protected by license and nondisclosure clauses. Any obligation on the part of the U.S. company to provide technical assistance should also be well-defined.

The agreement with the foreign manufacturer must also address the areas of price, payment, and delivery. A short-term agreement may have a set price, to be renegotiated following expiration. A longer-term agreement may provide for price adjustments on a periodic basis in accordance with a formula. Cost plus prices should normally be avoided. The price/delivery terms[1] should be clearly set forth to determine responsibility for transportation, insurance, duties, etc. as well as risk of loss. Payment terms and procedures, including currency of payment and the terms of any required letter of credit, should be provided for. Delivery specifications should include necessary packaging, marking, documentation and other requirements. If possible, the agreement should also allow the U.S. buyer sufficient time to inspect the merchandise, and set forth its rights for complete replacement of rejected goods on a duty-paid basis.

[1] See §8:04.

§5:05.   Entry Process.

Once production of the first shipment is completed, the goods are packaged and transported to a U.S. port for entry into the United States. While all or part of the transportation, insurance, and financing obligations may fall on the importer, in this part it is assumed that these have been borne by the exporter. This section deals with the procedures for bringing the imported merchandise through Customs at a particular port. Although the process is often delegated to a licensed customshouse broker who specializes in entering foreign merchandise, larger importers may undertake it directly.

The U.S. Customs Service is the governmental body principally responsible for regulating the entry of goods into the United States. The Commissioner of Customs, located in Washington, D.C., oversees a group of seven regional commissioners, each responsible for a region consisting of a number of the country's approximately 300 ports of entry.[2] The ports of entry, which include water, air, and land locations, are headed by a District or Port Director who coordinates the work of the various inspectors, import specialists (who classify and make other legal determinations with respect to the goods), and certain other personnel at the port.

When merchandise arrives by vessel, the local customs inspectors seal the hatches until the ship's manifest/cargo and passenger list are delivered to Customs. Customs then supervises the unloading of the cargo, designating cases to be taken to the customs warehouse for inspection. Within five days, an authorized person must file the necessary documents to formally enter the merchandise. Goods may be entered by the owner, purchaser, cosignee, broker or anyone else having an interest in the goods. In most instances, the goods are entered by a person or firm certified by the carrier to be the owner for customs purposes. This is often a customshouse broker in whose favor a power-of-attorney has been granted by the importer. Goods which are not entered within five

---

[2] See 19 CFR Part 101.

days are stored in a customs warehouse at the owner's expense and are subject to forfeiture after one year.

Several types of entry can be made. Normally, the goods are entered for "consumption," meaning that the goods will be available for sale or use immediately. In such case, various documents, typically including the Entry Manifest (Customs Form 7533) or Application and Special Permit for Immediate Delivery (Customs Form 3461), evidence of right to make entry (such as Power of Attorney on Customs Form 5291), commercial invoice or pro forma invoice and packing lists, must be filed with Customs at the port. Surety bonds must also be posted to cover potential duties, taxes and penalties, although the broker normally will allow its bond to be used. Following acceptance of the standard consumption entry, the shipment is examined and released. Summary documentation must be filed and estimated duties deposited within ten working days of the release. In certain cases the merchandise can be released almost immediately after arrival where a Special Permit for Immediate Delivery has been filed and approved prior to arrival.

In addition to consumption entries, goods can be entered into a bonded warehouse where they can remain for up to five years, or placed in a foreign-trade zone. In both cases the goods may then be stored, displayed, cleaned, sorted, and manufactured or assembled into different products. The goods may then be re-exported without payment of U.S. customs duties or entered for consumption upon payment of duty at the rate applicable to the goods in their then-present condition. The ability to manipulate goods within bonded warehouses and foreign-trade zones thus presents opportunities for deferring or reducing customs duties.[3]

Prior to releasing the goods, Customs may designate representative samples for examination by port inspectors. Examination is intended to determine (i) the classification and value of the goods for customs purposes; (ii) whether the goods have been marked with their country of origin, if necessary, and comply with other applicable marking and labeling requirements; (iii) whether the

---

[3] See §6:09.

goods are correctly invoiced, including excesses or shortages of invoiced quantities; and (iv) whether the shipment contains prohibited articles. If packages are found to contain articles not included on the invoice and there is reason to believe that the omission from the invoice was intentional, the contents of the entire package are subject to seizure and possible forfeiture and the importer is subject to fines and other penalties.

The duties that are deposited within ten days after the release of the goods are only a preliminary estimate. The final duties are not determined until the entry is "liquidated," which may occur weeks or months later. During this period, the importer may receive a Notice of Adjustment, indicating that Customs proposes to liquidate the entry in a manner different from that indicated by the importer on the original entry documentation. Importers generally have an opportunity to supply information to avoid the proposed adjustment. In certain cases, the importer may challenge the adjustment by seeking a ruling from Customs headquarters.[4] Ruling requests must be submitted to Customs Headquarters in Washington or the Regional Commissioner, New York Region. Customs is also authorized to demand the redelivery of merchandise which is improperly marked or otherwise fails to meet applicable requirements.

After liquidation of the entry, the importer may also challenge the dutiable status of an entry by filing a Protest and/or Application for Further Review.[5] A Protest must be filed with the District Director within 90 days following liquidation. If certain issues are present, the Protest can include an Application for Further Review, in which case it is reviewed by Customs Headquarters in Washington. If the Protest presents questions concerning classification, Customs headquarters will frequently defer to its national import specialists in New York, a group of individuals working in teams to insure the uniform classification of imported merchandise through the country. If the Protest or Application for Further Review is

[4] 19 CFR §177.8.
[5] See generally 19 CFR Part 174.

denied, in whole or in part, the decision may be appealed to the courts. Original jurisdiction lies with the U.S. Court of International Trade (formerly, the Customs Court) located in New York with Appeals to the United States Court of Appeals for the Federal Circuit, in Washington.[6]

[6] 28 USC §1581 et seq.

CHAPTER 6

UNITED STATES CUSTOMS LAWS AND REGULATIONS

§ 6:01.　In General.

The restrictions or other impediments that governments impose on imports are typically grouped into two categories: tariffs and nontariff barriers. Tariffs include customs duties and similar forms of taxes on imported merchandise. Nontariff trade barriers include marking requirements; health, safety and other standards that imported goods are required to meet; quotas which limit the entry of goods in excess of a given quantity; preferences for domestic goods such as those imposed by "Buy-American" legislation; as well as certain other requirements. While this Chapter deals principally with tariffs, nontariff barriers to trade, which have received considerable attention in recent years, are also discussed.

§ 6:02.　Tariff Schedules of United States.

Import duties have a long and interesting history in the United States. The Tariff Act of 1789 was the second bill to be enacted by the U.S. Congress. Until the early part of this century, customs duties were the largest single source of revenue for the U.S. Treasury. The Tariff Act of 1930, also known as the Smoot-Hawley Act, set the framework for the current tariff system. The heavy rates of duty established by that Act are often blamed for aggravating if not precipitating the great depression.

The Tariff Act of 1930 has been amended several times, most recently as a result of multilateral trade agreements to which the United States is a party. In 1962, the system of paragraphs under which imports were classified gave way to a system now known as the Tariff Schedules of the United States (TSUS).[1] The Tariff Schedules, which are based in part on a European system called the Brussels Nomenclature, contain approximately 8,700 separate

[1] 19 USC §1202 et seq.

items, each having a corresponding rate of duty.[2] The original Smoot-Hawley duty rates have been dramatically reduced for non-Communist countries, primarily as a result of successive rounds of negotiations which have taken place under the auspices of the General Agreement on Tariffs and Trade (GATT).

The General Headnotes to the Tariff Schedules establish several important rules regarding U.S. customs laws. General Headnote 1 establishes the principle that all goods entering the United States are subject to duty or exempt therefrom in accordance with the Tariff Schedules. This principle applies regardless of whether the goods are of foreign or domestic origin, or if they have been imported previously. General Headnote 6 establishes the rules governing the dutiable status of containers. General Headnote 7 establishes the principle that where goods of various classifications are commingled, the highest rate will be applied for the entire package. General Headnote 9 contains important definitions, and General Headnote 10 sets forth certain interpretative rules. The General Headnotes, as well as the Headnotes to each Schedule, Part, and Subpart must be carefully considered before attempting to determine the rate of duty applicable to a particular import.

It should be noted that Congress currently has under consideration legislation that would replace the Tariff Schedules of the United States with a new code known as the Harmonized Commodity Description and Coding System. The Harmonized System was the result of an effort by the United States and its major trading partners to establish uniform import classifications as a means to facilitate international trade and the development of trade statistics. While the Harmonized System differs from the Tariff Schedules in many important respects, it will still require importers to classify merchandise using the fundamental principles and procedures which are applicable to the Tariff Schedules. The Harmonized System is also intended to be trade neutral, so that its implementation will not affect the duty or exemptions applicable

---

[2] An excerpt from the tariff schedules appears in Appendix 1.

under the Tariff Schedules. The Harmonized System may be adopted by the United States as early as 1988.

§ 6:03.   Classification of Imports.

In order to determine the tariff treatment of a particular import, the import must first be classified in accordance with the Tariff Schedules. The Tariff Schedules contain eight separate lists, each with a given group of merchandise, plus an Appendix which lists tariffs or quotas of limited duration. The Schedules also have an index that is sometimes helpful in locating the appropriate classification. Each product is designated by its common name, by its physical characteristics or by its use or function.

The majority of products are described in the Tariff Schedules by their common name. Examples include eyeglasses (Item 708.30) and telescopes (Item 708.47). This type of designation, which is known as eo nominee, uses the normal definition of the item in trade or commerce. For this reason, courts often resort to a dictionary to assist in determining the applicability of a particular classification to a given import. Eo nominee designations apply whether a particular item is finished or unfinished, but do not extend to parts of the item unless otherwise provided.[3] Furthermore, under the "more than rule, an eo nominee designation, such as a screwdriver, does not extend to an item that is more than such item, such as a screwdriver with a built in light.

A number of products are classified by their physical characteristics or by their physical characteristics together with an eo nominee designation. Examples include articles not specifically provided for, stone (Item 514.41), copper bearing ores (Item 605.25) and men's or boys' wearing apparel of man-made fibers (Item 381.87). The physical description may refer to size, weight, shape, composition or other distinguishing features.

Finally, an import may also be classified by use or function. Examples of this include articles chiefly used in the household for

---

[3] General Headnotes 10(h),(ij).

preparing, serving or storing food (Item 546.11) and machines used to prepare natural or man-made fibers for spinning (Item 670.06). Unless the context otherwise requires, use means the chief use of the article in the United States at or immediately after the time of importation. If the classification is controlled by actual use, the importer must intend and actually use the item for such purpose and later furnish proof of such use.

Certain other interpretative principles must also be considered in classifying imports. Under the "rule of relative specificity," a product which falls within two tariff provisions will be classified under the more specific one.[4] Thus, an importer may not obtain a lower rate of duty by classifying machines for manufacturing glass under a general provision for machines where there is specific provision for such machines. Moreover, General Headnote 10(ij) provides that a provision for parts does not prevail over a more specific provision for such part. Thus, a standard bolt which is classifiable under Item 646.54 cannot be classified as a part of an automobile even though it is intended for, and actually used on, an automobile.

Merchandise is classified in its imported condition. Thus, an imported vehicle on which a specialized drill has been mounted is classifiable under a provision covering vehicles so equipped even though the drill is removable and the vehicle suitable for other uses. A related interpretative principle is the "rule of entireties." Under this rule, an item may be dismantled for shipment or shipped prior to assembly and still be classified under the provision for the finished item provided (i) the parts are designed to be combined; (ii) the parts are packed separately and are part of the same shipment; and (iii) if assembled, the parts would fit together and the assembled item would be substantially complete. This rule allows the importer to ship a particular product in parts and still have it treated au a completed item for tariff purposes. If, on the other hand, the duty would be lower on the individual items, the importer could avoid having them treated as an entirety, perhaps by sending them in separate shipments.

---

[4] General Headnote 10(c).

In classifying merchandise, one is often able to argue the applicability of two or more provisions, usually with different rates of duty. In cases where the difference in duties between two potentially applicable provisions is particularly high or where repeated shipments of the same product are contemplated, it may be desirable to obtain a ruling from the Regional Office or Custom Headquarters in Washington, D.C. The Service's Office of Regulations and Rulings is staffed by government lawyers divided into teams who deal with specific areas. The importer or its counsel will typically send a letter arguing for a particular classification and include samples, literature and a detailed description of the item in question. The Customs Service lawyer will normally consult previous letter rulings, requests for internal review and rulings on protests. While some of these are published in the Customs Bulletin, most are available only through Freedom of Information Act (FOIA) requests. The Government Printing Office also sells microfilm indexes of these materials, which are available at many ports. The ruling is binding on Customs only with respect to the requesting importer and only until Customs is persuaded to change its determination.

§ 6:04. Rates of Duty.

The second step in determining the tariff treatment of a particular import is to determine the applicable rate of duty. This is a function of (i) the duty corresponding to the particular classification, and (ii) the origin of the product.

The rate of duty corresponding to a particular item in the Tariff Schedules may be an ad valorem rate, a per unit rate or a compound rate. Most rates are ad valorem. In such cases, the applicable duty is expressed as a percentage of the value of the import for customs purposes. Silk yarn, for example, is classifiable under Item 308.30 and dutiable at the rate of 5% ad valorem. On a $1,000 shipment, the applicable duty would be $50. Imports may also be subject to a unit rate based on gallons, pounds, units, dozens, etc. An example is certain wools which are classifiable under Item 306.10 and dutiable at the rate of $.02 per clean pound. A compound rate is a combination of an ad valorem and per unit rate. Certain perfumes, for example, are classifiable under Item 460.80 and dutiable at the rate of $.05 per pound plus 4.3% ad valorem.

The rates quoted above, however, are applicable only to imports from noncommunist countries not on the list of least developed countries. These are the so-called "most favored nation" rates listed under column 1 in the Tariff Schedules. Column 2 rates apply to products from the "communist" countries listed in General Headnote 3(d). A third set of rates, consisting of the accelerated Tokyo Round rates, applies to the "least developed developing countries (LDDC's)" listed in General Headnote 3(e)(vi) and appears under the column designated "Special."[5] In certain cases, Canada enjoys a special rate of duty. This is accomplished by special classifications, however, rather than a fourth duty rate. Special rules requiring goods to have a minimum local content or to undergo a "substantial transformation" locally prevent importers from achieving lower rates of duty by simply transshipping products through a country that enjoys a lower rate of duty.

§ 6:05. Valuation (Appraisement) of Imports.

Imports which are subject to ad valorem rates of duty must be valued in accordance with customs procedures in order to determine the applicable duty. Section 402[6] of the Tariff Act of 1930, as amended by the Trade Agreements Act of 1979, sets forth in detail the means of valuing imports for customs purposes. In general, the rules for determining the customs value of the imported merchandise are designed to establish the value of the merchandise in the country of exportation (i.e., F.O.B., the foreign port without ocean freight, marine insurance or other export charges). The customs value of most merchandise exported to the United States on or after July 1, 1980 is the "transaction value" of the goods. If the transac-

---

[5] See Appendix 1.

[6] 19 USC §1401a; see also 19 CFR Part 152.

tion value cannot be used, resort will be made to one of the secondary bases, in the following order of preference: (i) transaction value of identical merchandise, (ii) transaction value of similar merchandise, (iii) deductive value, and (iv) computed value.

§ 6:06. —Transaction Value of Goods.

The transaction value of imported merchandise is the price actually paid or payable for the merchandise when sold for exportation to the United States, plus the following if not included in such amount: packing costs and sales commissions incurred by the buyer, the apportioned value of any "assists," royalties or license fees required to be paid by the buyer as a condition of sale, and any proceeds accruing to the seller from the subsequent sale or disposition of the imported merchandise. The packing costs include the costs incurred by the buyer for all containers and coverings as well as labor and materials used in packing the merchandise, ready for export. Sales commissions include any compensation paid to the seller's agent, or anyone related to or controlled by the manufacturers.

An "assist" includes any materials, equipment or services that the buyer of the imported merchandise provides to the seller, free or at a reduced cost, for use in the production or sale of the imported merchandise. Thus, assists can include (i) materials, components, parts, and other items incorporated into the imported merchandise; (ii) tools, dies, molds, and similar items used in manufacturing the imported merchandise; (iii) merchandise consumed in producing the imported merchandise; and (iv) engineering, development, artwork, design work, etc. that are undertaken outside the United States. If assists are present in a given import transaction, they must first be valued in gross using specified rules. Such value must then be apportioned to the particular shipment of imported merchandise, or in certain other ways.

Where the buyer is required, as a condition to the sale, to pay any royalties or similar fees, these must also be apportioned to and included in the appraised value of the imported merchandise for customs purposes. These fees are sometimes encountered in the acquisition of large or complicated machinery and equipment where the buyer must pay a continuing technical fee, or in goods which carry a foreign trademark subject to a license fee. In certain other cases, the U.S. buyer may have acquired the goods with the understanding that upon their sale or disposition, additional amounts will be paid to the foreign seller. These amounts must also be included in the transaction value of the merchandise.

Because the valuation procedure attempts to establish the cost of the merchandise in the country of export, certain costs incurred by the buyer will not be included for Customs purposes. Among these are transportation and insurance between ports, U.S. customs duties or federal taxes, and costs associated with assembly, maintenance or technical services after importation. These charges should not be reflected on the invoice.

§ 6:07. —Secondary Bases for Valuation.

If Customs finds that there is insufficient information available to determine any of the elements which must be included in the transaction value of the imported merchandise, it will resort to one of the secondary bases for appraising the merchandise. This is particularly common where certain elements are variable or conditional, such as quantity rebates. Transaction value of the imported merchandise will also be deemed inapplicable where the disposition of the merchandise by the buyer is subject to substantial conditions or in certain related party transactions where Customs determines that the transaction was not at arms' length.

If determination cannot be made with respect to the transaction value of the imported merchandise itself, Customs will first resort to a determination of the transaction value of identical merchandise from the same country and from the same manufacturer. The third preference is for the transaction value of "similar" (i.e., commercially interchangeable) merchandise from the same country and preferably, though not necessarily, the same manufacturer.

If neither of these may be employed, the importer may elect to use deductive value or computed value. Deductive value is the price at which the goods are sold in the United States using the largest quantity discount, but deducting the importer's commission or profit, expenses, transportation and insurance and processing costs. Computed value, which is equivalent to "American selling price" used prior to July, 1980, attempts to calculate the value based on information as to the costs of materials and fabrication, customary profit and expenses, assists and packing costs. Finally, if none of the foregoing can be utilized, Customs will resort to derived value which allows it to employ any of the above with such adjustments as it deems necesary.

While customs appraisement procedures may appear somewhat complex, few problems are encountered in actual practice. The vast majority of imports are appraised on the basis of the commercial invoice which the seller provides to the buyer. Among the most frequent valuation problems are those associated with transactions between affiliates. In such cases, Customs may use one of the alternative valuation procedures to test the invoiced value. If the test is met, it will not inquire further into the influence that the affiliation had on the price. Occasional problems also arise where an assist may be involved. The consequences of an assist as well as the other factors that may impact on the appraisement of the merchandise should be considered before the price and other details of the purchase order are worked out whenever the imports will be dutiable.

§ 6:08. Special Exemptions.

The Tariff Schedules and other customs laws also contain a number of total or partial exemptions from duty for imports meeting certain conditions. These special provisions are generally designed to encourage imports which do not negatively impact on the domestic economy or imports from developing countries in accordance with foreign policy or other objectives.

§ 6:09. —Foreign-Trade Zones and Bonded Warehouses.

Foreign-trade zones[7] and Customs bonded warehouses[8] allow importers to bring foreign merchandise into the country and to defer the payment of duties thereon until such merchandise is removed from the zone or warehouse. Goods entered into a foreign trade zone or bonded warehouse can be stored, displayed, cleaned, sorted, and manufactured or assembled into different products. The goods may then be exported without payment of U.S. Customs duties or entered for consumption upon payment of duty at the rate applicable to the goods in their then-present condition. Zones and bonded warehouses can also be used to store quota merchandise while awaiting the next quota period or to comply with marking or labeling requirements.

§ 6:10. —Duty Drawback.

Where imported goods are intended to be manufactured or assembled into a final product which is then exported, the importer may receive a 99% rebate of the duties and other taxes paid thereon.[9] This rebate, known as "drawback," would allow manufacturers of a vessel, for example, to import foreign raw materials or components for manufacturing the vessel at a U.S. port, and receive a rebate of 99% of the duties paid when the vessel leaves the United States. Duty drawback may also be available where duty is paid on merchandise which is reexported because it fails to meet specifications or is shipped without the consent of the consignee. In such cases, the importer must redeliver the goods to Customs within 90 days after their release so that they may be

---

[7] 19 USC §§81a–81u; 15 CFR Part 400. See generally Note, "U.S. Foreign-Trade Zone Manufacturing and Assembly: Overview and Update," 13 Law & Pol'y Int'l Bus 339 (1981).

[8] See 19 CFR Part 144.

[9] 19 USC 1313(a); 19 CFR Part 191.

reexported under Customs supervision.[10] The 1% fee, intended to reimburse Customs for its expenses, can also be eliminated in certain cases.

Drawback is often compared with bonded warehouses and foreign-trade zones as a mechanism for eliminating the customs duties on foreign goods which are brought to the United States and manufactured into a product which is ultimately exported. In this respect, the drawback procedures present the advantage of allowing the goods to be located anywhere in U.S. Customs territory, and not only to bonded warehouses or foreign-trade zones. At the same time, however, use of the drawback procedures requires the importer to initially post the required duties and wait until the product is exported for reimbursement.

§ 6:11.   —Temporary Imports.

Selected goods may also be eligible for Temporary Importation under Bond (TIB) or may be imported free on a temporary basis using the ATA Carnet procedures. TIB entry, which is covered by Items 864.00 through 864.25 of the Tariff Schedules, extends to merchandise which will be repaired, altered or processed (including processes that result in the manufacture of a new product) as well as samples, tools, and various other items which are brought into the United States on a temporary basis. The goods may normally remain in the country for one year, with the possibility of two one-year extensions. The bond is generally equal to two times the estimated duties.

The ATA ("Admission Temporaire - Temporary Admission") carnet is an international customs document which may be used for the temporary import of certain goods into a country in lieu of local customs documentation. The carnet serves as a guaranty against payment of the customs duties which may become due if

---

[10] Extension of this 90-day period may be granted, and in many cases, rebates can be obtained for goods re-exported within three years after release.

the goods are not reexported. In the United States and most other countries, an ATA carnet can be used for the temporary admission of professional equipment, commercial samples and advertising material. The U.S. Council of the International Chamber of Commerce located in New York City has been designated by Customs to issue ATA carnets to U.S. residents.

§ 6:12. —Return of Unimproved Merchandise.

Items 800.00 and 801.00 of the Tariff Schedules exempt from U.S. Customs duties U.S. and foreign merchandise meeting certain conditions. Item 800.00 provides for the duty-free entry of U.S. merchandise which is returned to the United States after having been exported but which has not been advanced in value or improved in condition by any process of manufacture or other means while abroad. This exemption is applicable, for example, to goods which may be sent abroad for display or exhibition, whether or not for commercial purposes. Item 801.00, on the other hand, extends to previously imported merchandise which was subsequently exported for certain purposes and is reimported in its same condition by the same person who exported it. Thus, Item 801.00 may be employed where foreign merchandise upon which duty is paid is sent abroad to be used as a model or for any other purpose which will not advance its value or improve its condition, then subsequently reimported. Both of these items are subject to certain other conditions.

§ 6:13. —Articles Repaired, Altered or Processed Abroad.

Items 806.20 and 806.30 of the Tariff Schedules create partial exemptions for articles which are sent abroad to undergo repair, alteration or further processing. Item 806.20 extends to U.S. goods which are repaired or altered abroad. Item 806.30 pertains to nonprecious metal articles, either manufactured in or imported into the United States, which are exported for processing abroad and then returned to the United States for further processing. The duty under these items is applied only to the cost or value of the repairs, alterations or processing performed outside the United States.

§ 6:14. —United States Articles Assembled Abroad.

Item 807.00 of the Tariff Schedules is similar to Items 806.20 and 806.30, but extends to U.S. articles assembled abroad. In order to satisfy the requirements of Item 807.00, several conditions must be met. First, the article itself must be a "U.S. product," i.e., manufactured or processed in the United States wholly from U.S. components or materials, or if partially or wholly of foreign materials, has been "substantially transformed" into a new and different commercial article in the United States. Second, the U.S. product must be exported in a condition ready for assembly, without the need of further fabrication. Third, the U.S. product must not lose its physical identity in the assembled article by changing in form, shape or otherwise during the assembly process. This would, for example, exclude the mixing or combining of liquids, gasses, chemicals, and amorphous solids.[11] Fourth, the U.S. article must not be advanced in value or improved in condition while abroad except by the assembly operations and incidental processes such as cleaning, lubricating and painting. The assembly operations themselves are defined to include any method of joining or fitting together sold components, such as welding, soldering, riveting, force fitting, gluing, laminating, sewing or by the use of fasteners. If these and certain other conditions are met, duty will be assessed upon the full value of the imported article less the cost or value of the U.S. products and any U.S. components. Like Items 806.20 and 806.30, Item 807.00 is particularly important to

[11] See 19 CFR §10.16; TD 73–27, TD 75–230.

companies who send partially completed articles and components to Mexico, Asia and certain other locations for assembly.

§ 6:15. —Country-Based Tariff Exemptions.

Finally, U.S. legislation creates special tariff exemptions or preferences for products produced in certain countries. We have already discussed the preferential duty rates available to products from designated LDDC's.[12] Certain other country groups enjoy full tariff exemptions in certain cases.

The broadest of these exemptions is authorized under the Generalized System of Preferences (GSP).[13] The GSP, which was originally enacted as part of the Trade Act of 1974 and was renewed with amendments in 1984, provides for the duty-free entry of most products from 140 developing countries designated as eligible under Presidential Proclamation. The countries which are currently eligible under the GSP are listed in General Headnote 3(e)(v) of the Tariff Schedules. In order to be eligible for duty-free treatment under the GSP, the product must be imported directly from the designated country and have been "produced" in such country (or in two or more members of an association of developing countries such as ANCOM, ASEAN or CARICOM). A product is deemed to be "produced" in the country if it is either (i) wholly the growth, product or manufacture of the country or association of countries; or (ii) has been "substantially transformed" in such country or association into a new and different article of commerce and at least 35% of its value consists of materials and/or processing which took place in such country or association. Certain products are not eligible for duty-free entry

---

[12] See §6:04.

[13] 19 USC §2461; 15 CFR Part 2007. See generally F. Hirsch, "Renewal of the G.S.P.: An Explanation of the Program and Changes Made by the 1984 Legislation," 18 Vand J Trans L 625 (1985); Note, "GSP: A System of Preferences, Not a Bargaining Lever," 17 Law & Pol'y Int'l Bus 879 (1985).

under the GSP, so that one must consult the Tariff Schedules to determine applicability.

A second exemption was created in 1984 as part of the Caribbean Basin Economic Recovery Act (CBERA).[14] The CBERA created a 12-year exemption from customs duties for all but a few sensitive imports (textiles, footwear, watches, etc.) from designated Caribbean countries. Like the GSP, the CBERA requires that the products be imported directly and that at least 35% of their value consist of materials produced or processing carried out in one or more of the designated countries or Puerto Rico and the U.S. Virgin Islands. Unlike the GSP, however, the value of U.S. constituent materials or processing can be credited toward this 35% local content requirement to a maximum of 15%, so that the minimum local content may be as low as 20%. The list of countries currently eligible for the exemption created by the CBERA is set forth in General Headnote 3(e)(vii) to the Tariff Schedules.

A third group of countries accorded special tariff treatment are U.S. possessions. These include the U.S. Virgin Islands, Guam, American Somoa, Wake Island, Kingman Reef, Johnson Island, and Midway Islands. Under Headnote 3(a) of the Tariff Schedules, merchandise produced in and imported directly from U.S. possessions is exempt from U.S. customs duties. The rules described above with respect to the GSP and the CBERA for determining whether the item was produced in the possession are also applicable under General Headnote 3(a) except that there is no 15% U.S. credit and the local content requirement has been reduced to 30%.

Finally, as a result of legislation enacted in August, 1985, most products of Israel are or will soon be entitled to duty-free treatment into the United States.[15] In order to be eligible for such exemption, the imports must meet direct shipment and rule of origin criteria similar to that described above with respect to Caribbean basin imports (i.e., 35% domestic content but with a 15% credit for U.S.

[14] 19 USC §§2701–2706, 19 CFR §§10.191–10.198; see also T. Clasen, "The Caribbean Basin Economic Recovery Act and its Implication for Foreign Private Investment, 16 NYUJ Int'l L & Pol 715 (1984).

[15] See 19 USC §2112; Pres Proc 5365 (Aug. 30, 1985).

content). This benefit for Israeli imports is particularly important given the new provisions of the GSP which mandate the "gradua-tion" of some of the more industrialized developing countries out of the program.

Because of the many conditions to which the duty-exemptions described above are subject, companies who contemplate sourcing products from any of these countries and relying on the above-described exemptions should be advised to consult with legal counsel and to obtain a ruling from the Customs Service which confirms eligibility.

§ 6:16.   Nontariff Trade Barriers.

In addition to the import duties imposed under the Tariff Sched-ules, U.S. import laws and regulations also impose certain non-tariff barriers to trade. The most important of these nontariff barriers for purposes of this group are import quotas and marking requirements.

§ 6:17.   —Import Quotas.

From time to time, Congress or the President are pressured by certain local industries suffering from foreign competition to limit the quantity of imports of a particular type. These quantitative limitations or "quotas" are presently in effect with respect to dairy and certain other agricultural products under Section 22 of the Agricultural Adjustment Act, coffee and rubber under interna-tional commodity control agreements, textiles and wearing apparel under the Multifiber Arrangement, and various other products. Quotas of this type are either "absolute" or "tariff rate." Absolute quotas prohibit the importation of any imports above an estab-lished quantity. Tariff rate quotas allow the entry of a specified quantity of the goods at a basic rate of duty and impose a higher rate on all such goods in excess of the quota amount.

It should also be noted in this context that from time to time informal quotas may be established under bilateral "orderly marketing agreements." Countries may also "voluntarily" limit their exports of a particular product under the threat of mandatory quotas. These mechanisms have been used recently with respect to televisions and automobiles from Japan.

§ 6:18. —Marking Requirements.

United States marking requirements are also often veiwed as a nontariff barrier to trade. Section 304(2) of the Tariff Act of 1930, as amended,[16] provides that with certain exceptions, every article of foreign origin, or in certain cases its container, imported into the United States be marked in a conspicuous place to indicate to the ultimate purchaser in the United States the English name of the country of origin of the article. The regulations applicable to country-of-origin marking set forth the required procedure for marking imported merchandise, list the exceptions from the marking requirements and explain where marking the container is permissible.[17] A special marking duty equal to 10% of the customs value of the imported merchandise is imposed on goods failing to meet marking requirements, unless they are exported, destroyed or marked under Customs supervision. In addition to country-of-origin markings, special marking and labeling requirements apply with respect to wool, textiles and fur, and other goods.

§ 6:19. —Preferences for Local Products.

United States federal and state legislation which impose preferences for local products over imports are also viewed as barriers to trade. The Buy American Act of 1933,[18] for example, created a

[16] 19 CFR Part 134.
[17] 19 CFR Part 134.
[18] 41 USC §§10a–10c.

preference for goods of domestic origin in government procurement programs. Under applicable guidelines, U.S. goods could be as much as 6% higher in cost than their foreign counterpart and still be purchased in a competitive bid. Similar "buy American" principles are included in the annual Defense Appropriation Act, the Merchant Marine Act of 1936[19] and federal housing legislation. While most of these preferences were reduced as a result of the procedures established under the Agreement on Government Procurement which emerged from the Tokyo Round of Trade Negotiations,[20] certain preferential practices continue. Moreover, states are increasingly adopting their own policies of providing preferences for local products.

§ 6:20.   —Health, Safety, and Other Standards.

An additional way that may be used by government to discriminate against imports is by imposing health, safety or other standards that may be costly for foreign products to meet. In the United States, for example, emission and safety standards for motor vehicles, purity standards for foods and testing requirements for drugs effectively prevent some imports from reaching the U.S. market. Japan has also been regularly accused of using such standards to block U.S. imports. This area was also addressed at the Tokyo Round of Trade Negotiations. The resulting agreement, known as the Standards Code,[21] seeks to discourage discriminatory manipulation of product standards, product testing and product certification without limiting the ability of countries to protect the interests of their citizens.

[19] 46 USC §1122.
[20] 19 USC §§2511–2518.
[21] 19 USC §2531 et seq.

CHAPTER 7

UNFAIR TRADE PRACTICES AND IMPORT RELIEF

---

§ 7:01. In General.

In addition to regulating the day-to-day import of foreign merchandise as described above, U.S. trade laws also attempt to protect domestic industries from what are perceived as unfair trade practices and, in certain cases, offer relief to industries suffering from competition from increased imports. While some of these remedies have been available for many years, they are being applied with increased frequency in recent years as more U.S.

companies battle foreign competition in the U.S. market. While the measures are generally designed to address specific practices or consequences, the situations that U.S. companies bring to their lawyers are rarely as well-defined. The lawyer's first responsibility, therefore, is to explain under what circumstances the remedies are available and then to proceed in recommending a strategy for obtaining relief, often by pursuing various remedies.

§ 7:02. Remedies Against Unfair Trade Practices— Antidumping and Countervailing Duties.

Among the remedies against unfair trade practices, the most important are the Antidumping Law and the Countervailing Duty Act.[1] These measures, which represent revisions to earlier legislation resulting from the Tokyo Round of Trade Negotiations, are similar in concept. Both provide for the imposition of a special duty to compensate for unfair pricing of foreign merchandise which injure or prevent the establishment of a U.S. industry. They are also procedurally similar, requiring decisions by both the Department of Commerce and the International Trade Commission.

The Antidumping Law[2] provides that when the Department of Commerce determines that a class or kind of foreign merchandise is being, or is likely to be, sold to purchasers in the United States at less than its fair value (a practice known as "dumping") it will advise the International Trade Commission (ITC). The ITC must thereupon determine whether, as a result of the dumping, a U.S. industry is materially injured or threatened with material injury, or the establishment of an industry in the United States is materially retarded. If the ITC determination is affirmative, Commerce publishes an antidumping duty order and importations of such merchandise become subject to special dumping duties. These duties

---

[1] See generally J Pattison, Antidumping and Countervailing Duty Law (1984).
[2] 19 USC §1673 et seq.

are equal to the amount by which the foreign market value or construed value of the foreign merchandise exceeds the purchase price or exporter's sales price.

The Commerce Department's determination as to whether the merchandise is being dumped in the U.S. market is ordinarily based upon a comparison between the U.S. price and the net, F.O.B. factory price to purchasers in the home market. If identical or similar merchandise is not sold in the home market, or is sold in insufficient quantities to be an adequate basis of comparison, other measures, including prices to purchasers in third countries or a construed value based on the cost of materials, labor, fabrication and overhead, packaging and usual profit, are employed. Special rules govern cases involving related party transactions, goods from nonmarket economies and other special situations.

The ITC injury finding also presents certain issues. ITC must first define the industry in question. As in antitrust proceedings, the determination of the industry is often controversial. The law also requires that the injury be "material." However, the definition of material injury—"harm which is not inconsequential, immaterial or unimportant"—is not particularly helpful. The injury must also occur "by reason of imports of that merchandise" so that a causal connection must also be established. These issues, and those regarding the definition of the merchandise and the basis for comparison of prices in the Commerce Department determination, are the key aspects of an antidumping case.

The Countervailing Duty Act[3] authorizes the Department of Commerce to investigate charges of bounties, grants and other types of export subsidies made by any foreign government or political subdivision thereof, or any other group, legal entity or person, with respect to articles or merchandise exported to the United States. The law extends to any type of payment, whether direct or indirect, made upon the manufacture or production of the merchandise, as well as its exportation. The law contains an extensive list of examples of proscribed subsidies, including the provision of capital, loans or loan guarantees on terms more favorable

[3] 19 USC §1671 et seq.

than prevailing market practices, the provision of goods or services at preferential rates, grants, forgiveness of debt and assumption by the government of certain costs or expenses in a given industry.[4] Commerce Department decisions, which are published in the Federal Register, illustrate other examples of prohibited subsidies.

If the Commerce Department makes a positive finding on the subsidy issue, the ITC must make an injury determination as described above if the country involved is a member of GATT or is a party to a bilateral agreement which accords it an injury test. If the ITC determination is also affirmative, a countervailing duty will be imposed in an amount equal to the net subsidy determined or estimated by Commerce. Like antidumping duties, the countervailing duties are reviewed annually by the Department of Commerce to determine whether adjustments or revocation are appropriate.

Complaints under the Antidumping and Countervailing Duty Laws may be initiated by private petitions or by the participating government agencies. Private petitions, which are submitted to both agencies, must set forth the allegations in detail and contain supporting information. Commerce has 45 days (which may be extended in difficult cases) to make a preliminary determination. If the Commerce Department finding is positive, the ITC has 45 days, unless extended, to make its determination. A positive preliminary determination by Commerce also means the importer is required to post security for the estimated antidumping or countervailing duties. Throughout the proceedings, the respective determinations and any other legal issues are subject to interlocutory review by the U.S. Court of International Trade whose final decision may be appealed to the Court of Appeals for the Federal District.

§ 7:03. —Section 337 of the Tariff Act of 1930.

If the foreign practices do not fall within the scope of the antidumping or countervailing duty laws, relief may be available under the provisions of Section 337 of the Tariff Act of 1930.[5]

---

[4] 19 USC §1677 (5)(B).

[5] 19 USC §1337(a).

Section 337, as amended by the Trade Act of 1974, declares unlawful all "unfair methods of competition and unfair acts in the importation of articles into the United States, or in the sale by the owner, importer, consignee, or agent of either, the effect or tendency of which is to destroy or substantially injure an industry, efficiently and economically operated in the United States, or to prevent the establishment of such an industry, or to restrain or monopolize trade and commerce in the United States. . . ."[6] While the 1974 amendments broadened the scope of Section 337 to encompass such practices as price-fixing, improper marking, deceptive advertising, predatory pricing, passing off and refusing to deal, ITC investigations under Section 337 continue to be primarily confined to patent infringement by imports to which it has always extended.

Petitions for relief under Section 337 are filed with the ITC who makes a determination as to the validity of the claim. The petitioner must establish three elements: (i) the existence of unfair methods of competition or unfair acts in the importation of merchandise, (ii) that such unfair methods or acts destroy, substantially injure or prevent the establishment of an industry, and (iii) that such industry, if it exists, is efficiently and economically operated in the United States. Preliminary decisions by the ITC must usually be issued within nine months following initiation of the proceedings, with final decision due within a year. The relief that may be granted includes prohibiting the enfringing merchandise from being imported into U.S. Customs territory.[7]

---

[6] 19 USC §1337(a).

[7] See also 19 CFR Part 133 authorizing the Customs Service to seize imported merchandise bearing U.S. trademarks or subject to U.S. copyrights pursuant to Section 526(a) of the Tariff Act of 1930 (19 USC §1526(a)) and Section 602(b) of the Copyright Act of 1976 (17 USC §602(b)). There is still a significant debate as to the extent to which these provisions and certain other laws are intended to extend to "gray market" goods—genuine merchandise manufactured abroad by a foreign trademark owner or licensee but imported through unauthorized distribution channels. See, e.g., Knoll, "Gray-Market Imports: Causes, Consequences and Responses," 18 Law & Pol'y Int'l Bus 145 (1986).

§ 7:04.   —Section 301 of the Trade Act of 1974.

Section 301 of the Trade Act of 1974[8] also provides a form of relief against certain unfair trade practices. It authorizes the President to take retaliatory measures to counter "unreasonable, unjustified or discriminatory trade policies" enacted by other countries that have an adverse impact on U.S. commerce. These may include unreasonable tariffs, import quotas, export subsidies or preferences which discriminate against U.S. imports. The available relief includes the suspension of trade concession benefits or the imposition of special duties or import restrictions.

Section 301 has been relied on in the past to impose tariffs on certain EEC products in retaliation for EEC tariffs on unrelated U.S. poultry. In the majority of the cases where the U.S. Trade Representative agreed with the complaint, subsequent negotiations led to an easing of the unfair trade practices so that no retaliation was taken. While most complaints under Section 301 have been initiated by private petitions, in recent times, the President has initiated his own actions under Section 301 to challenge Brazil's informatics policies, Japan's restrictions on U.S. tobacco products, and Korea's restrictions on foreign insurance carriers.[9]

§ 7:05.   —United States Antitrust Laws.

Recent judicial decisions which extend the application of U.S. antitrust laws to foreign firms illustrate another remedy that may be available with respect to unfair practices in international trade. In Continental Ore Co. v. Union Carbide and Chemical Co., for example, the Sherman Act was relied on to render unlawful the actions of another U.S. company to monopolize foreign suppliers

---

[8] 19 USC §2411 et seq.; see generally Fisher & Steinhardt, "Section 301 of the Trade Act of 1974: Protection for U.S. Exporters of Goods, Services and Capital," 14 Law & Pol'y Int'l Bus 569 (1982).

[9] 50 Fed Reg 37608, 37609 (1985).

of particular minerals.[10] While it is still difficult to predict to what extent courts will extend U.S. antitrust laws abroad, this remedy should not be neglected in considering a strategy to assist U.S. companies suffering from practices by foreign firms which would violate such laws if performed in the United States.[11]

§ 7:06. —Proposed Legislation.

Both the House (HR-3) and the Senate (S-1420) versions of the omnibus trade bill—the proposed Trade and International Economic Policy Reform Act of 1987—contain measures which would add to the arsenal of the U.S. laws against unfair trade practices. The House bill, which was adopted in April, 1987, requires the imposition of tariffs or quotas against countries that violate negotiated agreements unless the President determines such action would not be in the national economic interest. It also requires negotiations, and eventually retaliation, to eliminate unfair trade practices in countries deemed to have excess trade surpluses with the United States. Under the controversial Gephardt Amendment, if the practice persists, the President would be required to take action to reduce the surplus by 10% per year, unless it is not in the national economic interest.

The Senate bill, which was passed in July, 1987, requires the President to identify countries with a consistent pattern of trade barriers, and negotiate for their removal. If such negotiations fail, the President would be required to retaliate, but is given considerable latitude in determining the nature of the retaliation. The President's waiver authority is restricted where the country's trade practices violate a trade agreement. Finally, the bill authorizes the House Ways and Means Committee and the Senate Finance Committee to file petitions seeking investigation of a foreign country suspected of a pattern of import barriers.

[10] 70 US 690 (1962).

[11] See generally Davidow, "Extraterritorial Application of U.S. Antitrust Law in a Changing World," 8 Law & Pol'y Int'l Bus 895 (1976).

The President has threatened a veto over the House language. The administration also objects to the Senate version. At the time of this writing, it is unclear what compromises could be worked out in conference. It seems likely, however, that a comprehensive trade bill will be enacted in 1987 or early 1988.

§ 7:07.   Relief from Increased Imports.

Even where injury from increased imports cannot be shown to be the result of unfair trade practices, relief may still be available under certain circumstances. The principal sources for such relief are found in the Trade Act of 1974. Because the remedies available under these provisions require Presidential approval, they are much more political than the more self-operative remedies for unfair trade practices. Nevertheless, they have become increasingly important as more U.S. firms, as well as labor organizations and even municipalities, seek temporary relief from the effect of foreign competition.

§ 7:08.   —Escape Clause.

The most important of these measures is commonly known as the "escape clause." Under Sections 201–203 of the Trade Act of 1974,[12] a domestic industry may be accorded relief when "an article is being imported into the United States in such quantities as to be a substantial cause of serious injury, or the threat thereof, to a domestic industry producing an article like or directly competitive with the imported article." Petitions for relief under the escape clause are filed with the ITC which determines whether the conditions have been met. Questions often arise as to the definition of the industry, the seriousness of the injury and the causal connection between the increased imports and the injury.

[12] 19 USC §§2251–2253.

If the ITC makes a positive determination, it must recommend a form of relief to the President. The President must thereupon determine whether to accept the proposed relief, to impose an alternative form of relief or to deny any form of relief. The authorized remedies under the escape clause include increased duties or the suspension of duty-free status, the imposition of quotas, and the creation of orderly marketing agreements to restrict imports. Such relief may not extend beyond a five-year term with a possible three-year extension, during which time the U.S. industry will be expected to have adjusted to the import competition.

§ 7:09. —Increased Imports from Communist Countries.

A second statutory provision, similar to the escape clause but slightly less restrictive, applies in the case of injury to a U.S. industry as a result of increased imports from Communist countries. Under Section 406 of the Trade Act of 1974[13] the President is authorized to impose certain restrictions on imports from Communist countries if the ITC finds that such imports are a significant cause of material injury or threat thereof to the U.S. industry producing a like or directly competitive product. According to the statutory history, Section 406 reflects congressional concern over the perceived ability of a Communist country, through its nonmarket economy, to flood domestic markets within a shorter time period then could occur under free market conditions.[14]

Section 406 proceedings can be commenced by the President, the U.S. Trade Representative, Congress or certain private entities by petition to the ITC. If the ITC makes the necessary findings, it must make recommendations to the President who has sixty days to implement or reject the ITC's recommendations. Relatively few cases, however, have been brought under Section 406.

[13] 19 USC §2436; see generally Note, "Relief from Imports from Communist Countries: The Trials and Tribulations of Section 406," 13 Law & Pol'y Int'l Bus 617 (1981).

[14] Id.

§ 7:10. —Trade Adjustment Assistance.

Finally, Title II of the Trade Act of 1974[15] authorizes workers and firms to receive direct government assistance from the adverse affects of import competition. Petitions for trade adjustment assistance may be filed with the Department of Labor or the Department of Commerce and must show that increased imports "contributed importantly" to loss of jobs or lower sales or production. Workers are entitled to increased unemployment benefits and various job training, relocation and employment services. Private firms are eligible for loans and technical assistance. Communities were originally eligible for adjustment assistance but were excluded under the Trade Adjustment Assistance Reform and Extension Act of 1986. Communities may still be able to obtain relief under Title IX of the Public Works and Economic Development Act of 1965.[16]

§ 7:11. —Proposed Legislation.

The 1987 trade bills passed by both the House and the Senate and currently scheduled for a conference committee authorize increased assistance for industries which are hurt by imports. The House version (HR-3) automatically entitles all workers and businesses to certain benefits upon a finding by the ITC that the industry has been injured. The Senate version (S-1420) requires the ITC to recommend relief for industries found to be injured by imports and requires the President to provide relief unless he finds it would not be in the national interest. The measure also increases cash benefits to workers.

[15] 19 USC §2271 et seq.; 29 CFR Parts 90–91.
[16] 42 USC §§3241–3245.

PART II—SUGGESTIONS FOR FURTHER READING

Books

Feller, P., U.S. Customs and International Trade Guide (1987).
Serko, D., Import Practice, Customs and International Trade Law (1985).
Stowe, A., U.S. International Trade Laws (1985).
Sturm, R., Customs Law and Administration (1987).

Articles

Bellow & Holmer, "The Trade and Tariff Act of 1984: Principal Anti-dumping and Countervailing Duty Provisions," 19 Int'l Law 639 (1985).

PART III

EXPORT
TRANSACTIONS

CHAPTER 8

STRUCTURING THE EXPORT TRANSACTION

§ 8:01. In General.

The export transaction and the import transaction are, of course, one and the same. The two terms simply represent the two perspectives from which the transaction can be viewed.

In Part II, we examined the transaction from the perspective of an importer seeking to bring foreign merchandise into the United States. While the importer may undertake various responsibilities in such transactions, we assumed for purposes of our analysis that the importer's obligations commenced when the goods arrived at the U.S. port. Thus, our inquiry was generally limited to the U.S.

laws and regulations which govern the entry of foreign goods into U.S. customs territory.

This Part will consider the transaction from the perspective of a U.S. seller. But by continuing the assumption that the exporter has undertaken to deliver the goods to the foreign port, the analysis will present an entirely new set of considerations. Moreover, while many of these considerations are also based on U.S. laws and regulations, the prospect of selling and shipping goods abroad, even in the most basic transaction, requires an understanding of foreign business practices and procedures with respect to such matters as transportation, export documentation and international payment. As these transactions become more involved, such as where the exporter engages a foreign agent or distributor to handle sales in a particular country or region, where the transaction may require certain action under U.S. export regulations, or where the exporter seeks to provide financing or to insure payment, additional issues are presented.

§ 8:02.   Alternatives to Direct Exporting.

Before looking at the more standard export transaction where the seller undertakes responsibility for selling and shipping its goods to a foreign buyer, a word should be said about certain alternatives to such direct involvement. In many cases, U.S. goods which are destined for export are sold and delivered in the United States. United States export trading companies (ETC's), for example, which were authorized under legislation enacted in 1982,[1] typically take title to goods locally and arrange for their sale, shipment, financing, etc. Sales to resident buyers of foreign companies, U.S. offices of foreign trading companies, export merchants, and trading houses are often structured on a similar basis. In other cases, a local agent or company many assume some or all of the tasks associated with an export transaction on a fee or commission basis, without actually buying for its own account.

[1] Export Trading Company Act of 1982, 19 USC §4001 et seq.

Export management companies (EMC's), for example, perform a role similar to a larger company's export department, soliciting orders from abroad and arranging for the sale and shipment of the merchandise in the name of the manufacturer.

Selling through these intermediaries advances the U.S. manufacturer's objective of increasing revenues through export sales without requiring it to incur the costs or bear the risks associated with developing and supplying a foreign market. At the same time, the extent to which a company can generate export revenues through such indirect exporting is obviously limited. Not only does it rely on a much more limited number of buyers, but it must also share a portion of its profits with these middlemen.

§ 8:03.   Export Sales Agreement.

Like any contract, the export sales agreement basically serves to record the manner in which the parties have allocated the obligations and risks of the particular transaction. The principal obligations, of course, relate to the terms and conditions governing delivery of the merchandise and payment therefor. Because of the international nature of the transaction, however, these delivery and payment terms and procedures take on an added significance.[2]

Another risk presented by an export sale relates to the currency in which the purchase price is quoted. The party which is forced to accept or provide payment in a foreign currency must either assume or properly protect itself against a devaluation of its own currency against such foreign currency.[3]

An additional issue presented in the export sales agreement is the law under which the instrument will be governed. United States lawyers will often mindlessly insist on the applicability of U.S. law, principally because they are unaware of how the instrument would be interpreted under the laws of a foreign jurisdiction.

[2] Delivery terms are summarized in §8:04 while international payment procedures are discussed in §§8:07–8:10.

[3] This risk, and the means available for managing it, are discussed in §8:11.

This is often true even though such foreign laws may be more beneficial to the U.S. seller than U.S. law. It should be noted that under the laws of certain countries, local law will apply regardless of a contrary choice of law by the parties to the agreement.

The United Nations Convention on Contracts for the International Sale of Goods (CISG) must also be considered when analyzing the applicable law in the case of an export sale. The CISG was ratified by the United States in 1986 and will enter into force on January 1, 1988. After that date, contracts between parties with a place of business in different contracting states will be governed by the CISG unless the parties expressly agree to a different governing law. While the CISG is remarkably similar to the U.S. law under the UCC, there are important differences in terms of the formation of contracts, the obligations and rights of the buyer and seller, and the remedies for breach. Thus, the effect of the CISG on a proposed transaction should be carefully reviewed to determine the desirability of opting out in while or in part.[4]

Another issue requiring consideration is the mechanism for resolving disputes arising out of the export sales agreement. While there are circumstances in which arbitral proceedings may not be appropriate, binding arbitration proceedings are generally in the interest of both parties, providing a more expeditious and less costly means of resolving disagreements than the courts in any jurisdiction. The ability to select arbitrators who have particular expertise or experience is also advantageous where the disputes involve complex technical issues. In appropriate circumstances, the parties may wish to reserve certain issues from arbitration.[5]

Finally, a word should be said about the form the export sales agreement should take. In most circumstances involving inexperienced exporters, the legal instrument governing the sale, if any

[4] See generally Honnold, Uniform Law for International Sales under the 1980 United Nations Convention (1982); see also Note, "A Practitioner's Guide to the United Nations Convention on Contracts for the International Sale of Goods," 16 Int'l L & Pol 81 (1983); Winship, "A Bibliography of Commentaries on the United Nations International Sales Convention," 21 Int'l Law 585 (1987).

[5] See Part IX for a discussion of arbitration in international commercial disputes.

at all, is the firm's standard sales from. However, a standard purchase order for domestic transactions is seldom adequate to protect the seller from the special risks presented by an export sale. In many cases where a domestic sale of the merchandise can be handled by a standard form, a similar form can be developed to cover most of the company's export sales. In other cases, however, a customized agreement may be required to deal with special requirements under applicable local law or to provide necessary protection for the seller. Moreover, where a long-term, multi-shipment arrangement is contemplated, a specially-drafted agreement may be appropriate.[6]

§ 8:04. International Trade Terms.

One of the most important aspects of the export sales agreement are the provisions governing delivery and payment. To a large extent, these provisions define the principal obligations and risks that are assumed by the parties. An exporter, for example, who seeks to minimize its risks and obligations with respect to a certain transaction, may seek to sell on an "ex factory" basis, meaning that its obligations cease, and its right to payment commences, once the goods have been manufactured and are ready for shipment from its factory. Likewise, an importer who is interested in minimizing its responsibility, may insist that the transaction be structured on a "duty paid" basis, where the exporter assumes all costs and risks associated with the delivery of the goods to the importer's domestic warehouse. Between these two extremes lie a number of compromise positions in which both parties assume costs and risks with respect to the transaction.

The terms "ex factory" and "duty paid" are two examples of international trade or price-delivery terms that have been developed over the years. Other examples of trade terms include "free alongside ship," "free on board" and "cost, insurance and

---

[6] Special consideration should be given to issues raised in §5:04 with respect to foreign sourcing.

freight,"which are more commonly seen using their initials F.A.S., F.O.B. and C.I.F. A contract or price quotation that includes the term "F.A.S. (named vessel)" means that the price includes the price of the goods themselves as well as the cost of transporting them from the exporter's factory or warehouse to a point alongside the designated ship. It also means that the exporter's obligation ends with the delivery of the goods to such point and that thereafter the risk of loss is borne by the importer. If, on the other hand, the contract or quote specified a price "C.I.F. (name port of designation)," such price would include the cost of the goods as well as freight and insurance to such destination. In a C.I.F. transaction, the exporter's obligations are complete once the goods are delivered to the carrier with maritime insurance prepaid.

An instrument which employs a trade term should also clearly set forth the body of rules that defines the rights and obligations of the parties under such trade term. In a purely domestic transaction subject to Article 2 of the Uniform Commercial Code, the responsibilities of the parties may be found in Section 2–319 of the UCC, where certain of these trade terms are defined. While the parties to an international transaction may elect to use the UCC definitions, it is more common to use the terms as defined in one of two other publications. The American Foreign Trade Definitions, which was modified and reissued as the Revised American Foreign Trade Definition—1941, was developed by a joint committee of the U.S. Chamber of Commerce, the National Council of American Importers and the National Foreign Trade Council. The International Chamber of Commerce has also developed a set of uniform definitions, the most recent revision of which is known as Incoterms 1980. While both of these sets of definitions are found incorporated by reference in many export contracts, Incoterms 1980, because it is more detailed, is perhaps more common.

§ 8:05. International Transportation and Insurance.

As described in the previous section, the export sales agreement will normally allocate the responsibility of transporting the merchandise between the importer and the exporter. The agreement may also specify the form of transportation that will be used in shipping the goods either expressly or by implication (i.e., a short delivery time necessitating air transportation or an F.A.S. (named vessel) indicating sea transportation). While merchandise in international commerce may be shipped by sea, air, road or rail, most shipments to and from the United States involve sea or air transportation.

An exporter who desires to ship goods by sea may either charter an entire vessel or, more commonly, purchase space on a freighter following a fixed schedule. Space on an oceangoing vessel is usually reserved through an agent working for the shipping line at the port of embarcation. Freight forwarders, who specialize in the international shipment of merchandise, will normally assume responsibility for contracting space on an appropriate vessel as well as crating the goods and handling the export documentation. Often the goods are packed in large metal containers of standard dimensions which may be carried by truck or rail car to and from the port.

Once the goods are loaded on board, the vessel issues the shipper or its agent an ocean bill of lading. The bill of lading serves three important functions. First, it evidences the receipt of the goods by the carrier. If the contract calls for shipment F.O.B., the exporter must make sure the goods are on board, and will receive an "on board" bill of lading. If the contract is only F.A.S., the exporter need only deliver the goods to the dock, and will be issued a "received for shipment" bill of lading. The bill of lading will also be either "foul," indicating that the carrier has observed certain defects in the goods or their packaging, or "clean," if no such defects are noted.[7]

The bill of lading also serves as a contract of carriage. In order to prevent international carriers from disclaiming liability in contracts of carriage, Congress enacted the Harter Act[8] and the Car-

---

[7] These distinctions have particular significance in letter of credit transaction described in §8:10.

[8] 46 USC §§190–195.

riage of Goods by Sea Act.[9] The Harter Act represented an attempt by Congress to regulate the terms contained in bills of sale. The Carriage of Goods by Sea Act implemented the international convention on the relationship of the carrier and the shipper known as the "Hague Rules." These laws require the carrier to provide a seaworthy ship and to use reasonable care in handling the goods. Clauses in bills of lading that are not permitted under these laws or other international rules and conventions to which the United States subscribes are void.

Finally, the bill of lading may also serve as a title document. If it is issued in negotiable form, the bill of lading evidences the right of the holder to receive delivery of the goods. The bill of lading is thus typically forwarded to the buyer or its agent by air to allow it to claim the goods when they arrive at port. In transactions calling for payment by documentary collection or letter of credit, the negotiable bill of lading is presented to the buyer's bank with the other export documents in exchange for payment.

While the vessel is prohibited from disclaiming certain liabilities with respect to the carriage of goods, it is not always liable for loss or damage to the cargo. Accordingly, a marine insurance policy is normally obtained in connection with the shipment of goods by sea. The duty to purchase or arrange for such insurance is determined by the trade terms. In a C.I.F. transaction, for example, the exporter must arrange and pay for marine insurance; in an F.O.B. transaction, it is obligated to arrange for the insurance, but at the buyer's expense. Frequent shippers will typically purchase an "open" or "floating" policy, under which a certificate will be issued evidencing marine insurance on a particular shipment. This certificate, or the policy itself, is usually one of the export documents which the exporter must produce in order to obtain payment in a documentary collection or letter of credit transaction.

Goods which are shipped by air are governed by the Warsaw Convention if the ports of departure and destination are located in contracting states. The Warsaw Convention establishes the practices of documentation and allocates liabilities in the same manner

---

[9] 46 USC §§1300–1315.

as the Hague Rules do for sea transportation. In place of the bill of lading, the air carrier issues the shipper a non-negotiable "airway bill" which acts as a receipt and contract of carriage. The shipper may control the possession of the goods pending payment by consigning them to a third party, such as a bank, which may verify payment before releasing the goods to the buyer. The Warsaw Convention also limits the liability of the air carriers unless a higher value is declared by the shipper. Additional insurance coverage can usually be obtained at nominal rates under the carrier's open policy or from the shipper's insurer.

§ 8:06. Export Documentation.

Documentation plays a much more significant role in international trade than in purely domestic transactions. The special risks presented by export sales as well as the legal requirements imposed by the countries involved frequently require the preparation and exchange of a variety of documents which may be completely unknown to companies solely engaged in domestic sales. In general, these documents serve three functions: (i) to demonstrate the fulfillment of the underlying transaction (e.g., commercial invoices, bills of lading, and warehouse receipts); (ii) to satisfy government requirements (e.g., consular invoices, customs invoices, and certificates of origin); and (iii) to evidence the quantity or quality of the merchandise (e.g., packing and weight lists, certificates of inspection, and certificates of measurement and analysis).

The accuracy and completeness of the documentation with respect to a particular export transaction assumes added significance where payment is made on a collection basis or by means of a documentary letter of credit.[10] In such cases, a bank is used as the buyer's agent to determine that the shipment meets the buyer's requirements before payment is made. The bank's determination, however, is made solely on the basis of the documentation. Since

---

[10] See §§8:09, 8:10.

the funds are often required to be released to the exporter immediately after shipment and possibly several days or more before the buyer receives or inspects the goods, the buyer must carefully determine and require the exporter to deliver all documentation which may be necessary to insure that the merchandise has been shipped, that all government requirements can be satisfied, and that the goods meet the buyer's specifications.

The following are some of the most common documents used in export transactions:

(i) *Commercial Invoice.* The commercial invoice is the most basic of the export documents.[11] It sets forth the essential terms of the sale, including the names and addresses of the buyer and seller, the means of shipment, a brief description of the merchandise, and the purchase price. Depending upon the trade terms governing the sale, the commercial invoices may also itemize freight, insurance and other charges to be borne by the buyer. References to the buyer's purchase order and letter of credit, if applicable, are also commonly included.

Goods shipped to buyers in certain countries sometimes require the invoice to be visaed or consularized (to verify compliance with certain laws) or to contain certain additional information such as import license numbers, export permit numbers or additional itemization of prices for customs purposes. In other cases a Special Customs Invoice (Customs Form 5515) or Consular Invoice may be required. Where payment will be made through a letter of credit, the exporter should make certain that the invoice complies with the terms of the letter of credit and with the relevant provisions of I.C.C. Publication 400.

(ii) *Packing List.* The packing list describes the packages in which the goods are shipped, including their weight and measurements and outside markings, and itemizes the contents of each package.[12] The packing list aids in the entry of the merchandise

---

[11] See Appendix 2 for an example of a commercial invoice.
[12] See Appendix 2 for an example of a packing list.

through customs and facilitates the addition of the merchandise into the buyer's inventory.

(iii) *Insurance Policy/Certificate.* As discussed above, the insurance policy or certificate is issued by an underwriter to evidence insurance against specified losses during shipment. A policy is a separate contract normally covering a particular shipment.[13] A certificate is issued under a general policy to extend the policy's coverage to the shipment.[14] The contract of sale or letter of credit normally requires that the insurance policy or certificate meet specified risks; be at least for the value of the shipment and in the same currency; be in negotiable form; be signed, countersigned or endorsed as needed; and show coverage as of a certain date. A letter of credit may also require the delivery of original and duplicate copies.

(iv) *Bill of Lading.* Bills of lading and the various functions they perform were discussed previously.[15] As indicated, bills of lading are issued by a carrier for merchandise to be delivered to a part at a named destination.[16] The characteristics of the bill of lading (i.e., "on board" versus "received for shipment" and "clean" versus "foul") and the number of copies to be delivered are often dictated by the contract of sale or the letter of credit. Letters of credit may also require an "order" rather than a "straight" bill of lading. An order bill of lading is a negotiable instrument providing for delivery to a named party or to order (i.e., anyone the named party may designate by endorsement). A straight bill of lading is non-negotiable and provides for delivery only to the named party. Letter of credit transactions typically require an order bill of lading endorsed in blank.

(v) *Certificate of Origin.* A certificate of origin is used to evi-

---

[13] See Appendix 4 for an example of an insurance policy.

[14] See Appendix 5 for an example of an insurance certificate.

[15] See §8:05.

[16] See Appendix 6 for an example of a bill of lading.

dence that a particular shipment of merchandise originated in a particular country.[17] Such certificates are required where special tariff exemptions, such as the Generalized System of Preferences, may be applicable to the merchandise, or where quotas or other non-tariff barriers may apply to merchandise from certain countries. Certificates of origin are normally authenticated by the local U.S. Consulate, Chamber of Commerce, trade association or government agency.

(vi) *Measurement and Inspection Certificate.* Because payment in an international sale is often made before the buyer has an opportunity to ascertain whether the shipment is consistent with the invoice and meets its specifications, foreign buyers often require that the goods be weighed, measured, analyzed or inspected by an independent third party at the port of shipment prior to the release of funds. In such cases, the contract of sale and letters of credit, if applicable, must set forth in detail the nature and content of the certificates to be delivered by the exporter prior to obtaining payment.[18]

(vii) *Draft.* A draft or bill of exchange is a negotiable instrument containing an order to pay a fixed amount at a specified time. A draft is used by the exporter to request payment from the buyer either directly or under a letter of credit. A draft may call for payment immediately upon presentation ("sight draft") or within a specified period thereafter ("time draft").[19] Once a time draft is accepted for payment, it becomes a "banker's acceptance" and may be sold at a discount as a financing technique.[20]

§ 8:07.   Payment Procedures.

Perhaps the principal factor that causes companies to resist selling their products abroad is fear of nonpayment. Even com-

[17] See Appendix 7 for an example of a certificate of origin.

[18] See Appendices 8 and 9 for examples of such certificates.

[19] See Appendix 10 for examples of a sight draft and a time draft.

[20] See §8:09 for a fuller discussion of using drafts in export sales.

panies who do not appreciate many of the risks associated with export trade understand that they are usually in for a costly and drawn out fight when trying to force a foreign buyer to pay for or return merchandise. Moreover, the risk of nonpayment is more substantial in an export sale independent of the buyer's credit-worthiness. Perhaps currency fluctuations have made the purchase uneconomic from the buyer's perspective. Factors outside of the buyer's control, such as government impediments or inavailability of foreign exchange, may also result in nonpayment.

§ 8:08. —Alternative Methods of Payment.

Fear of nonpayment has caused many companies to continue to resist exporting, even though a number of payment methods have been developed to reduce substantially the risk of nonpayment. While each of these methods of payment has certain costs or other disadvantages, they are often acceptable alternatives to both parties. Thus, an understanding of these methods of payment is often the key to a company's successful entry into export sales.

(i) *Cash in Advance.* The first and most attractive method of payment from the exporter's perspective is payment in advance. This shifts all of the risk of nonperformance on to the buyer. While it may therefore be inappropriate in many cases, payment in advance is not unreasonable where the buyer's background and financial condition are unknown or cannot be easily ascertained. Cash in advance is also appropriate where political and economic conditions in the buyer's country make payment uncertain. However, in order to control cash flow and foreign exchange, governments may sometimes limit the amount that their importers may pay in advance.

(ii) *Open Account.* An open account sale is the direct opposite from cash in advance. Here the exporter, in effect, finances the transaction for the buyer and relies on the buyer's ability and willingness to pay on the due date. All risk of nonpayment is borne by the exporter. While sales on open account are common in domestic transactions, they are employed in international sales only where the exporter faces little or no risk of nonpayment, either because of a long standing relationship between the parties or in transactions between affiliates. In such cases, the transaction can proceed without bearing the costs associated with documentary collections or letters of credit.

(iii) *Documentary Collections.* Payment on a collection basis, which is discussed more fully below, presents certain of the advantages of a letter of credit transaction without requiring the buyer to incur the costs associated with posting a letter of credit. Under this method, the exporter forwards all the export documents along with its draft to the buyer's bank overseas with instructions to release the documents upon payment or acceptance of the draft. The exporter thus maintains title to the goods until payment is made or the draft is accepted. At the same time the buyer is not obligated to pay until it receives the documents or within a certain period thereafter.

(iv) *Letters of Credit.* Payment by means of a documentary letter of credit is similar to payment on a collection basis. In both cases the exporter obtains payment for the merchandise by presenting the export documents together with its draft. In a documentary collection, however, the bank acts solely as an agent in the collection process and the exporter is still relying on the ability and willingness of the buyer to make payment. Where payment is made against a letter of credit, however, the bank's credit is substituted for that of the buyer, so that the exporter can look directly to the bank for payment. A documentary letter of credit thus assures the exporter of payment if the terms of the letter of credit are satisfied. At the same time, to the extent that the documentation evidences fulfillment of the seller's obligations, the buyer is assured of performance by the seller before the funds are released.[21]

[21] In addition to documentary credits, standby letters of credit are sometimes used where the parties have developed more mutual trust. In such cases, a single letter of credit is posted in favor of the exporter and is drawn on only if payment is not made. This eliminates the need of obtaining a separate letter of credit for each transaction.

§ 8:09.   —Documentary Collections.

Payment on a collection basis normally involves four players: the buyer (importer) and its bank and the seller (exporter) and its bank. When the buyer and seller agree that payment will proceed on a collection basis, they should also agree on what documents will have to be produced by the seller in order to collect payment. Once the seller completes production of the goods, it delivers them to the carrier for shipment. The corresponding bill of lading, together with the invoice, insurance certificate and any other export documentation required by the terms of the export sales contract are then presented by the seller to its bank together with its draft for the agreeed purchase price drawn on the buyer. The seller's bank will then forward these documents to the buyer's bank with instructions to deliver the documents only upon payment or acceptance of the draft. Since the documents are typically shipped by airmail, they normally arrive before the goods. The importer must obtain the documents from its bank in order to claim the goods when they arrive at the port.

The next step in the collection process depends on the nature of the draft. In the case of a sight draft, payment is due immediately upon presentation of the draft. Thus, the buyer's bank may not release the documents to the buyer unless and until the importer authorizes payment of the draft. Sight draft collections thus protect the exporter by allowing it, through the agency of the bank, to retain title to the goods until it has been paid. At the same time, the buyer is assured of receiving the goods once payment has been made. Sight draft collections are customarily abbreviated "D/P" for "documents against payment."

Where the exporter has agreed to extend terms to the buyer, a time draft is employed. A time draft calls for payment at a specific time in the future or within a certain period (such as 30, 90 or 180 days) after the draft is presented to the buyer's bank. In order for the buyer to obtain the documents, it must "accept" the draft, meaning that it agrees to pay it when due. A time draft collection, however, is considerably less advantageous to the exporter than a sight draft collection. Not only does the exporter have to wait for payment, but it has given up title to the merchandise and is relying solely on the buyer's willingness and ability to pay when the draft is due. There is no liability on the part of the collecting bank if the buyer should fail to honor the draft. A time draft collection is customarily abbreviated "D/A" for "documents against acceptance." Time drafts are also sometimes referred to as trade acceptances.

It is also possible to use a "clean" draft in the collection process. Under this procedure, the export documents are forwarded directly to the buyer and only the draft is presented to the buyer's bank. Because this procedure does not provide for the control of the merchandise in the manner accorded by documentary drafts, it is not very common in international trade. Clean draft collections are only customary where the goods may have been sold on open account but where a draft is required for exchange control or other legal purposes.

Once the draft has been paid or accepted in accordance with its terms, the documents are released to the buyer or its agent, allowing it to receive delivery of the merchandise from the carrier and to clear it through customs. When payment is made, the funds are then transferred back to the exporter through banking channels in accordance with its instructions.

§ 8:10. —Documentary Letters of Credit.

As noted above, the principal disadvantage of payment by means of a documentary collection is that the exporter must still rely on the willingness and ability of the buyer to ultimately pay the draft. In many cases, particularly in the early stages of a commercial relationship between the exporter and importer, this credit risk is unacceptable. The ability of the exporter to control title to the merchandise under a documentary collection may be of little consolation where it has incurred all the costs associated with production and shipment, especially for customized goods which may have little or no other market.

The letter of credit was developed to deal with this risk. By definition, a documentary letter of credit is a commitment, usually expressed in a formal letter, in which a bank (the issuing bank), at the request of and in accordance with the instructions of its customer (the buyer), undertakes to reimburse or cause to be reimbursed a third party (the exporter) against presentation of documents and compliance with the terms and conditions of the credit. In effect, the issuing bank is substituting its own credit standing for that of the buyer, allowing the exporter to look directly to the bank for payment.

At the same time, the letter of credit does not guarantee payment; the exporter must comply strictly with the terms of the credit and do so prior to its expiration. The letter of credit also does not assure the buyer that the goods shipped will be those invoiced. Banks deal only in documents, not in the goods themselves, and if the documents are in accordance with the letter of credit, payment will be made regardless of the condition of the goods. While the buyer can partially protect itself against shortages or receipt of inferior merchandise by providing for the delivery of inspection certificates, it is still relying to some extent on the integrity of the exporter.

Letters of credit may be revocable or irrevocable. A revocable letter of credit may be modified or canceled by the issuing bank at any time without notice to the beneficiary. Revocable letters of credit thus accord little protection to an exporter and are rarely used in international trade. An irrevocable letter of credit, on the other hand, cannot be altered or modified without the consent of both the applicant (the exporter) and the beneficiary (the buyer). Exporters relying on a letter of credit for payment must thus insist that the credit be issued in irrevocable form. Letters of credit are deemed to be revocable unless they expressly state that they are irrevocable.

Letters of credit are also either confirmed or advised. A confirmed letter of credit is one in which the exporter's local bank (the confirming bank) adds its own liability under the letter of credit. Thus, the exporter may look directly to the confirming bank for payment, and need not rely on the issuing bank in the foreign jurisdiction. If the letter of credit is not confirmed by the bank in the beneficiary's country, such bank merely advises the beneficiary that the credit has been opened in its favor. In such case, the advising bank is not liable under the credit and will make payment to the beneficiary only if the issuing bank has funds available or has made some other arrangement with the advising bank. From the exporter's perspective, a confirmed irrevocable letter of credit is thus most desirable in such transactions.

The life cycle of a letter of credit begins when the buyer agrees with the exporter to pay for a shipment of goods by means of a letter of credit. Once the price and other terms have been agreed upon, the buyer goes to its bank (the issuing bank) and completes an application for the letter of credit as well as a letter of credit agreement. The application includes the relevant information concerning the applicant (buyer) and beneficiary (exporter), the tenor of the draft (sight or time), a description of the merchandise, the price-delivery terms (e.g., F.O.B., C.I.F.,) and the point of shipment. The application must also set forth the amount of the credit, which must include not only the cost of the goods but shipping insurance, inspection and processing charges, agent fees, and other costs to be borne by the buyer. Since these additional costs are unknown at the time of the application, some importers customarily estimate these charges and add 10% to insure coverage. The application also calls for the expiration date, which is the last date on which the seller may present the documents for payment. If the credit calls for presentation of the documents at the counters of the issuing bank, they must be mailed in sufficient time to reach the issuing bank by such date. The letter of credit also normally states the number of days after shipment during which the documents can be presented. If no date is stated, the documents must be presented within 21 days of shipment.

After reviewing and approving the application, the issuing bank will issue the letter of credit in accordance with the application, and forward the same, by airmail or coded cable, to the beneficiary's bank.[22] The beneficiary's bank, whether acting in an advising

---

[22] See Appendix 11 for example of an export letter of credit.

or confirming capacity, will then forward on the original letter of credit to the seller. At that time, the seller should review carefully the terms of the credit to insure that they are consistent with the sales contract or accepted purchase order. Particular attention should be paid to whether the amount is sufficient, whether all the documents will be available and whether shipment can be made and the documents presented before the expiration date. Except for certain variances permitted under the Uniform Customs and Practices for Documentary Credits (Publication 400) with respect to the quantity of merchandise and certain other terms, the slightest discrepancy between the exporter's performance and the requirements under the letter of credit, such as shipment one day after a specified shipment date, entitles the issuing bank to refuse payment under the credit.[23]

Either the buyer or seller may request changes in the letter of credit prior to the presentation of the documents. The proposed amendments are transmitted between the banks for approval by both parties and, once approved, the amendment becomes binding.

Having satisfied itself with the letter of credit, the seller than ships the merchandise and assembles the export documentation called for by the credit. These documents are then presented to the beneficiary's bank which may have either advised or confirmed the credit, or may be simply authorized to negotiate the documents (a "negotiating bank"). The advising or confirming bank will review the documents to insure that there are no discrepancies with the terms of the credit. Prompt presentment of the documents may not only be required under the credit but gives the beneficiary more time to correct any discrepancies before expiration of the credit. If no discrepancies are discovered, the bank, if it has confirmed the credit, will pay the draft, forward the documents on to the issuing bank or the applicant in accordance with the credit, and obtain reimbursement from the issuing bank. Even if the local bank has only advised the credit, it will often pay the draft if it has a good relationship with the beneficiary and/or the issuing or

---

[23] See Appendix 12 for a list of common discrepancies.

confirming bank. Otherwise, it will merely pass the documents on to the confirming or issuing bank.[24]

The foregoing summary of the procedures involved in a letter of credit transaction does not include the many refinements that may come into play in a particular transaction or the special types of credits that may be appropriate in certain cases. There is an abundance of excellent literature which deals with these subjects in detail. One point that does warrant mention, however, is the use of letters of credit to provide financing to the buyer through bankers' acceptances.

By definition, a bankers' acceptance is a negotiable instrument created by a bank to provide credit for financing a specific commercial transaction. In the context of an import/export transaction, a bankers' acceptance is created when the beneficiary of the credit presents a time draft which is accepted for payment by the bank itself. When a bank accepts the draft or bill of exchange by making the appropriate notions on its face, the accepted draft becomes a binding obligation to pay on the part of the bank. While the beneficiary (seller) has agreed to give the buyer terms by using a time draft, once the draft has been accepted by the bank, it has the option of immediately converting the instrument into cash by selling it at a discount, usually to the accepting bank. Because of their flexibility, bankers' acceptances have become an increasingly popular way of financing international trade.

§ 8:11.   Foreign Currency Aspects.

One final aspect relevant to the structure of the export transaction relates to the risks presented by the use of a foreign currency. While many exporters, particularly in the United States, follow a strict policy of insisting on payment in U.S. dollars, this may not always be possible and in certain cases may not even be desirable.

[24] See Appendix 13 for an illustration of the complete life cycle of a confirmed letter of credit in an export transaction.

A company which insists on quoting prices in U.S. dollars may, for example, exclude many foreign buyers who are willing and able to purchase the goods but have the same policy of dealing only in their own currency. In other cases, the foreign buyer may concede to payment in U.S. dollars but only in exchange for a lower price which more than allows it to cover the foreign exchange risk.

Obviously, most small and medium-sized companies are not in a position to predict world currency fluctuations over the weeks or months between the time of their quotation and the time payment is ultimately received. A company which quotes a price of 90,000 Deutsche mark on January 1 expecting to receive the equivalent of U.S. $36,000 based on the then existing exchange rate of 2.5 to 1 may lose its entire profit on the sale when the DM 90,000 it receives on June 1 buys only U.S. $30,000 due to the depreciation of the German currency to 3 to 1. These companies should therefore generally refrain from accepting this risk. But that is not to say that they should insist on structuring the transaction in U.S. dollars. What is important is that if a foreign currency is employed, the seller adequately protect itself against the foreign exchange risk.

The most common way of hedging foreign currency exposure in the export/import context is through foreign currency forward contracts, futures and options. A foreign currency forward contract represents an undertaking to buy or sell an agreed amount of a specified foreign currency on a specified date in the future. In the preceding example, the exporting company may hedge its foreign exchange risk on the Deutsch mark by entering into a forward contract on January 1 that would allow it to sell the DM 90,000 on June 1 at the January exchange rate of 2.5 to 1. Many banks do not charge their customers a commission for the forward contract. To the extent that the foreign currency has a higher interest rate than U.S. dollars, however, the forward contract will require the U.S. exporter to deliver more Deutsche marks for the same number of dollars. Because the exporter knows the precise difference, it can build it into the quotation and often pass this cost on to the buyer.

A futures contract is much like a forward contract but is standardized. Futures contracts are sold on exchanges in specified amounts at predetermined prices. While a commission is required to be paid, the overall cost is usually competitive with forward contracts. Unlike forward contracts, future contracts are seldom actually performed. Rather, they are sold before maturity, resulting in a gain or loss intended to offset the loss or gain on the underlying transaction.

Foreign currency option contracts represent a right to buy or sell a foreign currency future at a specified time in the future. By buying a foreign currency option, the exporter can acquire the right to sell a foreign currency at a set price (the "strike price") at the end of the option period. If the foreign currency depreciates, the exporter can exercise the option and sell the future contract for a profit. If, on the other hand, the foreign currency actually appreciates in value, the exporter can simply let the option contract expire and sell the foreign currency at the then-existing market price. In this way, the option allows the exporter to take advantage of the potential appreciation of the foreign exchange, where forward contracts and futures do not. The option holder can determine how much exposure to accept by setting the strike price farther from the current exchange rate. The cost of an option hedge consists of the contract price itself (including commission) plus this additional assumed exposure.[25]

[25] See generally Riehl, Foreign Exchange Markets: A Guide to Foreign Currency Operations (1979).

CHAPTER 9

ADDITIONAL CONSIDERATIONS IN EXPORT TRANSACTIONS

§9:01.   United States Export Controls.
§9:02.   Export Finance and Credit Insurance.
§9:03.   Countertrade.

§ 9:01.   United States Export Controls.

The United States maintains a comprehensive legal scheme designed to regulate sensitive exports. This scheme is primarily[1] based on the Export Administration Act of 1985 (EAA) and the Commerce Department Regulations adopted pursuant thereto. In general, the EAA is designed to control exports from the United States for one of three purposes: (i) to further national security and

---

[1] In addition to the export controls of general applicability administered by the Department of Commerce and imposed pursuant to the EAA, an additional set of controls imposed pursuant to the Trading with the Enemy Act and The Emergency Economic Powers Act are administered by the Treasury Department's Office of Foreign Assets Control. These additional controls govern shipments to certain countries, including Cuba, North Korea, Vietnam and Kampuchea (Cambodia). They also extend to wholly financial transactions and imports of products from such countries.

foreign policy objectives; (ii) to protect the short supply of certain commodities; or (iii) to advance other policies, including combatting terrorism, opposing cartels and other restrictive trade practices and promoting respect for human rights. The EAA contains a number of significant provisions which may affect exports, including authority for export embargoes and other enforcement mechanisms, reporting requirements and the antiboycott law discussed above. The discussion here, however, is limited to its rather complex export licensing system.

The licensing requirements under the EAA extend to the export of all[2] commodities from the United States to any foreign destination, as well as the re-export from foreign countries of any such commodities.[3] The term "commodity" includes "any article, material or supply except technical date."[4] Thus, an export license is required for virtually every conceivable export of U.S. products.

Despite these broad licensing requirements, many U.S. companies have been exporting for years without applying for a license and in many cases without even knowing that a license is required. This is because the EAA regulations themselves grant a "general" license for most export transactions. A "general" license is one that applies generally to specified transactions and may be relied upon by the exporter without the need to apply to the Department of Commerce for a specific license. Where a "general" license is not available, however, the exporter must apply for and obtain a specific "validated" license.

Thus, the initial question that the U.S. exporter must face is whether it must apply for a "validated" license for a contemplated transaction or can rely on a "general" license. The answer involves

[2] Certain commodities, such as defense articles on the munitions list, narcotics, natural gas, electricity and endangered fish and wildlife whose export is controlled by special laws or regulations are exempt from the EAA requirements. 15 CFR §§370.3(a)(3), 370.10.

[3] As discussed in §17:02, the EAA also imposes licensing requirements on exports or re-exports of U.S. technical data or products produced using U.S. technical data.

[4] 15 CFR §370.2.

a three-step search. First, the schedule of "country groups"[5] must be consulted to determine to which Country Group the commodity will be exported.[6] Each country, other than Canada which is covered specifically in the regulations,[7] is assigned to a group designed by the letter Q through Z. The second step is to consult the Commodity Control List[8] to determine whether a validated license is required for the export of the particular item to the Country Group in question. The process of finding the particular item on the Commodity Control List is similar to classifying it under the Tariff Schedules. Once the item is located, refer to the heading marked "Validated License Required." If the Country Group to which the export is destined is listed under such heading, a validated license must be obtained.[9] The third step in determining the requirements under the EAA for a particular export transaction consists of a review of the regulations[10] which impose "special restrictions."

An application for a validated export license is made by submitting an application form to the Department of Commerce together with its supporting documents.[11] The application calls for detailed information including the name and address of the applicant, the foreign purchaser, the ultimate and any intermediate consignees

[5] Contained in Supplement 1 to 15 CFR Part 370.

[6] See Appendix 14 for the list of Country Groups.

[7] 15 CFR §370.3.

[8] The Commodity Control List is published as Supplement No. 1 to 15 CFR §399.1.

[9] In some cases, a limited amount of the particular commodity, such as a sample, may be exported to country groups T and V under a "General License Limited Value (GLV)" despite the need for a validated license for larger commercial shipments. The dollar limit for such shipments appear in the Commodity Control List under the column entitled "GTV Value Limit, T&V." See 15 CFR §371.5

[10] 15 CFR Parts 376, 378, and 385.

[11] Application forms (Form ITA-6228) are available from any Department of Commerce District Office or from the headquarters in Washington, D.C. Instructions for completing and submitting the application appear in 15 CFR Part 372.

and the end user, as well as the description, quantity and net value of the merchandise. While the documents required by the application depend on the particular license requested,[12] the applicant must normally submit one or more destination or end-user certificates designed to prevent the merchandise from being resold to a prohibited end-user. Special documents are also required to be submitted for computer equipment, machine tools, and certain other commodities.[13] In other cases the exporters are required to maintain certain records.[14]

While most applications for validated licenses are processed within one or two months, those requiring review by the other U.S. agencies or by the Coordinating Committee (CoCom) may take considerably longer. Denials may be appealed following the procedure described in the regulations.[15] Failure to comply with the EAA's export licensing requirements may result in the imposition of criminal or civil sanctions, including suspension of export privileges.

§ 9:02. Export Finance and Credit Insurance.

In many cases, a producer of a competitive product may be able to sell successfully abroad without offering terms to the foreign buyer. As competition increases, however, the sale may go to the seller who offers the most generous financing. Financing is also

---

[12] The regulations under the EAA create various types of both general and validated licenses. Individual validated licenses cover particular transactions. Where related exports are contemplated as part of an entire project, as an arrangement with a particular distributor, or as part of a supporting services agreement, consideration should be given to an application for a Project License, Distribution License or Service Supply License, respectively, which authorize a number of related exports over a period of time. These and other special licenses are discussed in 15 CFR Part 393.

[13] See generally 15 CFR Parts 375 and 376.

[14] See 15 CFR Part 387.

[15] 15 CFR §389.2.

important in the case of buyers located in developing countries where local credit is expensive, if not completely unavailable. In some countries, local exchange control regulations may require the seller to grant terms as a condition of the sale. For these reasons, the exporter's ability to provide favorable financing is often critical to its success in generating foreign sales.

In the discussion of documentary collections and letters of credit,[16] the use of time drafts as a means of extending terms to the buyer as well as their convertion into bankers' acceptances in order to obtain the funds immediately was mentioned. However, while these are effective measures for extending short-term financing (i.e., up to 180 days), they are rarely used for medium or long-term arrangements. Moreover, as the volume of export sales expands, even the provision of short-term financing can become an economic burden on the exporter.

In such cases, the exporter may look to its bank to provide the financing. Normally the exporter will provide the bank with various information about the sale and the purchaser. The bank will also develop its own information about the purchaser's financial condition, using such sources as International Dun & Bradstreet Reports and World Traders Data Reports, bank references, trade references and financial reports. In some cases, financing may be denied not on the basis of the creditworthiness of the purchaser but as a result of the bank's internal country exposure limits. Where country limits are not a problem and the bank is satisfied as to the buyer's creditworthiness, the financing may be provided, either directly or through the purchase of the receivable from the exporter.

Where the bank determines that the buyer's creditworthiness, considered by itself, does not warrant the extension of credit, several options exist to obtain the financing. One possibility is to obtain guarantees from the buyer's local bank, from a parent or other affiliate of the buyer or from a governmental agency in the buyer's country. In other cases the bank may require that the receivable be purchased with recourse to the exporter. Still another

[16] See §§8:09, 8:10.

alternative, and often the most desirable both to the exporter and its bank, is having the credit guaranteed by a U.S. government agency and/or insuring the credit against nonpayment.

The furnishing of a loan guarantees and credit insurance in the context of export trade are two of the principal functions performed by the Export Import Bank of the United States (Eximbank) and its affiliate, the Foreign Credit Insurance Agency (FCIA). Eximbank was organized in 1934 as a wholly-owned government corporation to facilitate and finance U.S. exports. The FCIA is a private association of more than 50 U.S.-based property and casualty insurance companies which provides export credit insurance to exporters of U.S. made goods and services. Participation in both Eximbank and FCIA programs is available for all types of goods or services (other than military equipment), provided they meet domestic content requirements.

Coverage under both the loan guarantees and insurance against nonpayment is usually less than 100% of the contract price, so that the exporter and its commercial bank normally maintain some risk. In addition, coverage normally extends only to designated political risks (i.e., nonavailability of foreign exchange; war, revolution and civil disturbance; import or export permit revocation; diversion of goods; and expropriation or confiscation) or commercial risks (i.e., insolvency or bankruptcy and protracted default). Other common reasons for nonpayment, such as product disputes or warranty claims, nonacceptance of shipment or nonenforceability of the debt instrument, are risks still borne by the exporter or its bank.

Eximbank offers a number of programs or facilities to finance exports. Under its Commercial Bank Guarantee Program, for example, Eximbank will guarantee commercial bank loans made to finance exports of capital goods for between 180 days and five years (seven years for certain goods). In sales to private sector buyers, Eximbank will require a down payment of 15% from the buyer, and after the exporter retains an additional 10%, will cover 85% of the commercial risk and 100% of the political risk on the remaining contract price. An application for an Eximbank guarantee under this program is made directly to the exporter's bank who forwards it on to Eximbank to issue the commitment. In some cases, the commercial banks have been delegated authority to automatically secure Eximbank guarantees. Eximbank charges a flat fee on the guaranteed portion of the financial obligation which is based on the terms of the loan.

Other Eximbank programs include a Bank-to-Bank Guarantee Program to cover U.S. bank credits extended to local banks to be used for local purchases of U.S. products, a Discount Loan Program providing U.S. banks with funds to be made available to foreign purchases of U.S. goods at favorable rates, and a Direct Credit and Financial Guarantee Program for long-term financing of major (i.e., $5 million or more) exports. Eximbank has also recently introduced a Working Capital Guarantee Program which guarantees loans of up to twelve months for specific export-related activities by exporters who would not otherwise be eligible for such loans from banks. By providing financing in anticipation of export sales for such activities as design and engineering expenses, raw materials and manufacturing costs, this new program fills an important gap in the area of export financing.

The FCIA offers a variety of insurance policies covering non-payment by foreign purchasers due to the political and commercial risks described above. The policies correspond generally with the programs offered by Eximbank. While policies may be issued directly to banks, they are more commonly obtained directly by the exporter who assigns the proceeds to its commercial bank as a condition of such bank's purchase of the underlying receivable. FCIA insurance not only limits the exporter's exposure on financial export sales, but also frequently allows it to offer more attractive financing, since the insurance decreases the banker's commercial risk and country exposure. As suggested above, FCIA insurance may also be necessary to induce a commercial bank to extend financing.

The FCIA Short-Term Policy covers products such as raw materials, consumer goods and spare parts, which are traditionally sold on repayment terms of 180 days or less. Coverage extends to 100%

of the political risk and 90% of the commercial risk. Since no down payment is required under this program, coverage extends to the entire contract price but is subject to a first loss deductible for losses due to a commercial risk. In order to spread the risk, however, FCIA requires that the bulk of the insured party's export sales be included under the Short-Term Policy. This prevents the exporter from insuring only troublesome accounts or accounts in countries where the political risk is great. Short-Term Policies may be obtained directly from FCIA or certain private brokers and are renewable annually. Premiums vary with each exporter based on the terms of the sale, the exporter's collection experience, and the spread of country risk represented by the exporter's portfolio of foreign trade receivables.

The FCIA Medium-Term Policy is designed to cover the obligations arising out of the export of capital goods on terms of 181 days to five (and occasionally seven) years. Repayment terms, product eligibility and cost are identical to Eximbank's Commercial Bank Guarantee Program. Unlike Short-Term Policies, Medium-Term Policies are issued for individual transactions and there is no requirement for such policies to cover most of the exporter's foreign sales. FCIA also offers a Short-Term/Medium-Term (Dealer) Policy designed for exporters who maintain dealer or distributor networks abroad. The Dealer Policy contains elements of both the Short-Term and Medium-Term Policy that essentially allow the U.S. manufacturer to floor plan the foreign dealer's inventory for up to 270 days and convert the policy into medium-term insurance once the equipment is sold to a customer. Finally, FCIA offers a Master Policy which also contains elements of the Short-Term and Medium-Term policies but which can be designed to fit the particular needs of the U.S. exporter.

In addition to the Eximbank and FCIA programs, there are certain other sources of loan guarantees and credit insurance for export financing. The Small Business Administration offers bank guarantees for export credit and direct loans for export-related working capital under programs available to exporters falling within the definition of a "small business." Various state governments have also created facilities to provide export finance and related assistance to encourage export production by companies located within such states. The Private Sector Export Funding Corporation (PEFCO) is an additional source of financing for loans made under certain Eximbank programs, especially for long-term commitments where commercial bank financing is not available. Certain private insurance companies also offer policies covering nonpayment of export-generated receivables similar to those offered by the FCIA. Legal and other advisers in the area of international trade should become familiar with all of these programs in order to assist in structuring the most favorable arrangements for their clients.

§ 9:03. Countertrade.

In a $12 million sale of locomotive and diesel engines by GM to the government of Yugoslavia, GM reportedly agreed to purchase $4 million in Yugoslavian cutting tools that it exported and sold to a U.S.-based tool manufacturer for cash. A U.S. jeans manufacturer sold the Hungarian government equipment and designs necessary to manufacture blue jeans, and agreed to purchase a portion of the jeans produced in the plant. The firm reportedly buys approximatley 10% of the output of the plant for resale around the world. The Yamal pipeline in the U.S.S.R. involves a consortium of Western companies who are supplying pipe, production equipment and technology in exchange for natural gas rights. Each of these is an example of countertrade, an increasingly popular technique which companies use to enhance their export sales.

Countertrade can generally be defined as any means of trade in which the seller agrees to purchase goods from the party to which a sale is made. It includes any commercial arrangement in which purchases offset sales. Modern countertrade began to emerge in Europe after World War I as Germany tried to rebuild with an unstable currency. Many experts now estimate that more than one-third of the dollar volume of all international trade is done through countertrade. The U.S. Department of Commerce estimates that the amount will increase to one-half by the end of the century.

Before the beginning of this decade, countertrade was largely confined to the U.S.S.R. and Eastern Europe where state-operated trading houses found it to be one of the only means of creating an export market for local production. In recent years, however, countertrade transactions have experienced dramatic growth in the developing countries. This is particularly true in Latin America where servicing of enormous external debts consumes much of the foreign currency required to purchase imports in a conventional transaction. In China, efforts to develop in the areas of agriculture, industry, national defense, and science, combined with the absence of substantial hard currency reserves and a general aversion to foreign debt, have resulted in increased use of countertrade transactions.

Countertrade presents a number of advantages both to the buyer and to the seller. From the buyer's perspective, it preserves hard currencies, improves the domestic balance of payments, allows the buyer to gain access to new markets for its products and creates opportunities to upgrade manufacturing facilities and obtain new technologies. From the seller's perspective, countertrade creates sales opportunities in markets which are closed to traditional export sales, creates economical sources of supplies (through compensation trading), allows the seller to gain prominence in new markets, and creates new sources of revenue (e.g., income from the sale of goods purchased in a countertrade transaction).

The most common forms of countertrade include counterpurchase, compensation trading, and barter. Counterpurchase normally involves an agreement on the part of the seller to sell products to the buyer and to purchase from such buyer goods which are totally unrelated to the items which it is selling. It is exemplified by McDonnell Douglas' sale of commercial aircraft to the government of Yugoslavia and agreement to purchase substantial quantities of Yugoslavian glassware, cutting tools, leather coats, and canned hams. The seller is actually paid in currency and given a period of time (three to five years is common in Eastern Europe) to fulfill its purchase obligations. The seller is typically given a list of goods to choose from which are either of low quality or in excess supply. Sellers who do not have inhouse countertrading capability often resell the goods through trading companies or directly to customers.

In compensation or buy-back trading, a private firm agrees to sell equipment, technology or an entire plant and to purchase and export a portion of the output produced from such equipment or technology. A celebrated example of compensation trading is Occidental Petroleum's $20 billion transaction with the U.S.S.R. under which Occidental constructed and financed ammonia plants and agreed to purchase quantities produced in the plants over a 20-year period. Like counterpurchase, compensation trading usually involves the use of actual currency. These transactions, however, typically involve longer commitments (ten years or more) and greater funds than do counterpurchase transactions. In addition, compensation trading arrangements typically involve goods which are of marketable quality and are in international demand. The seller is normally able to negotiate a price which is below the world market so as to obtain a profit on the sale.

In a barter transaction, no currency is involved. The private firm sells specified goods or services and agrees to take payment in kind. This type of transaction is exemplified by Pepsico's sale of soft drinks in Korea, Thailand, China, and Poland in exchange for toys, glassware, cashmere, and beer. Barter is often used as a means of "liberating" blocked currencies or avoiding exchange controls, particularly in Latin America and Southeast Asia.

Certain companies have developed their own in-house countertrade trade expertise. These companies use countertrade divisions or subsidiaries to instruct international sales personnel, including distributors, of the advantages and risks of countertrade and to assist them in structuring transactions and disposing of purchased goods. They may also be operated as independent profit centers which provide countertrade and other international financial services to unrelated firms as well as their parents.

Those companies that engage in countertrade on a more infrequent basis typically use trading houses that specialize in structuring and financing countertrade transactions and in disposing of the goods which the foreign seller is obligated to purchase. While larger international trading houses handle commodities on a world-wide basis, often using three or more buyers and sellers in a single transaction, they may also be expensive. Although typical brokerage fees run from 5% to 10% of the purchase price of the goods, fees of up to 30% are not uncommon. For this reason, some companies choose to dispose of the goods internally, either as raw materials or components in manufacturing operations, or in non-productive capacities such as office furnishings, construction materials or employee incentives. The exporter should also consider requiring a subcontractor or supplier to purchase a portion of the goods or attempt to sell the goods to foreign importers, distributors and end-users.

Before entering into negotiations that may involve countertrade, the exporter should consider (i) the percentage of the original sale which can be covered by countertrade; (ii) the types of goods which will be accepted (e.g., only goods which will be used in the exporter's manufacturing operations); and (iii) how to use or dispose of such goods. Preparation should also include the study of prior agreements or consultation with experienced negotiators to learn what the particular government has required and what is subject to negotiation.

It is generally advisable to negotiate all other terms before the price is finalized to avoid being surprised by a countertrade proposal. One should also determine the cost of disposing of the goods (including transportation, storage, tariffs, taxes, and insurance) and include such cost in the price quotation. An attempt should be made to obtain the widest possible list of products to choose from to satisfy a counter-purchase obligation and, in the absence of guarantees on product availability and delivery schedules, to have the longest possible period to complete the purchases. If a penalty clause is included for failure to meet the purchase obligation, the agreement should specify that the payment of penalties will constitute a full release of the seller's purchase obligation. If acceptable pricing formulas for the products to be purchased are not available, prices should be based on acceptable international price, fair market value or most favored customer price. Acceptable quality guarantee provisions should be included which either allow return of products which are inferior or which impose penalties for shipment of nonconforming products. Care should be taken to insure that the sale of products in potential markets will not violate distribution rights of third parties. In some cases, it may be possible to obtain exclusive distribution rights for the products to be purchased. Finally, the countertrade transaction obligation should be transferrable.

While countertrade may pose a number of significant risks, it also offers an important new opportunity for exanding export sales. Careful negotiation and appropriate protections in the purchase agreements can minimize these risks and make countertrade an appealing option for any U.S. exporter.[17]

---

[17] For additional background on countertrade, see L. Welt, Trade Without Money: Barter and Countertrade (1984); T. McVey, "Countertrade: Commercial Practices, Legal Issues and Policy Dilemmas," 16 Law & Pol'y Int'l Bus 1 (1984).

PART III—SUGGESTIONS FOR FURTHER READING

Books

Dolan, J., The Law of Letters of Credit - Commercial and Standby Credits (1984) (1987 Cumm Supp).

Ezer, S., International Exporting Agreements (1987).

Liebman, J., Meyer, R., Johnson, R., Export Controls in the United States (1986).

Vishny, P., Guide to International Commercial Law (1984).

Articles

"Conference on Extraterritoriality for the Businessman and the Practicing Lawyer," 15 Law & Pol'y Int'l Bus 1095 (1983).

"Economics of the Application of Article 85 to Selective Distribution Systems," 7 Eur L Rev 83 (1982).

Liebman, "The Export Administration Act Amendments of 1985," 20 Int'l Law 362 (1986).

Sanders, "Trade Agreements: Selected Issues for Negotiating Terms: Including Issues of Payment, Countertrade, and the Use and Application of the International Sales of Goods Convention," in Negotiating and Drafting International Commercial Agreements (1986).

PART IV

FOREIGN AGENTS AND DISTRIBUTORS

CHAPTER 10

CONSIDERATIONS IN SELECTION OF FOREIGN AGENTS AND DISTRIBUTORS

§ 10:01. Decision To Engage Foreign Representation.

In many cases, the decision to engage foreign representation of one kind or another is part of a natural evolution of an exporter's activities in a foreign country. After repeated exports to the country, the seller may determine that the apparent acceptance of its product warrants appointment of a local representative who can develop the market much more effectively. The mere presence of a local agent or distributor who will be accountable to local customers is often a key to enhancing foreign sales. This local representative will also presumably advertise and promote the product and provide or facilitate provision of warranty and other services.

But the decision to establish local representation is not always based soley on marketing factors. In many countries, particularly in the Middle East, local laws prohibit the sale of foreign products other than through registered agents or distributors. Since these laws often require that the local representatives be nationals of the country or legal entities controlled by nationals, the selection of the local representative may also be partially dictated. Even where local law itself does not strictly require the use of local representatives, foreign companies often find that the complications of obtaining import permits or moving the goods through customs demands local assistance of some kind. Certain types of sales, such as those made to the local government, may also be possible, de jure or de facto, only through a local representative.

§ 10:02.   Distinctions Between Agents and Distributors.

The decision to engage foreign representation of some kind may thus be based on a number of different factors. Once made, however, the exporter must next consider the form that such local representation will take. Where the exporter is permitted and elects to organize its own subsidiary or branch to represent its interests, the legal arrangement between the parent and subsidiary is usually not particularly significant. Much more commonly, however, and particularly in the early stages of an exporter's development of a local market, the exporter will elect to engage an independent third party and to engage the same either as an agent or as a distributor. The legal distinction between these two is important.

In general, the sales representative or commission agent has four distinguishing characteristics: (i) it sells for the account of its principal and is compensated by a salary or by a commission based on the supplier's sales; (ii) it does not bear the economic risk of nonpayment, since the export sales contract is with, and payment made to, the principal; (iii) it does not usually inventory or deliver the goods but rather takes orders for shipment from the supplier directly to the customers; and (iv) it may or may not be authorized to bind the supplier depending on its authority. The distributor, on the other hand, usually: (i) buys and sells for its own account and is compensated by the markup it charges on the products it sells; (ii) bears the economic risk of sales and carries its customers' credit; (iii) warehouses and physically delivers the goods from its own inventory; and (iv) is an independent entity which has no power to bind the supplier.[1]

The foregoing characteristics suggest some of the advantages and disadvantages of both a foreign agent and a distributor. In general, an agent is significantly more under the control of the supplier. Its responsibilities are often limited to soliciting orders for the supplier's products and facilitating the movement of the merchandise through local customs once the order is accepted and the goods are shipped by the supplier. For tax reasons,[2] it is normally denied authority to bind the foreign supplier or to assume other responsibilities other than general promotional activities. At the same time, the fact that the representative does not bear the economic risk of nonpayment, that it does not maintain its own inventory, and that it can expose its principal to local liability are obvious drawbacks of this type of local representation. While foreign commission agents may be legal entities, just as often they are simply individuals who can also present certain problems under local labor laws.

The fact that distributors buy and sell for their own account, normally maintain their own inventories, and are legally distinct from their foreign supplier are important advantages of this type of local presence. Distributors also do not expose the supplier to the possibility of local taxation, and since they are normally legal entities rather than individuals, are rarely viewed as employees of the supplier protected by local labor law. Because of their typically greater size and resources, distributors commonly assume responsibility for servicing the products. On the other hand, a supplier loses some control when using distributors rather than agents. Distributors are normally free to develop the market in the manner and sell at the prices they deem fit. Distributors are also more likely to enjoy greater protections under special local laws.

[1] A. Saltoun & B. Spudis, "International Distribution and Sales Agency Agreements: Practical Guidelines for U.S. Exporters," 38 Bus Law 883 (1983).
[2] See § 11:05.

The terms "agent" and "distributor" are used where it is important to distinguish between these two types of foreign representation. For lack of a better term, "representative" or "dealer" are used to signify both agents and distributors.

§ 10:03. Selecting Foreign Representation.

The key to the successful utilization of any type of foreign representation is the selection of the proper person or entity. The business factors that go into this decision are the same as those in the case of a domestic agent or distributor: previous marketing experience, desire to promote the supplier's products, financial stability, reputation in the industry, adequacy of resources, etc. The problem in selecting foreign representation is first identifying who might be interested and then developing the relevant background information in order to qualify the potential candidates.

Identifying interested agents or distributors in a foreign jurisdiction can be much easier than is often perceived. As in the case of foreign suppliers discussed in Part II,[3] many trade publications regularly report on foreign representatives or distributors seeking to market specified types of foreign goods. Foreign representatives often advertise their availability in trade or other publications. Local chambers of commerce and the local branch of the U.S. Chamber of Commerce frequently act as a clearinghouse to put foreign suppliers together with local agents and distributors. The U.S. Department of Commerce, through its Agent/Distributor Service, also provides names and background information on local entities whom its foreign commercial service has identified as potential representatives.

Usually much more difficult than locating interested representatives is qualifying them by developing important background information. Even though the candidates can be presumed to cooperate by providing financial and other information of their own, it is often difficult to verify any of this information. At a

[3] See § 5:03.

minimum, foreign suppliers should satisfy themselves of the financial stability and resources of any serious candidate by checking bank references, obtaining audited financial statements, credit and other reports, such as Dun & Bradstreet profiles, if available, and by personally inspecting the proposed dealer's existing or proposed facilities. Dealers with an existing business in the industry may also show the exporter customer lists or provide other information evidencing their knowledge of and access to the market. Serious candidates may also have prepared business plans which demonstrate their desire to carry the products and their proposed marketing approach. In the end, however, nothing will substitute for the purely subjective evaluation a supplier can make by actually meeting the candidate or its personnel and spending a reasonable amount of time discussing each other's objectives and plans of action.

CHAPTER 11

LEGAL ASPECTS OF FOREIGN REPRESENTATION

§ 11:01. Local Laws Affecting Foreign Agents and Distributors.

In addition to the antitrust and tax laws discussed below, there are two principal types of laws that must be considered in preparing an agreement with a proposed local agent or distributor: those

123

governing their use generally and those governing their termination.[1]

Local laws governing the use of dealers or agents are mostly confined to the Middle East and certain socialist countries. Their objective is to protect the public from unscrupulous dealers who are compensated not so much for the services they perform but for sales they can create by using their political influence. In some cases these laws prohibit the use of dealers altogether. More commonly, however, these local laws prohibit their use or restrict their compensation only with respect to sales to government agencies. These laws may also prohibit the use of foreign nationals (including legal entities with a majority of foreign ownership) and/or prescribe registration and disclosure requirements for dealers. Local laws may also regulate a supplier's right to appoint exclusive dealers in a particular geographical location or impose substantive requirements, such as an obligation for the dealer to maintain an adequate inventory of spare parts. Many of these laws have complicity provisions which render the foreign supplier liable for the dealer's failure to comply. For these reasons, lawyers should review the local law applicable to any new sales agency or distribution arrangement, and encourage their clients to resist the temptation to simply use a standard agreement with prior consultation.

Far more common than the laws regulating the use of dealers are those governing their termination. These laws may be encountered anywhere in the world, including Europe, Asia, the Middle East and Latin America.[2] In general, they are designed to prevent foreign suppliers from using dealers to develop a local market and then to substitute their own local subsidiaries once a customer base has been established.

The most important of these laws are the specific statutes or policies requiring indemnification for agents or distributors which are unjustly terminated. These laws typically specify limited grounds under which a dealer may be terminated for cause, and

---

[1] See Appendixes 15 and 16 for a representative list of these local laws.

[2] A. Saltoun & B. Spudis, "International Distribution and Sales Agency Agreements: Practical Guidelines for U.S. Exporters," 38 Bus Law 883, at 914 (1983).

prescribe substantial prior notice of termination and/or compensation in the event of termination for any other reason. In some cases, the supplier's obligation may be limited to the repurchase of the dealer's inventory. In others, the supplier will be obligated to indemnify the dealer for lost profits and to reimburse it for various costs incurred in preparing for the acting as the supplier's representative. The calculation of lost profits is commonly based on the dealer's average profits in prior years, with consideration given to the length of time it served as a dealer and the amount that would have been earned during the statutorily prescribed notice period or the unexpired term of the contract. If the supplier is required, for example, to reimburse the dealer for substantial expenditures, such as a new warehouse used to maintain inventory of the supplier's products, this cost together with a penalty of three or four years of anticipated profits can reach substantial proportions.[3]

Even if a particular jurisdiction does not have specific legislation protecting local dealers, care should be taken to insure that the representative is not covered by local labor laws which may have a similar effect. In some countries of Europe and Latin America, labor laws have been construed to extend to representatives under certain circumstances, requiring severance pay in the event of unjustified termination as well as payment of social security, disability, pension, health or other benefits. In general, these laws are applicable only where the representative is an individual and where certain other factors such as the degree of the supplier's control over the representative and the manner of compensation render the relationship similar to employment. For these reasons, agents rather than distributors usually present a greater risk of being protected by local labor laws.

§ 11:02. Antitrust Aspects.

Foreign representatives will often seek the exclusive right to sell a supplier's merchandise in a particular country or other geograph-

---

[3] Chapter 12 discusses some of the contractual strategies, such as the use of short-term, renewable contracts in lieu of a longer term agreement to limit the supplier's exposure under these laws.

ical territory. At the same time, the supplier may insist that the foreign dealer handle no other goods which compete with its merchandise. These geographical exclusivity and noncompetition provisions, and certain other terms sometimes included in international sales agent and distributor agreements, raise certain questions under U.S. and other applicable antitrust law.

§ 11:03.   —United States Antitrust Law.

The initial question under U.S. antitrust law is jurisdictional: will the proposed restraints have a demonstrable "effect" on U.S. commerce. If the effects test is met, the law may be applied to activities taking place outside U.S. borders. A helpful resource in considering the treatment of dealer agreements and other foreign arrangements under U.S. antitrust law is the Antitrust Guidelines for International Operations published by the U.S. Department of Justice in 1977.[4]

The granting of exclusive geographical territories by U.S. exporters rarely presents a problem under U.S. antitrust law. Even the appointment of an entire network of foreign distributors with exclusive rights in their respective territories normally would have no effect on U.S. commerce. On the other hand, where the supplier seeks to enforce this exclusivity by imposing restraints on its U.S. distributors from exporting to the territory, there is an effect on U.S. commerce. These restraints can normally be justified, however, based on the need to develop a particular market and to maintain quality control and goodwill.

The noncompetition provisions present slightly more problems but are also usually permissible under U.S. antitrust law. Since the prohibition may foreclose U.S. competitors from selling into the foreign market, an effect on U.S. commerce can often be found. The key issue is then whether "the foreign distributor were such an important outlet in its own country that the product exclusivity

---

[4] U.S. Department of Justice, Antitrust Guidelines for International Operations (1977) (hereinafter cited as the "Antitrust Guide").

feature of the agreement necessarily restricted in an important way the ability of other firms to export to the market."[5] In general, any foreign market with a sufficient size to effect a U.S. supplier's business will have more than one dealer. The noncompetition clause should thus present an obstacle under U.S. antitrust law only in exceptional circumstances.

United States antitrust law may also come into play with respect to cross appointments, tying arrangements and restrictions on foreign distributors importing to the United States. Cross appointments, where a foreign or U.S. manufacturer appoint each other as exclusive dealers of the other's products in their respective jurisdictions, are sometimes viewed as agreements not to compete. In an international context, however, the Justice Department has indicated that such arrangements are permissible where they are designed to assist in the establishment of the manufacturer in a new market overseas and are of limited duration.[6] Tying arrangements, where a representative's right to sell a given product is conditioned on its selling certain other goods, may also be justifiable, under "rule of reason" analysis, for business necessities. It may, for example, be necessary from the supplier's perspective that the sale of a finished product be tied to the acquisition of certain spare parts in order to insure the availability of service parts in the foreign jurisdiction. Restrictions on resales back into the United States are normally permitted in order to develop or preserve the supplier's domestic market, provided they are not part of an overall price-fixing scheme.

§ 11:04.   —Foreign Antitrust Law.

While U.S. antitrust law often extends to international sales agency and distribution agreements, it seldom presents major obstacles to the U.S. supplier. This is not always true, however, with respect to foreign antitrust law, the most important of which

---

[5] Antitrust Guide at 47, n 80.

[6] Antitrust Guide at 47.

is contained in the competition rules of the European Economic Community (EEC) and in the Japanese Monopoly Law.

Under Article 85(1) of the Treaty of Rome, practices or agreements which materially prevent, restrict or distort competition, including arrangements which limit or control markets, are prohibited. Article 85(1) thus prevents U.S. supplier from restricting its distributor within the EEC from selling competing products or selling outside an exclusive territory. Prohibited agreements are void, and the parties could be subject to substantial fines. There are, however, a number of situations in which an agreement apparently falling within the scope of Article 85(1) may be exempt from its prohibitions. Under the so-called de minimus rule,[7] an arrangement affecting less than 5% of the market between parties whose combined annual gross revenues (including affiliates) are under 200 million European Units of Account (approximately U.S. $180 million) are exempt. Such arrangements are deemed to have no material effect on market conditions. Second, the parties may apply to the EEC Commission for an exemption under Article 85(3). Finally, the Commission has published a block exemption pursuant to Article 85(3) under which exclusive distribution agreements with the EEC are permitted provided they do not contain certain restrictions. A reciprocal undertaking by a distributor not to manufacture or distribute competing goods and to purchase the relevant goods only from the supplier is permitted. In addition, while the supplier cannot completely restrict the EEC distributor from selling abroad, restraints can be included in the agreement which prohibit it from seeking customers, establishing a branch or maintaining a distribution depot outside its assigned territory. The Commission has also indicated that distribution agreements relating to consumer goods which do not offer customers a Europe-wide warranty could violate the Treaty. It should also be noted that Article 85(1) has consistently been applied only to independent distributors and not to commission agents.

Japanese antitrust law also impacts agreements with a Japanese

---

[7] Notice Concerning Agreements of Minor Importance, J.O. Comm. Eur. (No. C86)(231/02) (September 3, 1986).

distributor. Exclusive agreements between competitors may have the effect of dividing markets which could violate the prohibitions on private monopolization (Article 3), unreasonable restraints on trade (Article 6) and unfair business practices (Article 19) of the Japanese Antimonopoly Law.[8] Agreements of this type which result in the Japanese party achieving a 25% or greater market share may also constitute an unfair business practice.[9] Moreover, the Import Distributorship Agreement Guidelines under the Antimonopoly Law generally prohibit a foreign supplier from restraining a Japanese distributor from selling outside Japan or from purchasing or selling competitive products.[10]

While the antitrust laws in other parts of the world are ordinarily less developed as those in the EEC and Japan, proposed agency distribution arrangements that contain territorial or product exclusivity provisions or other arrangements affecting competition should always be reviewed in accordance with applicable local law.

§ 11:05. Tax Aspects.

The U.S. Tax aspects of international business transactions are beyond the scope of this work. Exporting does present various tax issues that should be explored. Among these issues are domestic and foreign source income and the tax treatment of each. This is important in the export context since, by structuring the transaction to provide for passage of title either within or outside the United States, the U.S. exporter can often elect to realize domestic or foreign source income, respectively.[11] The exporter should also consider the use of Foreign Sales Corporations (FSC's). An FSC is a foreign subsidiary of a U.S. manufacturer which is accorded

[8] Antimonopoly and Fair Trade Maintenance Act, Law No. 54, 1947.

[9] Antimonopoly Act Guidelines for Sole Import Distributorship Etc. Agreements, November 22, 1972.

[10] Id. See generally Kitagawa, Doing Business in Japan Part IX, §7:03 (1984).

[11] IRC §§ 861(a)(6), 862(a)(6); Treas Reg §1.861-7.

special tax treatment allowing the manufacturer to substantially reduce its taxable income on export sales which are effected through the FSC.

What is important for purposes of the discussion of foreign agents and distributors, however, is the possibility that these foreign representatives may subject the U.S. supplier to local taxation. In general, a U.S. company will be subject to local taxation on the income generated in a foreign country only if it is deemed to have a "permanent establishment" in such country. In countries with which the United States has a tax treaty, the treaty will usually define the term "permanent establishment." Under the current model tax treaty, an independent distributor is not normally regarded as a permanent establishment of the U.S. supplier. An agent, on the other hand, will frequently be deemed a permanent establishment of its principal, thus subjecting the principal to foreign taxation, if it is authorized to accept orders or assume other obligations on the part of its principal, in some cases even where it has no fixed place of business in the foreign country. Where no treaty exists, these same factors are generally analyzed to determine whether the supplier will be subject to local taxation.

While most foreign taxes paid by a U.S. company are creditable against its U.S. tax liability, this is not always the case. Moreover, depending on its other international activities, the U.S. taxpayer may find itself in an excess tax credit posture where the full credit cannot be taken as a result of the foreign tax credit limitation. The necessity of filing tax returns and obtaining tax receipts in the foreign jurisdiction presents additional problems.

For these reasons, it is generally advisable to structure the supplier's relationship with its foreign representative in such a manner as to avoid the possibility of a permanent establishment. This can ordinarily be done by utilizing an independent distributor with no authority to bind the supplier, or by insuring that the foreign agent is authorized only to solicit orders on the part of the supplier which must be sent to the supplier's offices in the United States for acceptance. In some jurisdictions, however, the mere appointment of a representative or its performance of certain activities may trigger local taxation. Accordingly, the local law governing taxation of foreign entities should be reviewed whenever a new foreign representative is contemplated.

§ 11:06. Other Laws and Regulations—United States Export Controls.

Three other legal and regulatory schemes must be considered in drafting agreements with foreign agents and distributors. The first consists of the licensing and other requirements with respect to U.S. exports imposed under the Export Administration Act and similar laws.[12] In the context of agent and distributor agreements it is only important to note that such agreements should contain an undertaking on the part of the agent or distributor to comply with such laws and the regulations thereunder, to cooperate in furnishing the U.S. supplier with the necessary information and certificates in order to obtain the required license, to indemnify the supplier from any liability as a result of the dealer's noncompliance, and to exempt the supplier from any liability by reason of any delay or failure to ship merchandise due to its compliance with these laws and regulations.

§ 11:07. —Antiboycott Law.

A second regime that warrants some discussion in the context of international agent and distribution agreements is the U.S. Antiboycott Law and the regulations thereunder. The Antiboycott Law was enacted in response to the Arab boycott of Israel and is designed to discourage compliance with such boycott by U.S. firms. It is contained in the Export Administration Act and its implementing Commerce Department Regulations and the Internal Revenue Code and its implementing Treasury Department Regulations.

Under the Export Administration Act, U.S. persons or firms are prohibited from taking or agreeing to take certain action in fur-

---

[12] § 9:01 discusses these regulations in general terms.

therance of an unauthorized boycott. Such action includes not only refusing to do business with the subject of the boycott, but also furnishing information about a company's business activities with a boycotted country or paying a letter of credit containing certain prohibited conditions. Violations of these provisions are punishable by criminal and civil penalties and administrative sanctions, including suspension or revocation of authority to export. The Internal Revenue Code provides for additional penalties against taxpayers who comply with unauthorized boycotts, including loss of foreign tax credits and other favorable tax treatment for international operations.

Under the Commerce Department Regulations, a U.S. person includes foreign subsidiaries, affiliates or establishments which are "controlled in fact" by a U.S. resident or national or a domestic concern.[13] In some cases, such as where a foreign agent or distributor is acting exclusively for the U.S. supplier or where the underlying agreement grants the supplier extensive control over the activities of the foreign representative, such representative may be subject to the antiboycott provisions of the Export Administration Act. The tax code prohibitions will extend to the representative if at least 10% of its voting stock is owned by a U.S. person. Even where the dealer is completely independent of the supplier, however, there is also a risk of indirect application of the antiboycott provisions if the representative is supplying prohibited information on behalf of the U.S. supplier. For these reasons, agency and distribution agreements entered into with representatives in the Middle East should emphasize the independence of the foreign representative and then U.S. supplier and prohibit the representative from taking any action proscribed by the Antiboycott Law.

§ 11:08.   —Foreign Corrupt Practices Act.

The Foreign Corrupt Practices Act (FCPA)[14] prohibits any person subject to U.S. jurisdiction from making payments to foreign

[13] 15 CFR §369:1.

[14] 15 USC §78dd-1.

government officials, political parties or candidates to influence any act or decision of such official, party or candidate in order to obtain or retain business. The FCPA also prohibits such persons from making indirect bribes through payments where the payor knows or has reason to know that all or part of the payment will be passed on to such officials, parties or candidates for such purposes.[15] The FCPA's complexity and uncertain application have been discussed extensively.[16] It is perhaps sufficient to note that the law is apparently not intended to extend to facilitating or "grease" payments made to hasten or encourage the performance of a purely administrative function which is required by statute and does not involve discretion. These might include payment to customs officers to expedite the clearance of imports or to other government officials to speed processing of licenses or permits. In addition, the FCPA extends only to payments in a governmental or political context. Purely commercial bribes or similar payments are not prohibited by the FCPA.

While a U.S. supplier must insure its own compliance with the FCPA, it must also take certain steps to insure that its foreign agents and distributors are also complying. The key question relates to the phrase "knows or has reason to know." While there have been little litigation under the FCPA, it has generally been suggested that the law would require a U.S. supplier to inquire into any suspicious behavior which might suggest that part of the commission paid to its foreign agents is being passed on to government officials. This supicious behavior may include an agents' request for commissions substantially in excess of the going rate or that commissions be paid to an unusual account. Even where distributors are involved so that no commissions as such are paid by the U.S. supplier, the supplier may be held to have made an indirect bribe by granting a distributor an unusual discount suggesting that a payment was being made. Obviously, greater care must be taken in the context of governmental officials or political

[15]15 USC §78dd-2(a)(3).

[16]See, e.g., Baruch, "The Foreign Corrupt Practices Act," 57 Harv Bus Rev 32 (1979); "Foreign Corrupt Practices Act: Domestic and International Implications: A Symposium," 9 Syracuse J Int'l L & Com 235-378 (1982).

parties often have extensive influence in the private sector, however, this is not exclusively so.

In addition to inquiring into suspicious behavior, it is generally recommended that agreements with foreign agents and distributors contain appropriate provisions restraining the representative from taking any action in violation of the FCPA. While the text of these clauses depends on the particular circumstances, they should generally include (i) a representation on the part of the agent or distributor that neither it nor any of its employees, agents or beneficial owners or immediate relatives is a government official or political candidate as well as an undertaking to disclose any change in such representation to the supplier; (ii) an undertaking on the part of the representative not to make, offer or agree to offer anything of value to any government official, political party or candidate and to comply with all other terms of the FCPA; and (iii) the right to terminate the agreement in the event of a breach or violation of the FCPA (which would also constitute a breach of the agreement) and an undertaking on the part of the representative to indemnify the supplier for any losses suffered as a result thereof.

CHAPTER 12

INTERNATIONAL SALES AGENT AND DISTRIBUTOR AGREEMENTS

§12:01. In General.
§12:02. Standard Clauses Included in Agreement.

§ 12:01. In General.

Because of the potential pitfalls that are presented by foreign representation, it is almost always essential to have a written agreement between the supplier and its foreign representative. It is important that these agreements be prepared in light of the particular problems presented by the applicable law in the local jurisdiction as well as in the United States. This is true even though the agreement may be governed by U.S. law since the choice of law provisions is not always respected abroad.

§ 12:02. Standard Clauses Included in Agreement.

(i) *Appointment.* The appointment should make clear whether the representative is acting as an agent or distributor and should define precisely the products and territory to which the appointment extends. It should also state whether the appointment is exclusive or whether the supplier reserves the right to appoint other representatives or distributors in the territory or to sell directly into the territory itself. The supplier's right to sell directly into the territory itself is often reasonable even in exclusive agreements, particularly if limited to sales to government agencies, to sales of products outside the territory which may subsequently be used in the territory, and to sales to central purchasing offices within the territory where the goods will subsequently be used elsewhere. Preference should be given to appointment of legal entities rather than individuals in order to avoid the applicability of local labor laws.

(ii) *Relationship Between the Parties.* In distributorship agreements, the contract should recite that the parties are independent and that the relationship is that of a buyer and seller of goods. Even in sales agency agreements, a provision should be included to the effect that the relationship does not create a general agency. In both cases the absence of any authority on the part of the representative to bind the supplier as well as the representative's responsibility for its expenses and employees should be clearly set forth. An undertaking on the part of the representative not to take any action which would render the supplier a "permanent establishment" or otherwise subject it to local taxation may also be included.

(iii) *Duties of Representative.* The duties of the representative should be carefully considered and clearly set forth. In most cases, a specific list of marketing activities including research and advertising to be undertaken is preferable to a general obligation to promote the products. The representative's obligations to provide engineering and technical support and warranty or other servicing and to maintain an inventory including spare parts should also be set forth. The representative may also be responsible for obtaining all necessary import licenses, exchange control or other governmental approvals, to assist in the entry of the merchandise through customs and to insure that the merchandise complies with local safety and other standards. The agreement should contain undertakings on the part of the representatives to comply with antiboycott and FCPA requirements. A general obligation to indemnify the supplier for any damages resulting from breach of its obligations negligence or other tortious acts and violations of law should also be included. The agreement should specify whether the representative must refrain from handling competing products for other suppliers. Any minimum performance obligations should also be included.

(iv) *Duties of Supplier.* In the same way, the duties of the supplier should be provided for. In addition to its obligation to furnish the goods, the supplier may undertake to provide technical and sales training to the representative and its personnel as well as advertising and promotional materials.

(v) *Sales Terms.* In the case of distributor agreements, the contract should prescribe the terms of sale, including the price (or discount from current prices), credit, currency, allocation of risk of loss, and delivery terms. The agreement should specify the need to submit purchase orders for acceptance by the supplier at its U.S. offices. The agreement should also set forth any price protection accorded to the distributor and any minimum sales requirements. In the case of a sales agent, the agreement need only provide that sales will be made at the supplier's prices and upon its other terms and conditions. While the warranties may be set forth in the sales documents, an undertaking should be obtained that the agent or distributor will not extend additional warranties on the product.

(vi) *Patents, Trademarks, and Confidential Information.* The representative should acknowledge the supplier's ownership of all patents and trademarks pertaining to the products and that it will acquire no interest in such intellectual property rights by reason of the agreement. The representative should also acknowledge the supplier's exclusive right to apply for local patents or trademark registrations in the foreign jurisdiction and to sue for infringement thereunder. In this connection, the agreement should contain an undertaking from the representative to assist in such applications and law suits and to inform the supplier of any known infringement. Where required, the agreement should contain an undertaking on the part of the representative to secure registered user certificates or comply with similar requirements. The representative's right to use the intellectual property rights should be limited to activities related to the promotion of the goods, and the representative should covenant not to disclose any confidential information obtained during its performance of the agreement except as previously authorized by the supplier or after it otherwise becomes publicly known. Such nondisclosure obligations should survive the termination of the agreement. The agreement should expressly define the representative's right to use the supplier's trademarks and trade names, and contain an undertaking on the part of the representative not to utilize confusingly similar trademarks or trade names and not to deface or alter the product packaging or marks. Finally, where the foreign representative insists on indemnification for patent of trademark infringement, such indemnification should be conditioned upon the representative's obligation to immediately inform the supplier of any such infringement action or threat thereof and to assist in the suit and should be limited so as not to extend to consequential damages.

(**vii**) *Term and Renewal.* In jurisdictions with laws governing termination of a representative the agreement should usually have a fixed, definite and relatively short (one or two years) duration, even where a long-term relationship is contemplated, so as to reduce the risk and extent of liability for unlawful termination. Automatic renewal should usually be avoided since they may imply an agreement of indefinite duration.

(**viii**) *Premature Termination.* In jurisdictions regulated by dealer legislation, the law should be reviewed to determine the justifiable causes for termination and any required prior notice. These provisions should be carefully followed in drafting the termination clause of the agreement. In other jurisdictions, the causes for immediate termination or for termination after failure to cure a default should also be clearly defined. The agreement should also recite that it will be terminated immediately upon the enactment in the foreign jurisdiction of any law requiring compensation of the dealer upon termination. In all cases, the causes for premature termination should be reasonable to avoid judicially determined compensation for the dealer. A minimum notice of 90 days should precede termination other than for cause, and upon such termination, the supplier might undertake to repurchase the distributor's inventory or reimburse it for other expenses in lieu of any other obligation. The representative should acknowledge that it has no expectation of compensation for termination beyond what is provided in the agreement, should expressly waive any additional rights it may have to additional compensation under local law and should indemnify the supplier for severance or other claims by its employees or agents.

(**ix**) *Governing Law.*[1] While the supplier may hope to avoid local laws protecting representatives by providing that the agreement will be governed by the supplier's local U.S. law, this choice of law and jurisdiction will often be ignored abroad. The supplier should also ascertain that the chosen law will not be worse, as it may be, for example, in states with protective dealer legislation.

(**x**) *Arbitration.*[2] Another way to reduce the risk of an award of compensation for unlawful termination under local law is to provide for resolution of disputes by arbitration. The rules, place, language, law, and number of arbitrators should be stipulated. An obligation to resolve disputes through arbitration will not only be less costly to the supplier but also discourage the foreign representative from raising frivolous disputes and encourage the use of the supplier's local law. Where both parties are in jurisdictions which are signatories to a convention on the recognition of foreign arbitral awards, the arbitration should be structured to fall within its terms. The supplier may wish to reserve certain disputes from arbitration, allowing it to proceed directly into court for injunctive relief in the event of the disclosure of confidential information or a distributor's failure to pay the purchase price for goods shipped.

(**xi**) *Force Majeure.* Since the supplier may encounter numerous obstacles in filling orders and shipping goods abroad, a broad force majeure clause would normally be in its interest.

[1] See §29:02.
[2] See §29:02.

PART IV—SUGGESTIONS FOR FURTHER READING

Books

Foreign Distributors and Sales Agents Manual (1986).
Vishny, Guide to International Commerce Law (1981).

Articles

Herold & Knoll, "Negotiating and Drafting International Distributing Agency and Representative Agreements: The United States Exporter's Perspective," in Negotiation and Drafting International Commercial Contracts (1986).

Saltoun & Spudis, "International Distribution and Sales Agency Agreements: Practical Guidelines for U.S. Exporters," 38 Bus Law 883 (1983).

Toepke, "EEC Law of Competition: Distribution Agreements and their Notifications," 19 Int'l Law 117 (1985).

PART V

INTERNATIONAL LICENSING AND TECHNOLOGY TRANSFERS

CHAPTER 13

ADVANTAGES AND RISKS OF INTERNATIONAL LICENSING

---

§ 13:01.   In General.

In Parts II and III, certain legal and other aspects of importing to and exporting from the United States were examined. Importing and exporting are often referred to as "international trade" and, constitute the most fundamental of international business transactions.

In this Part, the discussion will move up the hierarchy of international business transactions to explore certain aspects of foreign licensing and technology transfers, those transactions in which a manufacturer or other owner of patents, trademarks or non-patented know-how elects to make such intellectual property available to a foreign manufacturer for certain purposes, either under a license or in some other form of transfer. A license implies an authorization to use or exploit the subject matter of the license for a

143

specified purpose and for a certain period of time. Unless otherwise granted, however, all other rights are maintained by the owner of the intellectual property. Patents, trademarks and non-patented technology may also be transferred outright or may be made available in some other form, such as in the case of technical or managerial assistance.

Traditionally, licensing is viewed as an alternative means for a manufacturer to generate revenue from a foreign market where export sales or local production through a subsidiary or joint venture are impracticable. While this is often the context in which a licensing transaction arises, this view ignores a number of important aspects of international licensing.

First, licensing is not always a viable alternative for a U.S. manufacturer. In order for the arrangement to be attractive for a foreign licensee, the licensor must be able to offer some valuable rights that are not available elsewhere. A potential foreign licensee will not pay for nonpatented technology which is easily susceptible to reverse engineering or a manufacturing process which can be discovered from other sources. Thus, before attempting to engage in international licensing, a prospective licensor should examine the reasons for its domestic success to determine if it is attributable to licensable technology or trademarks or merely to a well-developed marketing network or other factors which could not be easily transferred.

Second, international licensing is not limited to manufacturing technology as such. In many cases, such as in the designer clothing industry, a trademark may be significantly more valuable than any underlying technology. While trademark licenses present particular licensing problems, and are even prohibited in some jurisdictions, they can often generate significant royalties from foreign markets. Moreover, as a result of developments in the information, financial management, and other service industries, a new "technology" is emerging that has nothing to do with manufacturing. In many cases the best means of exploiting this new technology abroad is through management assistance and service agreements which represent a form of technology transfer.

Finally, the traditional view of licensing ignores the fact that licensing is now commonly combined with other types of international business transactions. In many joint ventures, one party will often furnish the relevant technology and technical assistance under a licensing and technology transfer agreement, and provide managerial or other services during an initial start-up phase under a servicing agreement. License and technology transfer agreements are also becoming common between U.S. companies and their foreign subsidiaries for tax purposes and to confirm that the proprietary rights to the subject matter of the license are owned by the parent. Even in the import/export context, agreements with foreign agents and distributors often contain technology licenses or obligations to provide technical or other forms of assistance.

§ 13:02. Advantages of International Licensing.

Licensing is often viewed as an alternative to exporting or direct investment to be used only where such options are impossible or undesirable. The use of licensing as a means of generating revenue from a foreign market in such cases illustrates some principal advantages.

Exporting may be impractical for many reasons. Perhaps the bulk or weight of the product would add transportation costs which make the foreign selling price uncompetitive with local products. In certain cases, the U.S. manufacturer may not have additional productive capacity in the United States to allocate to export production. In many developing countries, high tariffs or absolute prohibitions on certain imports may foreclose the market to foreign-manufactured goods. Moreover, local preferences or requirements to use locally produced goods may operate as a de facto prohibition on imports.

Direct investment is also undesirable in many circumstances. The first and most obvious drawback of direct investment is the capital expenditure that is required to commence local production. While direct investment normally presents a greater potential profit, it also normally requires the investor to commit a substantial amount of funds under considerably greater risks and to wait for a return until the enterprise becomes profitable. A license agreement, on the other hand, can often be structured with an initial lump-sum fee plus certain minimum royalties based on sales. This assures the licensor a certain minimum income from the technology without a substantial expenditure. Licensing is also more attractive than direct investment in smaller markets which do not warrant large capital expenditures, and in rapidly changing technologies where advances may make the technology unmarketable in a short time. Licensing may also present a more attractive means of penetrating a foreign market whose local laws prohibit or disfavor foreign-owned subsidiaries.

Licensing also presents certain advantages in itself. Because license agreements often contain "grant-back" clauses which require the licensee to share any innovations or other developments with respect to the technology with the licensor, licensing can create opportunities for the licensor to benefit from its licensees' research and development activities. In some cases, parties will execute cross licenses, under which they share with each other a given technology with or without compensation.[1] Local laws in many countries require the owner, of a patent or invention to actually exploit them locally or risk cancellation or the grant of compulsory licenses. The granting of a license in such cases may be the only means of protecting the rights of a licensor who is unable to exploit the invention locally itself. Finally, licensing presents a means of generating revenue from technologies which the licensor has no intention of pursing itself, perhaps because of the costs involved or because the technology is unrelated to the company's general business.

§ 13:03.   Risks of International Licensing.

Despite its advantages, licensing also presents certain risks. Foremost among these is that the disclosure of the technology to

---

[1] See §§16:02 and 17:03 for a discussion of the local law and antitrust implications of grant-back clauses and cross license agreements.

the licensee will create competition from the licensee or from others to whom the licensee may disclose it. While a well-drafted license agreement will contain restrictions designed to limit the licensee's sales to a particular geographical territory and prevent disclosure to others, the licensor's right to sue the licensee for breach of these obligations is often of little solace. Moreover, antitrust and other laws sometimes prevent the licensor from enforcing export restrictions.

In addition to the potential problems created by the licensee's failure to observe the territorial restraints and nondisclosure provisions of license agreements, licensors often complain of cheating by licensees on the computation of royalties or their failure to make timely payments. The agreements themselves can decrease the risk of cheating by requiring the licensee to maintain complete records and by allowing the licensor and its representatives to examine these and to have access to other information to determine their accuracy. Prompt termination and penalties for delayed payment may also be incorporated into the license agreement, both of which are more effective if a substantial up-front royalty was required.

Ultimately, however, the best means of reducing the risks associated with licensing is for the licensor to exercise extreme care in selecting prospective licensees. Choosing the appropriate foreign partner may even be more important in a licensing context than in a sales agent/distributor or joint venture transaction, since the licensor often has much more to lose and the licensee usually has less motivation to faithfully perform under the agreement. If at all possible, the appropriate licensee should not only be a company which has demonstrated a capacity to effectively manufacture and market its products, but which has also manifested its willingness to comply with contractual obligations. Finally, since agreements which are perceived to be fair and mutually beneficial are more readily complied with, the licensor should be careful not to force unreasonable terms on the licensee. The licensor's victory at the bargaining table may turn out to be pyrrhic.

CHAPTER 14

SUBJECT MATTER OF LICENSES AND TECHNOLOGY TRANSFERS

§ 14:01.   In General.

License and technology transfers may extend to any type of knowledge or practice which may be useful in the conception, design, fabrication, sale or maintenance of a product or in the organization, provision and marketing of a service. Basically, any means of accomplishing anything which may be useful to another party may be the subject matter of a license or other form of transfer. Such knowledge and practices are commonly referred to as "intellectual property" or "industrial property," or by the more generic "intangible property." As these terms suggest, it is viewed by the U.S. and most other legal systems as a form of property which may be owned or transferred, in whole or in part, to others.

149

At the same time, not all knowledge or information is proprietary. Nonproprietary knowledge or information—that which is already freely available in books, trade publications, etc.—is, of course, not susceptible to licensing.

Intellectual property is commonly divided into two categories, statutory and nonstatutory. Statutory industrial property encompasses patents, trademarks, copyrights and certain other items, the rights of which are governed by statute. Nonstatutory industrial property is often referred to as "know-how," and consists of all other nonpatented technology or information which is proprietary. License and technology transfer agreements may encompass statutory and nonstatutory industrial property. A license agreement from a company such as Xerox, for example, may authorize a German licensee to use Xerox' patents and nonpatented know-how to produce a certain copier in Germany and to market it, using Xerox' trademarks in Germany and certain other countries. In other cases, the license agreement may extend to particular types of statutory and nonstatutory rights.

§ 14:02. Patents.

A patent is a privilege, granted by a government, which protects an invention by entitling the holder to exclude others from exploiting the invention for a certain period of time. The value of a patent consists, therefore, not in the holder's exclusive right to practice the invention, but in its right to prevent others from utilizing the discovery without the holder's consent. In this way, U.S. and other patent laws provide an incentive for research and development of commercially useful science and technology.

Not all technology is patentable or patented. Under the U.S. patent law,[1] patents may be granted only with respect to a new and useful "process, machine, manufacture or composition of matter."[2] Many valuable practices and procedures for producing a

[1] 35 USC §§1–376.
[2] Id. at §101.

product or providing a service either do not fall within this definition or fail, after a search of the prior art, to meet the newness or inventiveness criteria. In other cases, an inventor may elect not to patent an invention which is otherwise patentable since to do so may in fact reduce the value of the invention. In the most celebrated example, if the Coca-Cola Company had patented its formula for Coke, its monopoly of the product would have ended after seventeen years rather than the more than a century which it has enjoyed by keeping the formula a trade secret. Some inventors also choose to rely on trade secret protection not because of the time limits of patents but because the publication required will result in more unauthorized use than can be reasonably remedied by infringement actions.

While patent laws are intended as a means of promoting the development of useful technology, the right of the inventor to prevent others from exploiting the patent means that the holder can effectively deny potential users the benefit of the invention if it fails to practice the patent itself or to authorize others to do so. For this reason, the patent laws of many countries impose an obligation on the patentee to practice or license others to practice the patent or risk loss of the patent rights. In certain countries, failure to exploit a patent will result in mandatory licenses. In other countries, "inventors' certificates" are issued in lieu of patents in certain areas. An inventors' certificate typically entitles the holder to royalties on an invention which is exploited locally but does not entitle the holder to prevent its exploitation as in the case of a patent.

§ 14:03. Trademarks.

A trademark is any word, name, symbol, device or combination thereof adopted and used by a manufacturer or merchant to identify its goods and to distinguish them from those manufactured or sold by others.[3] A trade name is descriptive of the manufacturer or

[3] 15 USC §1172.

merchant itself rather than a particular product or service. For example, "Minnesota Mining and Manufacturing" is a trade name, while "Scotch" is a trademark used on its brand of transparent tape. By designating the source or origin of a product or service, trademarks and trade names imply a particular standard of quality, symbolize the goodwill of the manufacturer, and protect the public from confusion.[4] For purposes of this discussion, both trademarks and trade names are referred to as "trademarks."

In most countries, including the United States, trademarks may be protected by registering them under applicable statutes. The statutory treatment of trademarks, however, differs from patents in several respects. First, whereas patents are valid for definite periods of time, trademark registrations, though issued for a term of years, are usually renewable forever. Second, whereas in the United States and certain other countries a patent is valid regardless of its exploitation by the holder, failure to use a trademark will usually result in its loss. Third, unlike patents whose ownership depends on government action, in most common-law jurisdictions, trademarks are created by their use, not by their registration. Registration in such jurisdictions serves only to perfect one's ownership rights if the same are not challenged by a prior first user within a prescribed period of time. In most civil law jurisdictions, on the other hand, trademarks are more similar to patents since ownership itself is determined by registration. Finally, while patent rights are normally licensable, many countries prohibit local entities from paying license fees for trademarks.

§ 14:04. Copyrights.

Copyrights are rights granted by statute to the author or originator of certain literary or artistic works, investing him or her, for a limited time, with the sole and exclusive privilege of copying the same and publishing and selling such copies. Copyrights are rele-

---

[4] 1 J Gilson, Trademark Protection and Practice §1.03.

vant in the context of licensing since the licensee often requires the use of manuals, specification sheets and other written documentation respecting the technology as well as advertising and sales literature, all of which may be protected by copyrights. Certain creative designs and artwork which may be the subject of a license agreement are also eligible for copyright protection under certain circumstances.

§ 14:05. Know-How and Show-How.

The term "know-how" in the context of licensing and technology transfers encompasses all knowledge, expertise and information which is useful in accomplishing the subject matter of the agreement. While know-how can be embodied in tangible form, such as in drawings, designs, models and blueprints, it may also consist of engineering, technical, managerial, and other expertise which is imparted to the licensee by means of training and technical assistance. The latter has recently become known as "show-how." Since the vast majority of valuable technology is not patented, nearly all technology transfer agreements include the transfer of nonpatented know-how, whether or not they also cover patents, trademarks or copyrights.

While know-how is thus the most pervasive subject matter of technology transfer agreements, it is also the most evasive. In the case of a patent, the law establishes an owner and grants the owner the exclusive right to practice the technology encompassed within the patent, regardless of whether it may be independently discovered by others. The legal protection for know-how in most countries, on the other hand, is founded in trade secret law, and is fundamentally limited to the enforcement of a contractual obligation not to disclose the know-how. Trade secret law allows the owner or other lawful possessor of a trade secret to invoke judicial action to prevent the use or disclosure of the trade secret by (i) a person who received the same under a covenant of nonuse or nondisclosure; or (ii) by any person to whom the trade secret was disclosed in violation of such a covenant. The owner of a trade secret may not prevent its use or disclosure by a person who received it accidentally or who discovered it, either independently or through reverse engineering.

CHAPTER 15

FOREIGN PATENTS AND TRADEMARKS

§ 15:01. National Character of Patents and Trademarks.

There exists a great deal of confusion among lawyers inexperienced in intellectual property as to the rights to patents, trademarks, and other statutory intellectual property abroad. Patents and trademarks exist as a result of national law. A valid U.S. patent or trademark creates rights only in the territorial limits of the United States. Without having created any rights to a patent or trademark abroad, the U.S. owner or authorized licensee cannot prevent the exploitation of the patent or the use of the trademark outside of the United States.[1] Thus, the only means of protecting one's patents or trademarks abroad is by taking the necessary action under local law to acquire the proprietary rights to the same in the local jurisdiction.

---

[1] See §§7:02-7:06, however, which discuss the right of the owner or licensee of certain U.S. intellectual property rights to prevent the importation of foreign merchandise which would enfringe such rights.

An example may help illustrate this point. Dupont invented and obtained a U.S. patent on the process for a new synthetic fiber which it called Mylar. Having concluded that the best way to market its invention was through licensing, it could then proceed with its domestic licensing program, since it alone could authorize the use of the patent and its Mylar trademark. Until it acquired the same patent and trademark protection in, say Germany, however, it could not enter into license agreements in that jurisdiction since anyone would be free to exploit the technology (which would have become publicly known through the publication of the patent) or use the trademark.

The national character of patent and trademark registrations has profound implications not only for licensing but for exporting and direct foreign investment as well. Where any of these transactions involve a product whose value is enhanced by a patent or trademark, that value will be lost (and possibly acquired by someone else) if the patent and trademark rights are not acquired locally. For this reason, any company which owns valuable patents or trademarks with respect to products which it may wish to sell abroad should develop a plan for acquiring the foreign rights to the same. There is also a certain urgency to acquiring such rights abroad, since the failure to do so on a timely basis may result in the loss of an important filing priority which international treaties accord to the originator of the invention or trademark.

§ 15:02. Securing Patents and Registering Trademarks Abroad.

In general, the only means of obtaining a foreign patent is to file an application in accordance with local law. In the case of trademarks, however, certain jurisdictions, including the United States, grant proprietary rights to the first person to use the trademark in commerce, regardless of whether such person has applied for registration of the mark. Even most of these so called "first-use" jurisdictions have a procedure for registering the mark which may have the effect of extinguishing the prior rights of the first users. It is therefore advisable to protect one's rights in a trademark not only by utilizing it within the country but also by applying for registration of the mark in accordance with local law.

Local law varies in terms of the criteria which must be met to obtain a patent or register a trademark and the rights which are conferred thereby. In most cases, however, the procedure involves an application to a governmental agency or authority who administers the applicable law and issues the patent or trademark registrations. Normally, the U.S. company will engage a foreign lawyer or other expert on local intellectual property to prepare and file the application on its behalf in each country in which patent or trademark protection is sought. While applications to register trademarks are usually routine, patent applications can be quite costly.

Various multilateral treaties have made some progress toward harmonizing the treatment of patents and trademarks in certain countries and the elimination of individual applications in each country. The oldest and most important of these is the Paris Convention for the Protection of Industrial Property. The Paris Convention, which the United States and more than 80 other countries have joined, created two important principles with respect to the treatment of intellectual property: national treatment and filing priority. National treatment means that each of the signatories must grant to nationals of other signatories the same rights and privileges with respect to patents and trademarks as they grant to their own nationals. The priority provisions of the Paris Convention stipulate that any patent application filed in a member state within twelve months of the original application made in a different member state will be deemed to have a priority as of the date of the original application. A similar provision extends to trademark registrations but with only a six-month priority.

The priority provisions of the Convention are significant for two reasons. First, they protect the patentability of inventions in jurisdictions which require absolute novelty. Absent the retroactive priority provisions, the mere application for a patent in one country might render the invention unpatentable in another country since it is no longer deemed novel. Second, the priority period protects the inventor while it considers the countries in which patents will be sought or negotiates with potential licensees. Since the patent will date back to the date of the original filing, the inventor is protected against others who may subsequently seek to acquire the patent abroad, even if they acquired the technology independently. If the patent application is not filed during this priority period, however, not only does the inventor lose this protection but the patent may be barred by reason of lack of novelty. It is therefore important to consider the international application for patents or trademark registrations immediately after the same are made in the United States.

Certain other multilateral conventions also warrant mention. Under the Patent Cooperation Treaty, an applicant may make a single filing for a patent in a number of countries. After such filing, which has the same effect in each country, the applicant has 20 months in order to comply with the national laws of each of the countries designated in the application in order to acquire a patent therein. The Patent Cooperation Treaty thus does not result in the issuance of an international patent, but only facilitates the filing for a patent and extends the filing priority period to 20 months.

A true "international patent" does exist on a regional basis in certain areas. The Convention on the Grant of European Patents created a European Patent Office which is empowered to grant patents applicable in any or all of the countries which are parties to the convention. Although an applicant must be a national of one of the member countries (which would include a wholly-owned U.S. subsidiary organized in one of such countries), this convention can reduce considerably the costs of obtaining individual patents in the member countries. When issued, a European patent has a duration of 20 years, but the rights thereto, including validity and infringement, are governed by national law.

As noted above, the Paris Convention also grants national treatment and a six-month priority period for trademarks. Under the Madrid Agreement, to which there are approximately 35 signatories, the filing and protection of a trademark registered in the country of origin can be automatically extended to one or more of the other countries by a single international application to the World Intellectual Property Organization in Geneva. While the United States is not a party to the Madrid Agreement, U.S. nationals can, in effect, benefit from its protection through a foreign subsidiary in a country which is a party.

CHAPTER 16

LOCAL LAWS AFFECTING INTERNATIONAL LICENSING AND TECHNOLOGY TRANSFERS

§16:01.   Patent and Trademark Law.
§16:02.   Antitrust and Special Transfer of Technology Laws.
§16:03.   Local Tax and Exchange Control Laws.

§ 16:01.   Patent and Trademark Law.

One must look to the national law of the relevant country in order to determine the rights and procedures governing intellectual property. Such law may vary significantly from jurisdiction to jurisdiction in terms of the standards which must be met in order to secure a patent or obtain a trademark registration. The rights or obligations accorded thereby also differ considerably among foreign countries. Local law also governs the procedures for applying for patents and trademarks, their duration and validity, and matters respecting infringement. Foreign laws governing patents and trademarks are summarized in various publications, including the Manual for the Handling of Applications for Patents, Designs and

Trade Marks Throughout the World, published by Octrooibureau Los Enstigter (Amsterdam) and Patents Throughout the World and Trademarks Throughout the World, both published by Clark Boardman (New York).

§ 16:02. Antitrust and Special Transfer of Technology Laws.

Local law may also affect the license or transfer of intellectual property to foreign licensees or recipients. It has already been mentioned that since nonpatented know-how is protected by contractual nondisclosure obligations (which have evolved in some jurisdictions into "trade secret law"), the lawyer must be satisfied that such obligations as well as the other provisions of the agreement are in fact enforceable. It is not enough to provide that the agreement will be governed by U.S. law, since the law in the local jurisdiction may preclude such a choice of law.

Local antitrust law, particularly in industrialized countries, can also affect the structure of a license agreement. In the discussion of foreign agency and distribution agreements in Part III, reference was made to Articles 85 and 86 of the Treaty of Rome which prohibits agreements that have the purpose or effect of preventing, restricting or dictating competition in the EEC. Article 85 specifically prohibits price fixing, limiting or controlling production and sharing or dividing markets, except when such practices improve the production or distribution of goods or promote technical or economic progress. Article 86 prohibits other abuses of one's dominant position.

In 1984, the European Commission adopted a block exemption under Article 85(3) for patent licensing agreements and ancillary licensing of trademarks and know-how.[1] Like the block exemption for distribution agreements, this block exemption contains a series of prohibited licensing practices which, if absent from the proposed license agreement, automatically renders such agreement

[1] Commission Regulation 2349/84 (July 23, 1984).

exempt from the notification requirements of Article 85. Among the provisions which cannot be used are restrictions on the licensee's right to challenge the validity of any patents or other industrial property rights of the licensor, production limitations, grant-backs on improvements by the licensee, field of use restrictions, tying arrangements, and territorial limitations.[2]

Japan's Anti-Monopoly Act of 1947 requires that all international licensing agreements to which a Japanese person is a party be reported to the Japanese Fair Trade Commission to insure that they do not violate antitrust law. Under the Fair Trade Commission's Guidelines for International Licensing Agreements, restrictions on dealing in competing products, tying, grant-backs, restrictions on resale prices, and certain other provisions in a licensing agreement could be deemed to violate Japanese antitrust law, and therefore preclude approval by the Fair Trade Commission. There are however, various exemptions which may allow the licensor to impose these restrictions under certain circumstances where they do not have a noncompetitive effect and have commercial justification.

In many developing countries, particularly in Latin America, special laws have been enacted to regulate the terms under which local companies may acquire foreign technology. These laws are designed not to insure competition but to enhance the terms and conditions under which the country will obtain the desired technology. In general, these laws require all license or other technology transfer agreements to be registered with a governmental authority in order to be enforceable, for payments by the licensee to be tax deductible, or for the licensee to obtain foreign currency to make such payments. The laws then set forth or authorize such authority to develop the criteria that must be met in order for the agreement to be registered.

The Mexican Transfer of Technology Law (TTL) is perhaps the most well-known of these laws. The TTL requires the registration of virtually every type of technology transfer agreement, including

---

[2] See generally Venit, "EEC Patent Licensing Revisited: The Commission's Patent License Regulation," 30 Antitrust Bull. 457 (1985).

patent licenses or sales, technical assistance agreements, management services agreements, and even computer software licenses. The TTL then lists seventeen different bases on which the Transfer of Technology Registry may deny registration. These bases include not only excessive license fees, but also certain restrictions or other provisions commonly included in license agreements such as limitations on the licensee's right to export licensed products, certain grant-back clauses, provisions requiring components to be purchased from the licensor, and provisions requiring the licensee to sell all of its products to or through the licensor. The TTL also establishes a maximum term of ten years for such agreements and provides that no obligations contained therein may extend beyond the term of the agreement. In the case of nonpatented know-how, this means that the licensee is free to use or disclose the technology after the expiration of the agreement. Finally, the TTL requires the agreement be governed by Mexican law and that any disputes arising thereunder be settled by Mexican courts or by international arbitration using Mexican law.

The registries in many countries have a staff of legal, economic and technical experts who evaluate the agreements in light of the criteria established under the applicable law as well as then-existing policy priorities. After evaluating the agreement, the registry will either approve it or make recommendations as to how it must be modified in order to be acceptable. Because the registries in many countries are now quite sophisticated in their analysis of these agreements, the negotiations with the registry are often much more rigorous than those with the licensee itself. In this way, the laws have the effect of substantially increasing the bargaining position of the local licensee vis-a-vis the foreign licensor.

Foreign antitrust laws and special transfer of technology laws often not only render noncomplying agreements unenforceable but may also create substantial sanctions against the licensor or licensee who knowingly or unknowingly violates the law. Whenever a foreign license or technology transfer agreement is contemplated, the lawyer should promptly determine whether any such laws may be applicable to the proposal and seek the assistance of local counsel in order to insure compliance while still obtaining the most favorable terms for the licensor.

Finally, depending upon the nature or extent of the activities to be performed by the foreign licensor, other steps may have to be taken under local law. In the case of management or technical assistance agreements, for example, the licensor may be deemed to be doing business locally, requiring it to register or obtain special permits. Where foreign personnel are required to be sent to the foreign jurisdiction, appropriate visas may have to be acquired in accordance with local immigration law. In certain areas, such as petroleum, transportation, pharmaceuticals, communications, etc., special laws may impact on the proposed transaction. All of these must be considered in the planning phase to insure that the proposal can proceed on an acceptable basis. The license agreement should provide that the licensor's obligations under the agreement should be conditioned on the receipt of all such necessary permits, visas and approvals, and require the local licensee to assist in securing the same.

§ 16:03.   Local Tax and Exchange Control Laws.

The local tax and exchange control laws, if any, must also be considered in contemplating a license or technology transfer. While merely entering into a license agreement and delivering patents or other technology pursuant thereto will not normally render the licensor subject to local income taxation, the transfer of the licensor's personnel to the licensee's local facility to provide managerial or technical services or training may be deemed to create a "permanent establishment" of the licensor in such jurisdiction, thereby rendering it liable to local taxation. There may also be income tax implications for the personnel transferred to perform such services. The impact of such tax laws must be carefully considered before a commitment is made to undertake any of these activities abroad.

Even if the arrangement does not subject the foreign licensor to local taxation generally, in almost all cases the licensor will be subject to tax on payments made by the licensee. Normally this takes the form of a gross withholding tax on all income payable to the foreign licensor, including royalties and any fees or other compensation for technical assistance or related services. The rate of tax may vary depending on the nature of the income or the existence of a tax treaty between the relevant countries. In Mexico, for example, which has no tax treaty with the United States, royalties on patents and trademarks are subject to a withholding tax of 42% while payments abroad for the use of models, plans and other know-how, and technical assistance are subject to a 21% withholding tax. In Italy, royalties are subject to a 21% withholding tax, but that rate is reduced under the U.S.-Italian Tax Treaty to 5% to 15% depending on the subject matter. Where no tax treaty is present, it may be desirable to transfer the technology to a subsidiary in a foreign jurisdiction which does have a tax treaty with the licensee's jurisdiction to obtain a reduction in withholding rates.

Even though these taxes are normally creditable in the United States, cash flow considerations or possible problems encountered under the foreign tax credit limitation usually dictate that the license agreement be structured in a way which minimizes foreign taxation. More advanced tax planning is appropriate where foreign affiliates are concerned in order to maximize income in low tax jurisdictions. In any case, the agreements should require the foreign licensee to promptly pay any applicable taxes, and if deemed paid by the licensor, to deliver tax receipts to the licensor in order to secure the available foreign tax credits.

Finally, if royalties or other compensation is to be paid by a licensee subject to exchange controls, the impact of these controls should be carefully considered. In most cases, the agreement would be structured in a manner in which all compensation payable by the licensee will be paid in the licensor's customary currency. In certain cases, the agreement may have to be registered with the central bank or other governmental authority in order for the licensee to acquire the foreign exchange to pay royalties at all or at a more favorable exchange rate. The parties should also consider and set forth their respective rights in the event of a delay or failure to obtain the relevant foreign currency for payments under the agreement.

CHAPTER 17

UNITED STATES REGULATION OF INTERNATIONAL LICENSES AND TECHNOLOGY TRANSFERS

§ 17:01.   In General.

United States law regulates international licenses and technology transfers, primarily by controlling the delivery of sensitive U.S. technology abroad and by insuring that the transaction will not have an anticompetitive effect on U.S. commerce. This chapter covers the impact of U.S. export controls and antitrust laws on these transactions.

§17:02. United States Export Controls.

The provisions of the Export Administration Act (EAA) and the need for a license for exports of any commodity from the United States were discussed previously.[1] The EAA also requires a license for the export of any "technical data" of U.S. origin. The term "technical data" is defined in the applicable regulations as "[i]nformation of any kind that can be used, or adopted for use, in the design, production, manufacture, utilization or reconstruction of articles or materials."[2] The regulations go on to provide that the data "may take a tangible form, such as a model, prototype, blueprint, or an operating manual . . . [or] may take an intangible form such as a service."[3] The regulations also provide that the export of technical data includes (i) the actual shipment or transmission of the technical data outside the United States; (ii) the release of technical data in the United States with the knowledge or intent that it will be shipped or transmitted from the United States to a foreign country; or (iii) any release of technical data, including by means of visual inspection, oral exchanges or application of personal knowledge or technical experience to situations abroad.[4] Virtually any type of license or technology transfer agreement would contemplate the "export" of "technical data" within these definitions, and thus would require a license.

As in the case of commodities, however, the export of certain technical data may be eligible for a "general" license, thus obviating the need to apply for and obtain a specific "validated" license. A General License GTDA covers technical data which is generally available to the public as well as scientific and educational data not directly or significantly related to industrial production.[5] A General License GTDR allows the release of most types of technical data not covered by the General License GTDA to destinations in Country Groups T, V and Canada (e.g., free world nations) pro-

[1] See §9:01.
[2] 15 CFR §379.1(a).
[3] Id.
[4] 15 CFR 379.1(b).
[5] 15 CFR 379.3.

vided "written assurances" are submitted to the Department of Commerce which state that neither the technical data nor the product thereof are intended to be shipped to certain prohibited countries.[6]

If a general license GTDA or GTDR is not available for the contemplated transaction, the licensor must apply for a validated license. The application form and procedures are similar to those described in Part III with respect to commodities. The supporting documents include a letter of explanation describing the proposed transaction in some detail. Special follow-up reports are also required.[7] Part 379 of the Export Administration Regulations contains certain special requirements with respect to specified types of technical data such as computer software. A detailed set of interpretations pertaining to the license requirements for technical data is contained in Supplement No. 1 to Part 379.

§ 17:03.   United States Antitrust Laws.

United States antitrust laws may also affect the structure of an international license agreement, particularly with respect to the restraints and limitations imposed on the licensee to limit its use of the intellectual property or to otherwise maximize the benefits of the arrangement to the licensor. United States antitrust law will extend to the foreign transaction only if it is found to have an "effect" on U.S. commerce. In the licensing context, the "effects" test might be met where the foreign licensee is precluded from selling its products freely in the United States, thereby reducing competition, or where the licensee is required to purchase all its raw materials or components from the licensor, thereby limiting other U.S. suppliers' opportunity to compete abroad.

The Department of Justice's Antitrust Guide for International Operations, though somewhat dated, provides some assistance in

[6] 15 CFR §379.4.
[7] 15 CFR §379.6.

predicting what types of restraints the Justice Department might consider violative of U.S. antitrust law. Both the Guide and the few decisions in the international area suggest that the courts would continue to distinguish between per se violations—which are necessarily anti-competitive—and conduct governed by the "rule of reason" in which an otherwise prohibited practice may be justified based on the surrounding circumstances. In applying the rule of reason test, the courts will normally conduct a detailed analysis of the restraint in light of the relevant industry and market. In order to avoid liability, the court must find that the main purpose of the restraint is lawful, that the scope and duration is no greater than necessary to achieve a lawful purpose and that the restraint is reasonable under the circumstances.

(i) *Territorial Limitations.* One of the most common provisions in license agreements involving patents and/or know-how are territorial limitations which restrict the right of the licensee to manufacture or sell the licensed products to a particular country or group of countries. While such limitations between competitors which have the intention or effect of dividing markets are per se illegal, other territorial limitations with respect to manufacturing or marketing are subject to the rule of reason. Territorial restraints in patent licenses are usually acceptable since the patent law itself contemplates the partial assignment of patent rights within a particular part of the United States.

(ii) *Field of Use Restrictions.* A field of use restriction is intended to limit the use of the licensed technology in some respects, such as to produce a particular product or to sell to a particular market (e.g., consumer and not commercial). Like territorial limitations, field of use restrictions may allow the licensor to multiply the value of the technology by executing separate licenses for each use. While field of use restrictions might be used unlawfully to allocate or divide markets or limit resales, these restrictions are usually acceptable under the rule of reason test.

(iii) *Tying.* A standard tying arrangement requires the licensee to accept a product it does not want as a condition to obtaining a desired product. Tying may occur where the licensor requires the licensee to acquire tools or raw materials and components in order to obtain the technology to produce a given product. It may also occur where the licensor requires the licensee to take additional technology, a practice known as package licensing. While these provisions have generally been found to be per se illegal in the domestic context, the Guide suggests that they may be justifiable in an international context where the undesired product or technology is necessary to insure proper production or marketing of the desired product. Moreover, the restraint may not meet the jurisdictional test if the arrangement does not effectively foreclose other suppliers from selling in the market.

(iv) *Tie-Out Provisions.* Tie-out provisions require the licensee to refrain from purchasing products from the licensor's competitors. Like tying provisions, tie-outs have been held to be per se illegal in the United States but may be acceptable in an international context where they do not have the effect of limiting the ability of U.S. competitors to sell in the relevant foreign market. The analysis would focus on the size of the market, the number of potential purchasers, and the dominance of the licensee in the market.

(v) *Grant-Back Clauses.* A grant-back clause requires the licensee to grant the licensor the right to use any improvements or modifications of the technology which it may develop on a royalty or royalty-free basis. Grant-back clauses are subject to the rule of reason test. Where the clauses are nonexclusive and thus allow the developments to be made available to the original licensor's competitors, they are normally acceptable. The Guide suggests that the validity of an exclusive grant-back clause will depend on the scope of the obligations and the competitive relationship between the parties. Where the licensee is obligated to grant back a broad range of developments, including those which are only remotely related to the original technology, or the parties are competitors, the provisions may have the unlawful effect of maintaining the licensor's dominant market position or otherwise limiting competition.

(vi) *Post-expiration Royalties.* The holder of a valuable patent may be tempted to extend the economic benefits therefrom by entering into a license agreement which requires the licensee to pay royalties after the expiration of the patent. This practice has been held to constitute a per se violation of the antitrust laws, since it is an attempt to extend the monopoly accorded by the patent laws. However, there is no similar limit on the payment of royalties for unpatented know-how even after it ceases to be a trade secret. Modern international license agreements rarely extend only to patents without some additional unpatented know-how. Where patents are an essential part of the total technology, however, it may be desirable to allocate a portion of the royalties to particular patents and provide that such royalties cease upon the expiration thereof. The prohibition of post-expiration royalties would not, of course, prohibit installment payments of royalties after expiration of the patents based on use prior to expiration.

CHAPTER 18

INTERNATIONAL LICENSE AND TECHNOLOGY TRANSFER AGREEMENTS

§18:01.   Types of Agreements.
§18:02.   Basic Provisions.

§ 18:01.   Types of Agreements.

Not all of the major issues discussed above are presented in every kind of agreement which might involve the grant of a license or transfer of technology. As this area has developed, companies which possess some type of valuable intellectual property rights have found that these rights may be made available to foreign companies in a variety of fashions, depending on the nature of the intellectual property and the needs of the parties. Among the types of agreements commonly used are straight licenses or assignments of patents or tradesmarks; license agreements covering unpatented know-how; technical assistance agreements; and service agreements. In certain transactions, two or more of these types of agreements may be executed among the parties, or they may be combined into a single agreement.

(i) *Patent and Trademark Licenses and Assignments.* A straight patent license would merely permit the licensee to utilize a patent in the manufacture or sale of a product, but not provide the licensee with any other know-how or technical assistance. In the international setting, such licenses are rare since the licensee normally seeks other technology or technical assistance as well as the patent license itself. Occasionally, however, a foreign firm may only require a license with respect to the patent itself in order to manufacture the product. This is particularly true where a foreign firm may have developed an improvement on the patented invention, but requires a license on the underlying patent in order to exploit the improvement.

A trademark license allows the licensee to utilize a trademark under specified conditions and for a definite period of time. In certain cases, such as where a trademark is being applied to a new product in which the owner may have no expertise, the trademark may be licensed independent of any know-how or other intellectual property. The Lacosta alligator, for example, appears on a host of products which benefit only from the familiarity of the trademark and not from any technology provided by the licensor. In most cases, however, a trademark license accompanies the transfer of the technology to produce the product. In some instances, the licensor of the technology may require the licensee to utilize the trademark as a condition to its acquisition of the technology, since it will benefit from the international enhancement of the mark. Other times, the licensee may seek the right to use a trademark since it may already have some local recognition that would assist the licensee in marketing a licensed product.

In certain cases, the holder of a patent or trademark may desire to assign these intellectual property rights rather than merely license them. An assignment transfers all of the holder's rights rather than merely the right of first refusal. Since patents and trademarks exist on a national level, a full assignment could be structured to extend, for example, only to the holder's French or Belgian rights without impairing its rights in other countries. It should be noted that assignments of trademarks without the underlying business can result in loss of the mark in some cases.

(ii) *Know-How License Agreements.* As already mentioned, a substantial quantity of valuable technology is unpatented, either because it does not meet the necessary qualifications or for other reasons. Yet this technology may be central to a patent licensee's effective exploitation of a patent. A foreign tool manufacturer, for example, may seek not only the right to manufacture and sell a newly patented hand tool, but also advice as to the layout of the manufacturing facility, information as to the equipment used to manufacture the product, specifications for parts and components, quality control and testing procedures, packaging procedures, and marketing methods. Even if the hand tool itself were not subject to a patent, a foreign manufacturer may still seek a license to obtain and utilize this know-how in order to increase its competitiveness.

(iii) *Technical Assistance Agreements.* As noted above, unpatented know-how may take some tangible form such as blue prints, specification and data sheets, drawings and models. In such cases, the tangible media can be physically delivered to the licensee. In other cases, the technology may be encompassed within the experience and expertise of the licensor itself and be imparted only through technical assistance. Such technical assistance may include training of the licensee's personnel, both at its facilities and at one or more of the licensee's facilities, engineering, design, production, quality control, testing and any other services which the licensee may require in order to effectively utilize a licensed technology.

In most cases, technical assistance is included in an agreement which provides for the grant of a license on patented or unpatented technology. In some instances, however, technical assistance may be provided independent from an explicit license of any technology. A U.S. company which is a leader in the production of a certain agricultural product, for example, may provide advice and training to a foreign company seeking to improve its productivity of such product, without actually granting an express license to any technology itself. Since the technical assistance consists of a transfer of valuable and proprietary information, the agreement should contain limitations on the foreign company's disclosure of the technical information both during and after the termination of the agreement. Moreover, because the agreement may in fact consist of an implied license to use the technology which is provided in the form of technical assistance, it may be desirable to formalize this arrangement by setting forth an actual grant of a license with appropriate limitations thereto.

(iv) *Service Agreements.* Like most technical assistance agreements, a service agreement does not involve an express grant of a license to the foreign party. Rather, the provider merely undertakes to furnish specified services to the foreign company for a given period of time. A services agreement of this type may include management and administrative services, marketing services, research and development services, etc. Services agreements of this type are particularly common in the context of a joint venture or other new enterprise where the provider of the technology also agrees to manage or furnish other services to the new company during its start-up.

§ 18:02. Basic Provisions.

(i) *Recitals.* Possibly more than in other commercial agreements, it is important that license and technology transfer agreements set forth in the recitals the background and intentions of the parties to the agreement. The recitals should clearly point out the owner of the intellectual property rights and the nature of the rights to be transferred. Where the agreement will be subject to review by a local government, it is often helpful to recite the licensor's recognized reputation in the industry and the broader economic benefits that will result from the proposed transfer.

(ii) *Definitions.* Many license agreements begin with a section setting forth certain defined terms used in the agreement. Where the subject matter of the agreement consists of technology for the manufacturer and sale of one or more products, the definition section would specify the product, often by reference to a list contained in an attachment to the agreement. If the agreement extends a license to patents or trademarks, the names, numbers and dates of issue or application of such patents or trademarks should be specified. In the case of know-how, the agreement should utilize a broad definition extending to all knowledge and information with respect to the design, manufacture, production, marketing, maintenance, and repair of the defined product.

If royalties are to be based on net sales, a definition of that term should be included. It is customary to use the invoice price, less certain elements including transportation and insurance; duties, tariffs and taxes; discounts and returns; amounts paid for components purchased from the licensor; and installation and maintenance expenses. If the license is limited to a specific geographical territory, the same may be defined with subsequent references to the "territory." An agreement which extends to improvements on the technology should include a definition thereof which distinguishes improvements from other developments. Agreements which are subject to certain conditions, such as the execution of related agreements or the receipt of necessary governmental approvals often define the term effective date in terms of when such conditions are satisfied.

(iii) *Scope of License.* In the case of license agreements, the precise scope of the license granted should be specified. In each case, the grant should stipulate whether it extends to manufacturing or sales, whether it is exclusive or nonexclusive and whether the grant is limited to a specific territory. If the grant is exclusive, it should be noted that the licensor is only agreeing not to grant similar licenses in the territory but shall not be liable for sales in the territory by third parties. The grant should also stipulate whether the licensor reserves the right to sell directly in the territory and whether the licensee has the right to assign or sublicense the rights granted under the agreement.

The license agreement should also state whether the license extends to any improvements on the licensed products or related technology developed by the licensor during the term of the agreement. If such improvements are to be provided without any additional charge, the licensor may wish to obtain similar access to the licensee's improvements on a reciprocal basis. The agreement might also grant the licensee a first right of refusal to any future licenses for related products which the licensor may elect to make available in the territory. This may be done on a to-be-negotiated, most-favored-licensee, or other basis.

(iv) *Patents, Trademarks and Copyrights.* In the case of licenses of patents or trademarks, the agreement should contain an acknowledgment on the part of the licensee that all proprietary rights thereto continue to be held by the licensor and that the licensee's sole right thereunder is to use the same in strict compliance with the license agreement. The agreement should state that the licensor has the sole right to obtain any patents or register any trademarks as well as the sole right to sue for infringement thereunder, but should impose an obligation on the part of the licensee to notify the licensor of any possible infringement and to assist in prosecuting the infringement action. The agreement should also state the liability and obligations of the licensor in the event that a patent or trademark is found invalid or is subject to a successful claim of infringement.

To the extent permitted by law, the agreement should restrict the licensee from challenging the validity of a patent or trademark registration.[1] It should also allocate responsibility for maintaining the validity of patents or trademarks by filing renewals and paying required fees. The licensee should also undertake to obtain, at its expense, any registered user certificates which may be required in the territory. In the case of trademarks, the agreement should require the licensee to utilize the same in strict compliance with the licensor's instructions. The agreement should also require the licensee to affix any patent numbers, nameplates, labels or other identifying marks to the licensed products as determined by the licensor.

In some cases, the licensee may desire to utilize one of the trade names as part of its corporate name. While such use can create certain advantages for the licensor by building up additional goodwill abroad and perhaps giving it bargaining power over the licensee, this practice also creates the risk that the licensee will not change its name in the event that the licensor desires to terminate

[1] But see §16:02.

the arrangement. If a licensee is allowed to use the licensor's trademarks as part of its corporate name, the license agreement should set forth a clear mechanism for changing the licensee's name in the event of the termination or expiration of the license agreement, and provide for liquidated damages and injunctive relief if it fails to do so. The licensee's charter or equivalent organizational documents should also provide for the taking of the necessary action to change the corporation's name if such license ends.

In perhaps the majority of cases, license agreements do not extend to the licensor's copyrighted materials. Instead, the licensor agrees to make these materials available to the licensee, so that it retains all rights to reproduce the same.

(v) *Know-How and Technical Assistance.* Agreements which extend to know-how provide for the licensor to furnish the licensee, promptly after the effective date of the agreement, with copies of the know-how which is in written form which the licensor deems necessary to manufacture the licensed products. The agreement should specify where such know-how will be made available, in what language, in accordance with what standards (e.g., metric or British measurements), and whether the licensee must pay for the compilation and delivery of such know-how. Some licensors follow the practice of numbering each item delivered to the licensee and recording such delivery in a log acknowledged by the licensee. This accounting will be helpful in obtaining the return of the technical data upon the termination of the license and, more important, proving what was actually provided by the licensor in the event of a subsequent dispute. The licensee may also be required to detail any related know-how that it possessed prior to such delivery.

Provisions on the supply of technical assistance are often included in this section. The agreement may specify the types of technical assistance to be provided, both at the licensor's and licensee's facilities, and the cost and other charges therefor. Often a specified amount of technical assistance (usually stated in terms of a number of mandays) is provided by the licensor at cost (travel and living expenses), with additional time chargeable at cost plus a specified per diem rate. While the licensor often prefers a general description of, and ultimate control over, what technical services will be provided, the licensee should insist on greater specificity, including such items as the designation of the personnel who will provide the services and some assurances that they will continue to be available until the training is satisfactory. Additional specificity, including the number and qualifications of personnel and the tasks to be performed, is required in technical, managerial and other services agreements.

In certain cases it might be necessary for the licensor to warrant that the know-how is current, that it is the same quality utilized by the licensor in its own operations and that the product resulting therefrom will not infringe the proprietary rights of others. A licensor should attempt to disclaim other warranties, however, including any guarantee as to the results which may be obtained by the licensee.

(vi) *Parts and Components.* In many cases, the licensee may desire, or the licensor may require, that the licensed products be fabricated using parts and components supplied by the licensor. These provisions may consist merely of the licensor's agreement to supply such parts and components, and/or the licensee's obligation to purchase the same, at the prices and on the terms and conditions as apply at the time an order is accepted. Alternatively, the agreement may set forth the prices or discounts and other terms which will apply to the sale thereof. In certain cases, a separate parts supply agreement which contains detailed terms and conditions of sale is entered into in connection with the license arrangement.

(vii) *Compensation.* In addition to the consideration for technical assistance, license agreements usually provide for running royalties. The royalty rate may be expressed on a per unit basis or as a percentage of sales. If on sales, the agreement should define when a sale is deemed to be made, i.e., either when the product is shipped and invoiced or when payment is received. The agreement should also require the licensee to maintain complete and accurate books and records of its production and sales and to allow the licensor and its representatives (including independent auditors) access to the same in order to verify the accuracy thereof. Running royalties are usually payable on a quarterly or other periodic basis and are accompanied by reports signed by a responsible officer and setting forth the basis for such quarter's royalty payment. If royalties are payable in a currency other than that in which sales are invoiced, the agreement must set forth the method for determining the applicable exchange rate for computing the royalties. The impact of any local currency controls should also be addressed.

In certain cases, the licensor may seek an initial "lump-sum" or "front end" royalty, prior to its delivery of the technology, either in addition to or in lieu of running-royalties. Lump-sum royalties are common where the licensor has made substantial investments in developing the technology and is unwilling to share it without some assurances of adequate compensation. Lump-sum royalties are also common where a particular technology can be readily transferred to and absorbed by the licensee without extended technical assistance or support or where the technology is deemed to have a limited life. While lump-sum royalties are usually fixed amounts, they may be payable in installments, possibly backed by a letter of credit. Lump-sum royalties are also sometimes treated as advances against future running royalties.

In order to insure a minimum level of compensation from the technology, licensors will often seek to provide for minimum royalties regardless of actual production or sales. Minimum royalties usually commence after a certain start-up period, and are sometimes increased over the course of the agreement to reflect the parties' expectation of growing production and sales. The agreement may provide that upon the failure of the licensee to pay the minimum royalties, the licensor may elect either to sue for damages, to terminate the agreement or to convert an exclusive license into a nonexclusive license that would allow it to license other manufacturers in the territory. It should be noted that local law in some countries prohibits minimum royalties. In these as in all cases, the agreement should contain an affirmative obligation on the part of the licensee to use its best efforts to meet the needs of the territory for the licensed product in order to maximize royalty income.

Finally, the section on compensation should allocate between the parties the responsibility for local income taxes on the royalties. Local laws often impose a withholding tax on royalty payments abroad which the licensee is responsible to withhold and pay to the governmental authorities. In such cases, the agreement should confirm this withholding tax obligation and provide that the licensee will promptly pay the tax and remit certificates evidencing such payment to the licensor to allow it to apply for a foreign tax credit. If the royalties are stated on an after tax basis, the taxes will be paid by the licensee. This net royalty approach insures the payment of a certain royalty regardless of changes in local taxation. However, since local taxes will often be deemed paid by the licensor, the licensor should "gross-up" its royalty income and apply for the foreign tax credit thereon.

(viii) *Confidentiality.* To the extent that the agreement calls for the transfer of nonpatented know-how, it must contain covenants on the part of the licensee to keep the same confidential and otherwise treat such know-how as a trade secret. If the prospective licensee requires access to the know-how prior to the execution of the agreement, it should be required to execute a secrecy agreement which will allow it to evaluate the know-how but prohibit it from using or disclosing the same except in accordance with a definitive agreement. Confidentiality clauses often limit the disclosure of know-how to such employees as may need to have access to the same in order to produce the licensed product and, to the extent permitted by local law, require such employees to execute a confidentiality agreement with respect to the know-how. The license agreement may also restrict the licensee's right to make copies of any documentation containing know-how.

To the extent permitted by local law, the confidentiality and limited use obligations contained in the agreement should survive the termination or expiration of the agreement. In order to avoid antitrust problems, the obligations should not continue if the know-how is found to be in the public domain prior to disclosure to the licensee or becomes publicly known thereafter without the negligence or fault of the licensee.

(ix) *Quality Standards and Warranties.* In addition to the other obligations imposed on the licensee, it should undertake to manufacture the licensed products in strict conformance with the licensor's quality standards and specifications. This is particularly important where the licensee has been authorized to sell the licensed products under the licensor's trademarks, since poor quality will impair the value of the licensor's trademarks. Provisions of this type often require the licensee to submit samples of its production for the licensor's approval prior to the commencement of its sale thereof and to periodically allow the licensor's representatives access to the licensee's facilities in order to obtain samples or to otherwise insure compliance with quality standards.

The agreement may also set forth the warranties which the licensee will be required to offer. If possible, the licensee should obtain an indemnification from product liability on products produced by the licensee, at least to the extent that they fail to meet the licensor's quality standards and specifications. Ideally, the licensee would be obligated to secure and maintain adequate liability insurance against such claims with the licensor expressly named as an insured thereunder.

(x) *Term and Termination.* A technology transfer agreement is often designed to continue for a term that is roughly equivalent to the expected useful life of the underlying know-how or actual life of the patent. Because of the investment usually required by the licensor to exploit the technology and the risk of its unauthorized use after disclosure, both parties normally prefer a relatively long term, generally five to ten years. At the same time, the agreement should contain the circumstances in which the licensor may terminate the agreement, such as failure to make required payments, any other breach which is not cured within a short default period, bankruptcy or insolvency of the licensee, and the imposition of governmental restrictions which affect the agreement or performance thereof by the licensee.

The agreement should also specify the consequences upon termination, including the immediate cessation of the licensee's manufacture of the licensed product and use of the patents, know-how and trademarks, the requirement to return any documentation containing know-how, the continuation of the licensee's obligation to pay accrued royalties and be bound by the nonuse and nondisclosure obligations and the disposition of any parts or components purchased from the licensor. In order to avoid confusion, the agreement should distinguish between premature termination and expiration and describe the rights of the licensee following normal expiration of the agreement (e.g., continued use of the know-how in the territory on a royalty-free basis, but subject to the limited use and nondisclosure obligations).

Where ongoing services are being provided, such as in the case of a technical assistance or management services agreement, the parties may wish to include a mechanism under which the agreement will be renewed.

(xi) *Miscellaneous Provisions.* Finally, the agreement should contain certain other provisions commonly included in international commercial agreements. While the U.S. licensor may prefer that the agreement be governed by U.S. law, this may be prohibited under certain transfer of technology laws. Arbitration or some other alternative mechanism for dispute resolution is often desirable, but the licensor may prefer to exclude the licensee's payment and nondisclosure obligations from such arbitration. A provision is also generally included for excused performance for reasons of force majeure, possibly excepting again the licensee's payment, nondisclosure and certain other obligations. Provisions rendering the licensor's performance subject to, and requiring the licensee to comply with, any applicable requirements under the Export Administration Agreement of 1979, the Trading with the Enemy Act of 1917, The Mutual Security Act of 1954, The Foreign Corrupt Practices Act of 1977, and similar laws, as well as any regulations thereunder should also be included. Restrictions on the assignment or transfer of the agreement or any rights thereunder should also be expressly stated.

PART V—SUGGESTIONS FOR FURTHER READING

Books

Echstrom, L., Licensing in Foreign and Domestic Operations (1986).

Goldscheider, R., & Arnold, T., The Law and Business of Licensing: Licensing in the 1980's (1986).

Lades, S., Patents, Trademarks, and Related Rights, National and International Protection (1975).

Melville, L., Forms and Agreements on Intellectual Property and International Licensing (1987).

Articles

Byington "Planning & Drafting of International Licensing Agreements," 6 NCJ Int'l L & Com Reg 1931 (1981).

Letterman, "U.S. Controls in Exporting Technical Data: An Analysis and Selective Practioners Guide," 9 Hous J Int'l L 59 (1986).

Note, "Territorial Distribution and Patent Licensing in the European Community: Towards a Rule of Reason," 20 Stan J Int'l L 503 (1984).

Safran, "Protectioc of Inventions in the Multinational Marketplace: Problems and Pitfalls in Obtaining and Using Patents," 9 NC J Int'l L & Com Reg 117 (1984).

PART VI

DIRECT FOREIGN INVESTMENT: BRANCHES AND SUBSIDIARIES

CHAPTER 19

FOREIGN INVESTMENT DECISION

§ 19:01. In General.

As noted in Part I, direct foreign investment encompasses those transactions in which an enterprise creates or acquires its own establishment abroad. This establishment may consist of a subsidiary—a separate and distinct legal entity—or simply a branch of the enterprise itself. If a subsidiary, it may be organized either locally or under the laws of another jurisdiction, and may be either wholly- or partially-owned. The local establishment may be a full-blown operation which manufactures and markets products locally and abroad, or may serve only certain limited functions, such as providing marketing services or acting as a holding company.

Despite all of these variables, there are several issues which are common to most foreign branch or subsidiary operations. These include the opportunities, risks and certain other considerations which are part of the foreign investment decision as well as the impact of special foreign investment laws on the proposed activities.

§ 19:02. Factors Motivating Direct Foreign Investment.

A company's decision to establish a foreign branch or subsidiary may be motivated by a number of factors. Among the most important are: (i) to enter a new market which cannot be served by export sales; (ii) to increase revenues or to respond to competition in a market currently being served by export sales; (iii) to obtain a more economical source of supply for products to be sold in other jurisdictions; (iv) to take advantage of tax or other incentives otherwise available only to foreign investors; and (v) to place certain activities outside of the jurisdiction of onerous taxes or regulations existing in certain countries.

Serving a foreign market by means of exports presents obvious advantages over local production. It allows the foreign manufacturer to avoid putting capital at risk in a jurisdiction whose political and/or economic stability may be doubtful. At the same time, export sales may not always be possible. In many foreign jurisdictions, particularly in developing countries, high tariffs or absolute prohibitions on certain imports may render exports uneconomical or altogether impossible. These import barriers are usually designed to encourage local production or to protect local industry by providing an economic advantage for locally-produced merchandise. The foreign manufacturer is then forced to establish its own local production facility to serve the market or to exploit the market through some other mechanism, such as licensing a local producer in exchange for royalties.

Even in jurisdictions in which exports are not legally barred by restrictive trade barriers, however, export sales have certain limitations. Production costs in the United States may be significantly higher than those present in the local market. These additional costs, together with transportation, insurance, tariffs, and other expenses associated with exports, may substantially reduce the exporter's profit margin. Moreover, if a competitor commences local production of the product, the foreign manufacturer may be unable to retain market share without responding with its own local production. A local branch or subsidiary may also increase revenue on the sale of the product by eliminating sales commissions for agents and discounts to distributors. A local branch or subsidiary may also increase sales volume, particularly for products which require the manufacturer to provide local technical support and maintenance.

Taking advantage of economical sources of supply is another major motivation for establishing a local enterprise. Prior to World War II, most direct foreign investment was confined to the extractive industries or agricultural production, providing items that were either impossible or impractical to obtain in the United States. High import duties around the world, such as the Smoot-Hawley rates in the United States, as well as transportation and communication difficulties prevented companies from taking advantage of lower labor rates in developing countries by manufacturing abroad for export to the United States. Although foreign mining and agricultural activities continue to represent a significant portion of U.S. foreign investment, reductions in tariffs for manufactured goods have resulted in a substantial increase in local investment for export production.

Another reason for establishing a local presence is to take advantage of tax holidays or other foreign investment incentives available under the laws of some jurisdictions. These incentives were traditionally available only in developing countries. Recently, however, even industrialized nations, or their political subdivisions such as the U.S. states, have begun to offer tax holidays, funds for infrastructural improvements, favorable financing or exemptions from certain restrictive regulations in order to attract foreign investment and the corresponding creation of jobs. Local production may also be necessary to take advantage of certain markets, such as a local government itself, which give preference to locally-produced merchandise.

An additional factor which has led to the movement of certain activities offshore is to avoid onerous tax and regulatory obligations. While the international tax systems of most countries are designed to prevent taxpayers from avoiding taxation by moving income-generating activities to other jurisdictions, the devices which are employed, such as Subpart F under the Internal Revenue Code, are not intended to extend to genuine manufacturing operations. Various types of regulatory measures, such as environmental protections, OSHA requirements, and labor law obligations can also be circumvented by means of foreign production. Foreign affiliates of U.S. banks can often provide less costly financing because they are not subject to U.S. banking regulations.

The foregoing represents some of the most common factors which motivate a company to create a foreign branch or subsidiary. There are, of course, many others. In planning a proposed foreign investment, it is obviously important for the attorney to understand the client's objectives so as to achieve the most favorable result.

§ 19:03. Special Risks Presented by Direct Foreign Investment.

Each of these motivating factors implies certain advantages of direct foreign investment. These advantages must, however, be weighed against the special risks presented by a foreign branch or subsidiary. These special risks are often classified as either political or economic.

Political risks arise from the submission of one's capital to the sovereignty of a foreign government, thus creating the opportunity for such government to seize such capital, or to take or refrain from taking some action which reduces the value of the investment. Expropriation is the most extreme of political risks; it is not, however, the most common. More subtle actions, such as the imposition of price controls which limit the foreign operation's profitability or exchange controls or other regulations which limit its ability to acquire foreign primary materials or to expatriate capital or profits, are considerably more common than the total confiscation of foreign assets. Other actions which may be taken

194

include the imposition of burdensome taxes, the enactment of new laws which force foreign subsidiaries to increase domestic content or reduce domestic sales or the promulgation of regulations which force the subsidiary to accept less attractive terms as a condition to retaining government or other major contracts. The failure of a government to protect foreign capital against a civil disturbance or to alleviate the impact of an action by a court, labor union or other body is also an important political risk.

The economic risks presented by direct foreign investment depend upon the nature and purpose of the investment. If the proposed foreign branch or subsidiary is designed to service a local market, the investor faces the risk that the market is economically inadequate to support the investment, that the product cannot be competitively priced or that it otherwise fails to meet with local acceptance. If the investment is designed to take advantage of low production costs, such as labor, primary materials or energy, to manufacture for export, the economic risks of the proposal would include the possibility of significant increases in these local production costs as well as costs for transporting the product to the foreign market. In both cases, inflation, exchange rate fluctuations, increases in interest rates and other economic factors may also affect the profitability of the foreign operation.

Before proceeding with a proposed investment, the investor and its counsel should attempt to identify these special risks and take steps to minimize them. Various resources are available to assist foreign investors in forecasting political risk and in developing reliable financial information to reduce economic risks. International banks as well as research and consulting firms develop information on the general political stability of a country from which they attempt to predict the likelihood of governmental action which would affect a proposed investment. These and other organizations also compile economic information, which often must be based on sources outside of the government itself, the analysis of which should reduce the risk of unforeseen conditions that may render the investment undesirable. Foreign investors may also be eligible for financial assistance in preparing a feasibility study analyzing the costs and benefits of a proposed foreign operation. Such studies are particularly important in determining whether a proposed location has the infrastructural facilities to support the proposed investment.

One of the most common means of alleviating the special risk associated with a proposed foreign investment is simply to share the risk with another investor. This is usually accomplished by structuring the investment as a joint venture with a local investor who agrees to contribute capital to the local company in exchange for a share in its profits. In some cases, the local government will assume the role of a co-investor. Another important mechanism for dealing with political risk is to structure the investment so that the foreign subsidiary is dependent on the parent for trademarks, technology, management, components or foreign marketing, thus discouraging the local government from taking any action which might cause the parent to cease providing such support. In certain cases, the investor may be able to obtain guarantees against governmental actions which might interfere with the branch or subsidiary's activities. Such guarantees, however, are of questionable enforceability, both with respect to a government itself and to its possible successor.

§ 19:04. Legal Form of Foreign Enterprise.

An additional issue that must be considered as part of the foreign investment decision is the legal form that the foreign enterprise will take. One option which is available under most circumstances is simply a branch or other extention of the company itself. A branch has, of course, no separate legal identity of its own. Thus, any activities undertaken by the branch will be attributed directly to the company itself. The alternative is to effect the investment through some type of distinct legal entity, such as a partnership or some form of corporation. For purposes of this discussion, this independent legal entity, whether in the form of a partnership, corporation or otherwise, is referred to as a subsidiary.

Numerous factors must be considered in determining whether to undertake an investment by means of a branch or a subsidiary. In some cases the foreign investment laws themselves will dictate the legal form of the investment. Many of these laws, for example, prohibit foreign investment other than through a locally-organized subsidiary or favor such form of investment by restricting eligibility for investment incentives or government contracts to local entities. Where laws require the investment to be made with local equity participation or mandate a gradual increase of local participation, a separate legal entity may be the only effective means of complying with the requirements. On the other hand, local laws in some jurisdictions require or favor branch operations in certain industries such as banking and mining.

In general, the legal treatment of the foreign investment under local laws will favor a local subsidiary rather than a branch. In most cases, a branch will subject all of the assets of the investing company to local jurisdiction, while a subsidiary would limit the investor's exposure to the assets of the subsidiary itself. While the parent will often have to guarantee the foreign subsidiary's performance of certain obligations, such as loans and major contracts, use of the subsidiary will often limit the parent's exposure with respect to product liability, employee termination and other claims. The corporate law in some jurisdictions also require that any company doing business locally must file or publish annually an audited balance sheet, and/or certain other information. By operating through a subsidiary, rather than a branch, a company which is not otherwise obligated to conduct an audit or disclose such information could limit the impact of such laws to the subsidiary itself rather than to the company as a whole.

In most cases, the use of a subsidiary for conducting foreign operations also facilitates transactions within the company group itself. The subsidiary will often make payments to the parent for supplies, technology, interest and dividends. It will also keep separate books which may be in a currency other than that of the parent. A domestic subsidiary can also be helpful in creating a local image for the foreign operation, thus diffusing possible prejudice against its products. Operating through a subsidiary rather than a branch also facilitates and limits the investor's exposure in the event it becomes necessary to liquidate the investment.

Finally, the tax treatment of the foreign investment, both under U.S. and local law, should also be considered in choosing between a branch and a subsidiary. While the income of a foreign branch of a U.S. corporation would continue to be subject to U.S. tax, the income (other then Subpart F income) of a foreign subsidiary would not, unless and until it is actually received by the U.S. parent. In most foreign jurisdictions, it is desirable to engage in business locally through a subsidiary rather than a branch. Taxes on local companies are often lower than on branches, even after adjustment for eventual withholding taxes on dividends. This structure will normally allow the parent to more effectively shield its income from local taxation, since only the local entity will be subject to taxation. On the other hand, where significant losses at the foreign level are anticipated, a branch structure would allow such losses to be used against the U.S. operation's income. A branch structure in several countries also would allow the enterprise to move funds from country to country without paying a withholding tax on interest, royalty, and dividend payments.

In most cases, the legal and tax treatment of the foreign operation favors the utilization of a local subsidiary as the vehicle through which the investment will be undertaken. While the domestic corporate structure of multinational corporations varies considerably, often including several divisions with different responsibilities, the international corporate structure is typified by a subsidiary in each foreign jurisdiction in which the nature of the company's activities would require it to somehow register or qualify to do business or, more importantly, subject it to local taxes. In some cases, these corporations may be owned indirectly through an international holding company which may also be organized offshore to facilitate financing or to secure more favorable tax treatment. In some instances, a multinational may have more than one local subsidiary, separating the activities of its overall divisions or dividing operations between manufacturing and sales for tax or other purposes.

CHAPTER 20

FOREIGN INVESTMENT LAWS AND REGULATIONS

§20:01. Purpose and Effect.
§20:02. Prohibitions and Conditions.
§20:03. Investment Incentives.

§ 20.01. Purpose and Effect.

A foreign branch or subsidiary will be regulated and affected by various local laws and regulations, including those governing taxation, labor relations, corporate structure, commercial transactions, real estate ownership, and foreign exchange. In addition to these general laws, however, many countries have enacted special laws or regulations governing foreign investment.[1] While the impact of all local law must be considered prior to instituting the proposed operations, this analysis should usually begin with these foreign investment laws since they may affect not only the structure of the proposal but also whether it will be permitted in the first place.

[1] Many of these laws are compiled in Investment Laws of the World, a publication of the International Centre for the Settlement of Investment Disputes (ICSID).

Although foreign investment laws may also be found in industrialized countries such as Australia, Canada and Japan, they are
most commonly encountered in developing countries. Their purpose is usually two-fold: to control the entry of foreign investment
and to provide incentives to encourage certain types of investments. In some cases, such as Mexico's Law to Promote Mexican
Investments and Regulate Foreign Investment, the control aspect
predominates. In other cases, such as the Dominican Republic's
Industrial Incentive and Protection Act, the purpose is primarily to
promote foreign investment by according it preferential treatment.
Developing countries employ these foreign investment laws as a
means of furthering their domestic, political, and economic objectives. Thus, where a country's national economic or development
plan may call for development in certain industries or geographical
areas, the investment law may implement this policy directly by
providing incentives for foreign investment in such areas or, indirectly, by restricting or discouraging investment in other areas.

Egypt's Law No. 43 is illustrative of the purpose and effect of
such investment laws. Enacted in 1974, the law was the cor-
nerstone of a new "open-door" policy toward foreign investment.
The law creates important incentives for foreign investment,
including guarantees against expropriation, tax holidays and
exemptions from certain labor, profit-sharing and other laws which
would be a nuisance to foreign investors. Special incentives are
offered in key sectors and geographical areas. At the same time,
the law also provides that all new investment expansions, remittances of profit and capital, employment of foreigners and certain
other actions taken by foreign controlled companies be approved
in advance by the Egyption General Authority for the Investment
and Free Zones. This allows the government to focus investment in
priority areas and to maintain overall control over the investment.

The Peoples Republic of China's Law on Joint Ventures Using
Chinese and Foreign Investment is another example of a specialized foreign investment law. In many socialist countries, foreign investment is virtually prohibited. While China's treatment of
foreign investment still cannot be characterized as an "open-door"

policy, the Law on Joint Ventures does allow for private investment under certain circumstances. As might be expected, however, all aspects of a joint venture are subject to government approval, in this case by the Foreign Investment Commission. The law also contains considerable protection for the Chinese participant, even though it allows majority foreign equity participation.

Latin American countries were among the first to enact comprehensive laws regulating foreign investment. Decision 24 of the Andean Common Market obligated ANCOM's member countries (Venezuela, Colombia, Ecuador, Chile and Peru) to enact specific laws which establish the conditions under which foreign investment would be permitted. One of these conditions called upon the investor to execute an agreement with the local government under which it agreed to "transform" the project into a local investment within a period not to exceed 20 years. This transformation was to be accomplished gradually selling off the equity to local investors and employing local managers and directors. While the member countries' enforcement of these agreements has waned as a result of economic and other problems and the weakening of ANCOM itself, the transformation concept has found favor in other countries who encourage it either by law or informal policy.

The foregoing examples also illustrate how foreign investment laws, or their implementation, change with changes in local policy toward foreign investment. Egypt's Law No. 43 and China's Law on Joint Ventures were designed to encourage foreign investment after periods in which those countries were virtually closed to foreign capital. Mexico's foreign investment law was a codification of policies which increasingly sought to limit foreign investment; its implementation in recent years, however, has been characterized by an easing of the restrictions on foreign-controlled investment in certain sectors. These changes may result from changes of or within the government itself or from general economic developments. It can probably be safely said that as a result of increasing competition for foreign investment on a world-wide basis, the current trend of such laws is generally toward encouraging rather than limiting foreign capital.

§ 20:02. Prohibitions and Conditions.

Despite this trend, however, most foreign investment laws still regulate foreign investment in some way. This is usually accomplished by (i) establishing absolute prohibitions on foreign investment in certain sectors; and (ii) creating certain conditions which affect the structure or operation of the proposed investment.

Absolute prohibitions on foreign investment are usually motivated by national security or defense considerations, by a perception that the prohibited area does not need foreign capital, or by a desire to prevent the area from being dominated or significantly influenced by foreigners. These prohibitions frequently extend, for example, to such industries as armaments, energy, banking, telecommunication, transportation, tourism, and mining. Occasionally the foreign investment laws or regulations promulgated pursuant thereto will specify precisely which industries are closed to foreign investment. In most cases, however, the law will contain general categories, allowing the regulators to determine whether a particular proposal falls within the scope of the prohibitions. This may be particularly troublesome in the case of those laws whose prohibitions are stated not in terms of particular industries but on the basis of whether the investment will meet certain economic criteria, such as maintenance of a favorable balance of payments or promotion of exports. Some laws expressly designate those areas which are open to foreign investment rather than those which are not.

In addition to establishing the areas which are open to foreign investment, many foreign investment laws set forth certain conditions which the investment must satisfy either to proceed at all or to obtain certain beneficial treatment. One of the most celebrated of these is the so-called "Calvo Clause" which requires the investor to agree not to resort to the protection of its government in the event of a dispute or other problem arising from the investment. Another common condition is that the foreign investor not control the investment, either through equity ownership or otherwise. This would normally require the investment to be made in the form of a joint venture with foreign equity participation limited to 49%.

The transformation arrangement arising out of ANCOM Decision 24 or a similar mechanism for gradually decreasing foreign influence over the investment appears as a condition in many foreign investment laws.

At times the conditions imposed on foreign investments do not appear in the investment laws or regulations but are the result of negotiations with the government to obtain approval for the proposed investment. These conditions may be quite detailed and include such commitments on the part of the investor as the employment and training of a minimum number of local workers, the use of local managers and technicians, the construction of infrastructural facilities such as roads or powerlines, or the making of contributions to local public projects such as housing, schools or hospitals. This undertaking by the investor may also be the quid pro quo that renders the proposed project eligible for certain investment incentives.

The foreign investment law or the administering authority may also impose conditions respecting the type of capital or other contributions made by the investor and certain performance criteria that the operation must satisfy. In some cases, for example, the investor will be required to provide foreign financing for the operation so that it will not compete for local credit. The host government may also require the technology and equipment used by the branch or subsidiary to be state-of-the-art. The performance criteria may require the operation to maintain a positive balance of payments or produce a minimum amount of exports, to utilize a specified minimum amount of local content, to employ a certain number of local workers or to generate a maximum rate of return to the parent. The governing authority may also specify the minimum amount of capital that must be invested during the start-up period or require that it be located in a certain underdeveloped geographical area.

In most cases, these conditions are not mandated by the investment law itself. The conditions are usually established through negotiations with the foreign investment authority and are contained in an overall investment plan which must be accepted by the authority and the investor before the investment may proceed. In preparing such a plan for submission to the authority, as well as for the subsequent negotiations, it is important to consult with local counsel to determine which, if any, of the conditions are mandatory and which are subject to negotiation. It is also important for the investor to review the government's current development plan or to consult other sources to determine its bargaining posture in light of the priority being given to investments of the type contemplated. Careful preparation of the investment proposal and the use of experienced and knowledgeable negotiators can often reduce significantly the conditions which may otherwise be imposed on the foreign investor.

§ 20:03. Investment Incentives.

In those countries seeking to attract rather than control foreign capital, the foreign investment laws may set forth a framework of incentives and guarantees designed to improve the local investment climate. These measures frequently include exemptions from taxes and customs tariffs, subsidies for raw materials, favorable financing for construction of plants and other facilities, guarantees against expropriation, assurances of availability of foreign currency, exemptions from restrictive local laws, assistance in site selection, etc. In many cases, the law itself will merely authorize the administering authority to grant such incentives on a discretionary basis. Accordingly, the impact of each of these measures on the particular investment must be carefully weighed in order to negotiate the most favorable treatment for the proposed operation.

The most common investment incentive is a temporary exemption from specified taxes, commonly known as a "tax holiday." The investment law may expressly exempt foreign investment projects from income, withholding, property and other taxes for periods extending for several years. In evaluating tax holidays, however, the investor should consider that the initial years of the operation may not result in the generation of taxable income at all, thus defeating the value of the income tax holiday for such years.

Moreover, most foreign taxes are creditable against U.S. taxes, so that a tax holiday may be significant only to the extent that the foreign taxes otherwise payable would be in excess of those payable in the United States or would otherwise fail to qualify for the foreign tax credit. Finally, since many foreign production facilities are operated as cost centers that generate minimal profits, the impact of an income tax exemption may be insignificant.

Another common investment incentive is an exemption from customs tariffs. Nearly all countries, including the United States,[2] provide some mechanism for rebating or reducing customs tariffs paid or payable on raw materials and components imported to undergo further processing or assembly and subsequently exported. Certain countries also offer whole or partial tariff exemptions on machinery, spare parts and equipment used for export production. These exemptions may be created under the host country's customs code rather than the foreign investment law. It should also be determined whether the tariff exemption would extend to any applicable export tariffs or taxes.

Another important category of investment incentives involves commitments on the part of the government to provide financial assistance to reduce the risks associated with foreign investments. The financial assistance may take the form of subsidies for materials and labor in the construction of an appropriate facility, for rent on existing facilities or for energy, transportation, and other costs. In certain cases, the government may offer favorable financing or provide guarantees to obtain bank financing at favorable rates. Occasionally, a government will act as a co-investor or will agree to purchase a minimum amount of the facility's production. Governments may also provide exemptions from restrictive labor, regulatory and other laws which would otherwise increase the investor's operating costs. In order to reduce risks, the government may guarantee that the project will have access to sufficient foreign currency for debt service, purchase of imports, payment of royalties and repatriation of capital. In appropriate cases, a govern

---

[2] For a discussion of the U.S. measures available for such purpose, see §§6:17-6:20.

ment may agree to provide the investor with a virtual monopoly for a given product by blocking imports or refusing to approve similar foreign investment proposals. In such cases, however, the government will usually impose price controls on local sales to prevent abuse. Some foreign investment laws also contain guarantees against expropriation. The enforceability of these and any other future commitments on the part of the government should, however, be carefully considered if they are deemed important to the success of the investment project.

The extent to which the investor will obtain such incentives is largely a function of the priority attached by the government to the investment proposal and the contribution which it is perceived to offer to the local economy. For these reasons, the ability to negotiate the most favorable package of investment incentives requires an investigation into the developmental priorities of the host country and the presentation of an investment plan which responds to these priorities in terms of job creation, export production, import substitution, technology transfer, etc.

Both the conditions and the incentives which have been negotiated between the investor and the government are often set forth in a formal authorization for the proposed investment. This authorization may take the form of a letter, resolution or agreement between the government and the investor. If in the form of an agreement, it may contain other contractual provisions such as a mechanism for dispute resolution to which the investor may resort in the event of a disagreement over the respective obligations of the parties. While the government's surveillance of the investor's compliance with its undertakings varies from country to country, it should be assumed that any investment incentives or other benefits accorded to the investor may be terminated or not renewed if the investor fails to comply with its undertakings.

CHAPTER 21

ORGANIZING A FOREIGN SUBSIDIARY

§ 21:01. Using Local Counsel.

Assume that the prospective foreign investor has considered the factors entering into a decision to invest abroad, has negotiated an acceptable investment plan which includes certain conditions as well as investment incentives, and has elected to proceed with the proposal through a wholly-owned subsidiary organized under local law. In most cases, the investor and its U.S. counsel would have already worked closely with local counsel in the host country to evaluate the investment proposal and to develop a structure and strategy which minimizes the risks of the investment while maximizing its potential benefits. Even if the foreign investor has not theretofore utilized local counsel, however, it will normally have to retain an attorney or other specialist in the host country in order to organize the local subsidiary.

Unlike in the United States where an individual can simply complete and file a simple form in order to organize a corporation,

207

the formation of corporations in many foreign countries is quite involved, requiring the preparation of long documents, the securing of approvals or certificates from various governmental agencies, and often formal appearances before notaries or other officers who review and witness the execution of the documents before they are filed to effect the final organization. While these procedures may be effected in some countries by nonlawyers, it is usually advisable to engage local counsel in order to assure that the corporation is validly organized and that the organizational documents provide maximum protection for the investor. This is particularly important where another party may be involved, such as a co-investor or a bank which is extending financing to the subsidiary.

§ 21:02. Company Laws Generally.

While most texts tend to emphasize the distinctions between the law governing U.S. corporations and that governing its foreign counterparts, given the range of possibilities the similarity is even more surprising. As in the case of Delaware, New York or similar corporation statutes, most foreign jurisdictions have specific laws (though usually on a federal level) governing the organization, operation and dissolution of various types of business organizations. These laws which are generally referred to as Company Laws or Acts, also contain provisions regarding the capital structure, organization, rights and liabilities of the partners or shareholders, and administration and management of the company.

Local company laws, particularly in civil law jurisdictions, often provide for various types of business organizations. In most cases, however, a foreign investment investor will find that only one or two offer an appropriate vehicle through which to conduct business abroad. An organization similar to a partnership is available under the company law—or separate partnership laws—of most jurisdictions. Except in the case of certain joint ventures or in unusual transactions where tax considerations favor the use of such a structure, however, a partnership-type form is usually undesirable since it fails to accord the partners the limited liability available to a corporation. In certain jurisdictions special types or cooperatives, associations or corporations are provided for where the business of the organization is confined to agriculture, mining or other areas, or where the enterprise will meet certain other conditions. Such legal organizations are rarely utilized in the context of foreign investment, however, unless they are accorded preferential treatment and the conditions can be readily satisfied.

In most cases, the foreign investor should seek to utilize a legal entity which offers most of the advantages available to a U.S. corporation—limited liability for the shareholders, perpetual existence, transferability of shares, broad corporate purposes, centralized management, etc. In most jurisdictions, whether following the common law or civil law traditions, there are two types of corporations: the private company, which corresponds roughly to the close corporation, and the public company, which closely resembles a standard U.S. corporation. While the distinction between the private company and the public company differs from country to country, in general a private company has a maximum number of shareholders (usually less than 100) and may not make a public offering of its stock or other securities. Public Companies, though not so restricted, are often required to conduct annual audits, to publish financial information and to meet certain other obligations. Other legal and nonlegal distinctions between such entities may make one or the other appropriate in given circumstances.

§ 21:03. Illustrative Jurisdictions.

While there are many similarities in the types of legal entities which are appropriate vehicles for foreign investment projects, there are also some important differences in the nature of such entities and the procedures for organizing the same. This section summarizes some of these differences in four important countries.

West Germany. West Germany is illustrative of the civil law jurisdictions. West German law provides for two forms of corporations, the Gesellschaft mit beschraenkter Haftung (GmbH), and the Aktiengesellschaft (AG). The GmbH is the entity best suited for family businesses and wholly-owned subsidiaries, while the AG is appropriate for public companies. Both corporations are formed by a notarial act in which the incorporators or their representatives adopt the articles of incorporation, subscribe to the shares, and conduct the first shareholder meeting. At such meeting at least one managing director (Geschaftsfuhrer) who has full power to represent the company is appointed. The managing director then applies for registration of the company with the Commercial Register Court. The managing director of the GmbH, or Board of Managers (Vorstand) of the AG is monitored by a Supervisory Board (Aufsichtsrat), whose approval may be required under the charter to take certain actions. Large GmbH's and all AG's must prepare annual financial statements which must be audited by independent accountants and published.

Japan. Japanese law provides for two major corporate forms, the limited liability company, Kabushiki Kaisha (KK), and the private limited company, Yugen Kaisha (YK). The KK closely resembles the U.S. and European corporation and is the vehicle adopted for most foreign investment. The YK, which is also a separate legal entity distinct from its shareholders, is generally used for small, family-controlled ventures where limitations on the transfer of shares and other restrictions on corporate management are sought. A KK requires at least seven shareholders, while a YK needs only two members for formation. A YK's membership is limited to 60; a KK can have any number of shareholders. Unlike YK's, KK's are also authorized to issue various classes of stock. Both companies are managed by a Board of Directors (Torishimariyaku), with representative directors performing the functions of officers of the U.S. corporation. A KK must also have at least one statutory auditor (Kansayaku), and in some cases an accountant auditor (Kaikei-Kansanin). The KK is also required to issue annual financial reports on operations and to comply with other formalities not applicable to the YK.

Saudi Arabia. Saudi Arabian Companies Law authorizes a number of forms of doing business, including the joint stock company, Sharika Musahma, the limited liability company, Sharika Musahama Mahduda, and the joint venture, Sharika Mahassah. The joint stock company is most similar to the U.S. corporation. It is formed by a minimum of five founders who must sign and register a memorandum of association, and who must contribute a minimum of SR 2 million. Their equity ownership is represented by negotiable shares of equal value into which the capital is divided. The joint stock company is administered by a Board of Directors, each member of which must also be a stockholder. The joint stock company must maintain prescribed capital reserve and is subject to certain requirements to maintain books and records and conduct an annual audit.

A limited liability company is perhaps more similar to a U.S. partnership than a corporation, though its "shareholders" do enjoy limited liability. It may have from two to fifty shareholders who must each contribute a minimum of SR 500,000. The capital is divided into shares of equal value which may not be negotiated. The limited liability is also precluded from offering its shares to the public. It is administered by one or more managers who may or may not be shareholders. Limited liability companies are required to appoint at least one auditor, but are subject to less stringent financial reporter obligations.

A joint venture is not technically a distinct legal entity but an association of two or more parties. Nevertheless, the joint venture can take on a legal identity similar to a partnership, with the joint venture agreement serving as the memorandum of association. The Companies Law also include certain requirements on the joint venture independent from the joint venture agreement.

Mexico. While Mexico's General Law of Mercantile Corporations, Lew General de Sociedados Mercantile, provides for a number of legal entities, the most important are the limited liability company, Sociedad de Responsabilidad Limitada (SRL), and the corporation, Sociedad Anonima (SA). Both are distinct legal entities whose members/shareholders enjoy limited liability.

However, whereas the capital of the SA is divided into shares which may be freely transferred (unless otherwise provided in the Charter) and publicly traded, an SRL's capital consists of participations or "quotas" which may not be freely transferred or traded on a public market. Neither may SRL's issue bonds or debentures to the public. Both entities are organized by executing a charter and bylaws (escritura constitutiva) in the presence of a notary and registering the same in the applicable public registry of commerce. The company law provides for ordinary and extraordinary meetings of members/shareholders, special quorum and voting requirements, and certain minority rights. The SA is administered by a board of directors (consejo adminstrativo) headed by a chairman (presidente) which usually appoints and delegates managerial authority by means of powers-of-attorney to a general director (director general) and/or a general manager (grente general). A SA must also appoint one or more statutory auditors (comisarios) to oversee the financial affairs of the company. The capital stock of both entities may be fixed or variable, the latter (abbreviated SA de CV or SRL de CV) allowing the entity to increase or decrease its capital without complying with the formalities of amending its charter.

In practice, an SRL is commonly used in Mexico only in the case of rural land and farming operations or for small ventures. The SA is considered a more appropriate vehicle for use by foreign investors.

CHAPTER 22

OPERATING A FOREIGN SUBSIDIARY

§22:01. Financing Foreign Subsidiary.
§22:02. Intercompany Transactions.
§22:03. Local Tax Considerations.

§ 22:01. Financing Foreign Subsidiary.

One of the most fundamental issues in the operation of a foreign subsidiary is the sources and manner in which it will secure its initial and ongoing financial requirements. The financial needs of the foreign operation will vary significantly depending upon its function: a company devoted solely to marketing a product line abroad may require only a small facility with few employees while an offshore production facility may have significantly greater capital requirements. In most instances, however, the subsidiary will need to be capitalized at some level and will require additional funds from time to time, either from its parent or from some other source.

While the term "foreign investment" may suggest the movement of capital across national borders, this does not always occur in the establishment of a foreign branch or subsidiary. The local branch or subsidiary may obtain its operating funds through borrowings from local or other sources. Among the most common alternatives currently employed to finance the activities of a foreign subsidiary are (i) intercompany financing from the parent company, a finance subsidiary or other affiliate, (ii) local borrowing from domestic commercial banks, (iii) Eurodollar financing, (iv) international capital markets, and (v) government supported financing from national or multinational sources.

(i) *Intercompany Financing*. The initial funds for capitalizing a foreign subsidiary will normally come directly from the parent corporation in exchange for all of the subsidiary's capital stock. In most cases, this can be accomplished on a tax-free basis in reliance on Section 351 of the Code. At the same time, the parent will usually attempt to minimize its equity contributions and instead finance the subsidiary through loans and credits. This allows the parent to repatriate the subsidiary's earnings in the form of interest (which is usually deductible for the subsidiary) rather than dividends (which are usually not). Moreover, the repayment of the debt would normally be tax-free to the parent, while payments on the stock would constitute a dividend.

Although parent financing may satisfy the needs of some foreign subsidiaries, it is often necessary or desirable to locate other sources of financing so as to reduce the subsidiary's consumption of the parent's resources or to take advantage of cheaper money elsewhere. One option is the foreign finance subsidiary. In general, foreign finance subsidiaries are organized in low tax jurisdictions which allow them to raise funds through the issuance of parent-backed bonds or debentures. Because of limitations on the tax payable with respect to interest on their securities, these finance subsidiaries are able to acquire less costly money than might be available elsewhere. The finance subsidiaries may then make the funds available through loans to, and equity investments in, their operating affiliates.

(ii) *Local Commercial Banks*. One natural source of financing for foreign subsidiaries is from commercial banks in the subsidiary's local jurisdiction. This source is particularly useful once the subsidiary has acquired its own assets and is operating on a profitable basis. While foreign banks often lend on an unsecured basis, preferring parent guarantees rather than risking the uncertainty of mortgages and liens, local banks are usually more comfortable with secured financing. Assuming local rates are competitive, given inflation and other economic factors, local bank financing can provide an independent source of financing for the subsidiary without drawing on the parent's resources.

(iii) *Eurodollar Financing.* A foreign subsidiary of a U.S. company could also borrow funds directly from a U.S. bank, usually on an unsecured basis with a guarantee from the parent. In most cases, however, these funds can be obtained more cheaply from the foreign branches or subsidiaries of such U.S. banks, or directly from foreign banks which function in the Eurodollar market.

A "Eurodollar" is simply a U.S. dollar deposited in a bank account outside the United States. The Eurodollar market developed as a result of various capital reserve and other requirements imposed on U.S. banks by the U.S. government. The effect of the regulation was to make U.S. based financing of foreign operations more costly. Because these regulations do not apply, for the most part, to U.S. dollar deposits abroad, Eurodollars could be loaned at lower rates. The current differential between U.S. prime and the London Interbank Offered Rate (LIBOR), to which Eurodollar loans are frequently tied, can be up to 50 basis points (one-hundreths of a percentage point) on a one-year loan.

Smaller Eurodollar loans may be handled entirely by the foreign branch or bank using documentation, such as loan agreements, promissory notes, security agreements and guarantees, which is not significantly different from that utilized in a domestic loan in the United States. Larger loans may be syndicated, i.e., the funds are generated from various banks ("participants") who have responded to the lead bank or syndicate manager's offering memorandum. In such cases, the participating banks will usually execute an inter-agreement which appoints the lead bank as their agent to collect installment payments and take certain actions in the event of a default.

It should be noted that offshore financing such as that represented by the Eurodollar market is not limited to U.S. dollars. In appropriate cases, it may be desirable for the loan to be denominated in another currency or in a multi-currency unit such as European Currency Units (ECU's) or Special Drawing Rights (SDR's).

(iv) *International Capital Markets.* Where long-term financing is required, a foreign subsidiary may look to the capital markets to acquire funds for foreign operations. While the issuer may offer either debt or equity, in most cases the securities consist of notes, bonds or debentures which allow the parent to retain 100% of the issuer's equity. Such securities may be offered in the United States, the local jurisdiction or on a multinational basis depending on the size of the issue and the availability of investors. United States and foreign investment bankers are continually developing hybrid securities and financial strategies designed to raise funds as efficiently as possible.

(v) *Governmental Sources.* Governmental and quasi-governmental organizations, both on a national and multinational basis, represent an additional source of funding for foreign operations, particularly in developing countries. Many governments maintain developmental banks or agencies designed to provide financing for investment projects which fall within priority areas. The Overseas Private Investment Corporation (OPIC) is one U.S. agency who provides direct financing and loan guarantees to U.S. investors in developing countries. Regional banks, such as the Asian Development Bank and the Inter-American Development Bank, extend credit to private investors whose proposed activities will provide needed jobs or bring important technology to a given geographical area. Multilateral institutions, such as the International Finance Corporation, affiliate of the World Bank, also provides funds and financial assistance to approved private investment projects.

§ 22:02. Intercompany Transactions.

The operation of a foreign subsidiary, whether in a production, sales or other capacity, frequently raises issues concerning intercompany transactions. The manner in which these transactions are handled can have important implications on the multinational company as a whole, particularly with respect to its tax liability.

The most basic issue relates to intercompany pricing. Assume that a U.S. parent company has a production subsidiary in Costa Rica (where income on export sales is exempt from local taxation) and a sales subsidiary in Sweden (a relatively high tax jurisdiction). The U.S. parent supplies the Costa Rica subsidiary with parts and components which are assembled into a final product and shipped directly to Sweden. From a tax perspective, the group as a whole would benefit by maximizing the income in Costa Rica and minimizing the income in Sweden. If it were free to do so, the parent might sell the parts and components to Costa Rica at cost (thus recognizing no U.S. income or tax), have the Costa Rican subsidiary sell to Sweden at cost plus the entire profit margin (thus recognizing all the profit but still being subject to no tax), and having Sweden resell at its cost (thus recognizing no income, and hence being subject to no tax).

The opportunity to minimize taxes through carefully considered intercompany transactions also arises in the case of licenses and technical assistance agreements. A U.S. parent which is making its intellectual property rights or technical services available to foreign subsidiaries would seek to charge the subsidiary in a high tax jurisdiction more (thus the reducing the taxable income thereof but increasing its own U.S. taxable income) while charging the subsidiary in a low tax jurisdiction less (in order to decrease its own U.S. tax liability). While withholding taxes and foreign tax credits must also be considered, this over-simplified example illustrates the basic opportunity for tax savings through intercompany licenses.

Another area in which intercompany transactions can be adjusted to minimize taxes is in loans. The advantages of such loans over equity investments from a tax perspective has been alluded to. By charging high tax jurisdictions higher interest rates than low tax jurisdictions, the parent or its finance subsidiary can also minimize the taxable income of such subsidiaries.

There are numerous other areas in which intercompany transactions can be structured in a manner which minimizes taxes. In most cases, however, the extent to which the various companies can manipulate their recognition of income is subject to the scrutiny of local tax authorities who are authorized to adjust the intercompany charges in such a way as to represent an arm's-length transaction between independent parties. Section 482 of the Internal Revenue Code, for example, allows the Internal Revenue Service to examine and adjust intercompany transactions to insure they reflect the actual economics of the transaction. Because of the penalties that may result from such adjustment, as well as the potential for double taxation (since the income deemed to be earned has already been taxed abroad), U.S. companies are usually advised to structure their intercompany transactions on an arm's-length basis. However, since the tax authorities in many jurisdictions are often not in a position to identify contrived intercompany charges, this practice continues in many parts of the world.

§ 22:03. Local Tax Considerations.

In general, most foreign jurisdictions follow the U.S. practice of taxing locally-domiciled corporations on their world-wide income. An Italian subsidiary of a U.S. corporation, for example, will be subject to Italian taxes on all of its income whether or not generated from sources within Italy. The Italian subsidiary could not avoid Italian taxation on its sale of a widget to a German purchaser merely by executing the sales agreement abroad, collecting payment abroad or making delivery abroad. Italy would also tax all of the subsidiary's interest, royalty, capital gains and other income.

At the same time, the fact that the Italian subsidiary is 100% owned by a U.S. company would not grant Italy a sufficient nexus to tax any income of the U.S. parent. Under the applicable U.S.-Italian tax treaty, the ownership of a subsidiary organized and operating in Italy does not render the U.S. parent a "permanent establishment" in Italy. As we have seen, unless the "permanent establishment" nexus is present, a country lacks jurisdiction to impose its income taxes on the foreign entity. On the other hand, a branch of a foreign corporation would generally be deemed a

218

"permanent establishment," rendering the income which is "effectively connected" with such branch subject to local income taxes and possibly special branch taxes.

The foregoing suggests certain opportunities for tax planning for foreign sales. Where possible, it is desirable to locate a sales subsidiary in a low tax jurisdiction and to structure its sales activities in such a way as to avoid "permanent establishment" status in any higher tax jurisdiction in which it might have customers. This is particularly important with respect to sales in jurisdictions with tax rates which are higher than those in the United States, since the difference between the rates will not benefit from the U.S. foreign tax credit.

In addition to income taxation, most foreign jurisdictions impose withholding taxes on payments made abroad. This includes interest, royalties, dividends, etc. In many cases, these withholding taxes are reduced under tax treaties between the country from which the payments are made and the country to which the payments are made. For example, France imposes a gross withholding tax of 25% on dividends paid abroad. This rate is reduced to as little as 5% under the U.S. French Tax Treaty where the payment is made to a U.S.-domiciled corporation owning at least 10% of the stock of the French company.

There are numerous other taxes in foreign jurisdictions for which a branch or subsidiary of a U.S. corporation may be liable. These include value added taxes (similar to sales taxes), registration taxes, capital taxes (a percentage of a company's capital), stamp taxes (on certain transactions for which documents must be prepared and submitted), state, provincial, commercial and municipal taxes, etc. All of these taxes must be carefully considered in any decision to invest abroad.

PART VI—SUGGESTIONS FOR FURTHER READING

Books

Diamond, W. & Diamond, D., Capital Formation and Investment Incentives Around the World (1982).

Leksell, L., Headquarter-Subsidiary Relationships in Multinational Corporations (1981).

Meinhardt, P., Company Law in Europe (1980).

Simmonds, L., Multinational Corporations Law (1979).

Articles

Comment, "Foreign Investment in Japan: The Legal and Political Climate," 18 Tex Int'l LJ 175 (1983).

Juncadella, "The Foreign Investment Laws of Latin America: Present and Future," 16 Int'l Law 463 (1982).

Lassila, "Structuring Business Operations in Foreign Countries," 35 Tax Exec 185 (1983).

Lebkowski & Monkiewicz, "Western Direct Investment in Centrally Planned Economies," 20 J World Trade L 624 (1986).

Rose, "Foreign Investment in Canada: The New Investment Canada Act," 20 Int'l Law 19 (2986).

Thomas, "Host State Treatment of Transnational Corporations: Formulation of a Standard for the United Nations Code of Conduct on Transnational Corporations," 7 Fordham Int'l L J 467 (1984).

DIRECT FOREIGN INVESTMENT: JOINT VENTURES

CHAPTER 23

REASONS FOR UTILIZING THE JOINT VENTURE STRUCTURE

---

§ 23:01. In General.

The international joint venture presents an ideal review of international business transactions, since it frequently encompasses aspects of nearly all of the various types of transactions. A joint venture which is engaged in manufacturing often imports parts or components from one of the joint venture partners under a parts supply agreement. It also frequently exports finished or partially finished goods pursuant to a distribution agreement with the foreign joint venture partner or independent distributor. The joint

223

venture also commonly utilizes one of the partner's technology and trademarks, thus necessitating a technical assistance agreement and license. Finally, in as much as the joint venture is typically structured as a local corporation with the participants' interests represented by equity, the joint venture poses many of the issues discussed in Part VI regarding foreign subsidiaries.

But the international joint venture is more than the sum of these various types of international business transactions. Whether it is structured merely as a contractual arrangement to cooperate on a given project or as a distinct legal entity of which the participants are members or shareholders, the purpose and mode of operation of the joint venture, together with the contribution or role of its participants, must be clearly defined in one or more underlying documents. These documents, which generally take the form of a cooperation agreement in nonincorporated joint ventures or a shareholders' agreement together with a charter and by-laws in the case of an incorporated joint venture, must also deal with various other issues such as the management and control of the joint venture, the transferability of interests, the financial operation of the joint venture, the distribution of profits, the settlement of disputes, and the liquidation or termination of the joint venture.

In general, a joint venture encompasses any association of two or more persons who combine specified resources or assume certain responsibilities in order to carry out a single business enterprise. The distinctive characteristic of the joint venture structure is this participation by two or more independent persons in the administration and profits (or losses) of the enterprise. While the contributions or responsibilities of the partners are usually different, they each participate, to some degree, in the direction of the joint venture and share in its resulting success or failure.

This distinctive characteristic suggests the three major reasons for utilizing the joint venture structure in the international context: (i) to take advantage of complimentary strengths of the participants; (ii) to share the costs and risks of a new foreign enterprise; and (iii) to comply with local law which limits foreign equity or control of a domestic enterprise.

§ 23:02. Combining Complimentary Strengths.

The most common reason for a U.S. company to do business abroad through a joint venture is to take advantage of a local company's strengths in areas which compliment those of the U.S. participant. An example illustrates how the decision may be made. Assume that a U.S. company has developed an important technology and, while successful in manufacturing and marketing the product at home, has little or no experience in manufacturing or selling abroad. Under these circumstances, the U.S. company may elect to manufacture the product at home and to market it abroad through a local agent or distributor. But the transportation and import tariffs may render the product noncompetitive or the discount demanded by the distributor may be excessive. A second option would be to license the technology to a local manufacturer and receive royalties on such manufacturer's sales. This option may also be unsatisfactory, perhaps because local law limits the amount of royalties which can be paid or because the U.S. company is unable to find an acceptable licensee with sufficient capacity to manufacture the product. The U.S. company may also reject the idea of forming its own foreign subsidiary to manufacture and market the product due to its lack of experience and to difficulty in competing with a well-structured sales network which may already exist in the foreign market.

A joint venture with a local company which already has an established marketing network may be the most advantageous structure under these circumstances. Under the joint venture, the U.S. company may contribute half of the capital to establish a local production facility together with the technology and technical assistance to manufacture the product. In exchange, it might receive the right to half of the joint venture's profits plus a small royalty and technical assistance fee to cover certain costs. The local distributor would contribute the other half of the capital and agree to distribute the product through its extensive distribution network. In exchange, it would receive half of the joint venture's profits and a small discount on its wholesale purchase of the

225

product. The U.S. company's royalties and the local company's sales discount would be designed to offset each other. The real objective would be to build up profits within the joint venture which would, in turn, be distributed equally between the participants.

This example illustrates one of the most common objectives of an international joint venture: the ability to combine forces to provide a new product with immediate access into an important foreign market. The example, however, has myriad variations. Perhaps the U.S. company will also supply parts and components to the joint venture which are not available locally. It may also obtain the right to distribute the joint venture's products in the United States or other foreign markets. The local company may already have existing manufacturing facilities and agree to rent the same to the joint venture and provide workers on a contract basis. In some instances the local company may assume full responsibility for manufacturing the product for the joint venture so that the joint venture's activities would be confined to marketing. The only common characteristic of these variations is that the parties are taking advantage of each other's respective strengths by contributing them to the joint venture in exchange for a share in the joint venture's profits.

§ 23:03.   Sharing Costs and Risks.

The foregoing example also suggests another reason for using the joint venture structure: the opportunity to share the costs and risks of entering a new market. Assume, for example, that the U.S. manufacturer has decided against the export and licensing options, leaving it only with the direct foreign investment alternative. The financing of a foreign manufacturing facility, however, may be beyond its means. Moreover, if it has no previous experience with operating a foreign plant or with marketing goods abroad, the risk of proceeding on its own may be unacceptable.

Entering the foreign market by means of a joint venture with a local company reduces both the overall risk of failure for both parties as well as the costs of the proposal. Risk is reduced through the use of a partner who has experience with local manufacturing and who can insure immediate access to markets through an established sales network. Other risks which are present in purely contractual relationships, such as distribution or licensing arrangements, are also reduced since the emphasis is on mutual success rather than individual advantage. The U.S. partner's costs are obviously reduced since the local partner is expected to make a capital or other contribution that corresponds to its share in the profits of the joint venture.

§ 23:04. Compliance with Local Law.

A third general reason for doing business abroad through a joint venture is to comply with local law or to obtain benefits under local law which would not be available through another investment vehicle. Part VI discussed certain foreign investment laws which limit a foreign investor's ownership and control of a local enterprise. In Mexico, for example, foreign equity ownership and control of a local company is limited in most cases to 49%. India and the Philippines have enacted foreign investment laws which generally limit foreign participation to 40%. The result in such countries is that a foreign company seeking to do business in the country must often do so by means of a joint venture with a local investor. Local law in certain jurisdictions may also limit investment incentives or otherwise provide preferences to companies which are controlled by local investors.

CHAPTER 24

FORM OF THE JOINT VENTURE

§ 24:01. Equity versus Contractual Joint Ventures.

There are essentially two legal forms of international joint ventures. These have been characterized as equity and nonequity or contractual. The equity form, which is the most common, consists of a distinct legal entity (possibly a partnership but in most cases some form of limited liability company), in which the joint venture participants' interests are represented by equity (partnership interests or shares of stock). A contractual joint venture is one in which the participants agree to cooperate with each other with respect to a given project or business activity and to share in the results thereof. Thus, in a nonequity joint venture, the participants' interests are represented by contractual rights and obligations.

The equity joint venture presents a number of advantages over the nonequity joint venture for most marketing and manufacturing activities. First, it eliminates the need for each of the participants to form its own corporation in the local jurisdiction, a measure which it would otherwise have to take in most cases to minimize tax and corporate liability and/or to comply with local law. Second, the use of a distinct legal entity as the investment vehicle often simplifies the rights and obligations of the joint venture participants. While the joint venture will often maintain contractual relationships with its equity owners, it generally operates on a independent basis, with its own facility, management, budget and business plan. Since it maintains its own books and records, the joint venture partners can readily determine the results of its operations, share in its profits through dividends, and cover losses through additional capital contributions. Third, the separate identity of the joint venture facilitates its relationships with suppliers, customers and other third parties with whom it must deal. The entity also can assume a local identity which may be helpful in jurisdictions whose local customers may harbor some prejudice against foreign companies. Fourth, because the joint venture partners' interest is simply represented by equity, that interest can be easily accounted for on its own books and, if desirable, transferred to the other participant or to a third party. An equity joint venture also facilitates the pursuit of an enterprise on a long-term basis and at the same time simplifies the liquidation of the enterprise and the distribution of its assets to the participants.

The nonequity joint venture is more commonly employed in short-term projects, particularly in the engineering, construction, and extraction industries. The exploration, extraction, and processing of minerals and petrochemicals are often accomplished using nonequity joint ventures due to the financial requirements and length of the project as well as local law restricting foreign participation in such activities. In these cases, the parties (which may include the local government or a quasi-governmental company) agree to cooperate with each other in performing certain obligations in exchange for a share in the resulting product, profits or compensation. A nonequity joint venture resembles but should not be confused with other contractual relationships, such as supplier/distributor, licensor/licensee and consultant or services provider/customer, where both parties benefit by the success of the other but which do not involve a sharing of profits or management.

§ 24:02. Local Law Issues.

The local law of the foreign jurisdiction will often influence, if not completely dictate, the form of the joint venture. Local law will also frequently affect many other aspects of the joint venture's operation. While the impact of local law on direct foreign investment generally was addressed in Part VI, certain additional factors should be considered in the context of the joint venture.

(i) *Foreign Investment Laws*. As noted above, the decision to utilize the joint venture structure as a vehicle through which to conduct business in a particular foreign jurisdiction may result from local foreign investment laws which limit foreign equity participation and control of local enterprises or which directly or indirectly favor locally-controlled companies. In many cases, these foreign icvestment laws also dictate, directly or indirectly, the form of the joint venture. In those cases, for example, where local law effectively prohibits operations through a branch of a foreign corporation, the joint venture partners must either utilize an equity joint venture—using a local corporation—or form their own local subsidiaries to participate in a non-equity joint venture. On the other hand, there may be occasions where the foreign investment law does not have the same impact on a nonequity joint venture as it would on an equity joint venture. Thus, the impact of any foreign investment law must be carefully considered in determining the form of the joint venture.

(ii) *Joint Venture Laws*. A number of jurisdictions have enacted special joint venture laws in addition or as an alternative to foreign investment laws. In 1979, the Peoples Republic of China enacted a joint venture law following Yugoslavian, Romanian and Hungarian models. The Chinese law created various administrative bodies designed to regulate the formation and activities of joint ventures with foreign capital. The Chinese also have a special tax law governing joint ventures whose operation and effect depends on the form of the joint venture—equity, contractual or a special hybrid.[1]

(iii)　*Company Law.* Company law in the local jurisdiction is also important where an equity joint venture is contemplated. In most cases, the same kinds of considerations discussed in Part VI with respect to subsidiary operations will generally result in the decision to utilize a limited liability company as the vehicle for the joint venture. Certain legal characteristics of the company, however, such as limitations on in-kind capital contributions, special quorums, and super majority voting requirements for sharing control and restrictions on transfer of equity interests must be carefully considered in the context of joint ventures. In certain cases, tax or other considerations may dictate the use of a partnership entity or some alternative that may be available under local law. If no tax or other reasons compel the use of a certain type of legal entity, local custom would normally be followed.

(iv)　*Foreign Exchange Controls.* Foreign axchange controls in many countries regulate remittances in and out of the country for such items as capital contributions, imports and exports, royalties and similar fees, interest, dividends and repatriation of capital. The regulations may also establish preferential exchange rates for certain payments and restrict the local company's right to sell or hold foreign currencies and maintain foreign bank accounts.

While foreign exchange controls should always be examined in the context of direct foreign investment, they are particularly important where a joint venture is being contemplated. This is because the impact of the controls on the local joint venture partner may be minimal compared to the impact on the U.S. partner, who may contribute capital, sell components, license technology and trademarks, extend loans, and buy finished products for the joint venture all in U.S. dollars. If the documentation

[1] See Confe, "Joint Ventures in China and Their Tax Treatment," Int'l Fin L Rev January, 1985.

does not deal with the different impact of exchange controls, the U.S. participant's interest may be substantially prejudiced vis-a-vis its foreign counterpart. The parties should also employ an indexing mechanism to deal with such problems as inflation and unrealistic currency valuations in those jurisdictions in which these problems exist or are threatened.

(v) *Contract Law*. Finally, local contract law, and particularly issues surrounding the enforceability of contractual obligations, assumes a great deal of significance in joint ventures. Even in equity joint ventures, the basic understanding between the parties is usually contained in a joint venture agreement which may perform the role of a partnership agreement or a shareholders' agreement after the joint venture is formed. While nearly all jurisdictions recognize contractual undertakings as enforceable obligations, the U.S. partner who ignores local law or procedures may be surprised to find that it is unable to enforce share transfer restrictions or contractually-provided minority shareholder protections because they are not authorized under statutory law. Certain other jurisdictions, such as Japan, provide little protection against breach of a joint venture agreement due to lack of effective equitable relief.

One common means of dealing with this issue is to insist that the agreement be governed by U.S. state law. Even if the U.S. partner can convince its foreign counterpart to include such a provision in the agreement, however, such choice of law may not necessarily be respected by a foreign court. Moreover, foreign choices of law are often rejected by local foreign investment registries who must approve the agreement in order to render it valid and enforceable.

A better means of dealing with the problem of unenforceability is to create a structure in which the foreign joint venture partner has too much to lose by breaching the agreement. This starts by insuring that the foreign joint venture partner is happy with the arrangement in the first place. One might also attempt to encourage a dependency by the foreign partner on the continued good will of the U.S. partner, such as through the U.S. partner's supply of essential components, technology and management services, all provided under agreements containing broad cross default provisions.

§ 24:03.   Tax Issues.

A foreign joint venture presents a number of special tax issues.[2] First among these is whether the joint venture will be treated as a corporation or partnership for U.S. tax purposes. This issue is governed by U.S. tax law rather than the legal characterization of the entity under the local law. Distinguishing a partnership from a corporation involves an analysis of (i) whether the entity has limited liability, (ii) whether its equity interests are freely transferable, (iii) whether it has a continuity of life, and (iv) whether it has centralized management.[3] If the answer to three or more of these is yes, then the entity will be treated as a corporation for U.S. tax purposes.[4] The limited liability issue is normally governed by local law. Shares or interests in a joint venture usually are deemed freely transferable even though subject to a first right of refusal but not if the consent of the other joint venture partner is required. There is continuity of life even if the life of the entity is for a limited period of years, but not if the entity is automatically dissolved under certain circumstances rather than at the option of one party upon certain events of default. Centralized management is nearly always present in a joint venture.

Given the foregoing test, the parties may be able to structure the joint venture so as to cause it to be treated as a partnership or a corporation for U.S. tax purposes. The potential advantages of having the joint venture treated as a partnership are the avoidance of local withholding tax on dividends and the ability to flow-

[2] Generally Kleinbard, "United States and Foreign Tax Issues," 38 Bus Law 1048 (1983).

[3] Treas Reg §301.7701-2(a)(2).

[4] Treas Reg §301.7701-2(a)(3).

through early losses of the joint venture. There is also no tax on distributions in-kind upon the dissolution of a partnership. The principal disadvantage of a partnership structure is the lack of protection of the parent from local tax and other liability, though it may be possible (by failing two other prongs of the test) to achieve limited liability for local law purposes and still be taxed as a partnership. The second potential disadvantage is that providing a flow-through of early foreign forces will not create tax savings for the U.S. partner in the current year and may in fact accelerate problems for a company in an excess tax-credit position.[5] Moreover, under Section 904(f) of the Internal Revenue Code, a joint venture which is taxed as a partnership in early years to take advantage of initial losses will cause its U.S. participant to recharacterize some of its foreign-source income as domestic source income (thus reducing its available foreign tax credit) when the joint venture is converted into a corporation for tax purposes.

If the joint venture is treated as a corporation, on the other hand, the income generated by it will not be taxable to the U.S. participant until actually received so long as the joint venture is not a "controlled foreign corporation" (CFC) within the meaning of IRC §957(a). A CFC is a foreign corporation more than 50% of whose combined voting power is owned, directly or indirectly, by U.S. shareholders.[6] A 50-50 joint venture should avoid CFC characterization, and thus deemed distributions to its U.S. participant under the Subpart F rules, provided such U.S. participant does not have any unusual veto or other rights with respect to the operation of the joint venture. Avoiding CFC characterization for the joint venture also allows the U.S. participant to obtain capital gains treatment on the sale of its stock in the joint venture. In the case of a CFC, IRC §1248 would otherwise treat some of the income on the sale of such stock as ordinary income.

---

[5] See Kleinbard, "United States and Foreign Tax Issues," 38 Bus Law 1048 (1983).

[6] See Treas Reg §1.947-(b)(1); See also Estate of Weiskopf v. Comm., 64 TC 78 (1975) affd 76-1 USTC §9387 (CA2, 1976) (dependency of joint venture on U.S. shareholder for technology and components rendered it CFC despite U.S. shareholder's ownership of only 45% of joint ventures stock).

§ 24:04. Antitrust Issues.

An international joint venture frequently raises a number of antitrust issues.[7] Since the joint venture is often a cooperative arrangement between two competitors or potential competitors, there is a possibility of collusion. As in the case of any international activities, however, the antitrust analysis must also include the jurisdictional issue under the "effects" and "comity" tests.[8] Once again, the U.S. Department of Justice's Antitrust Guide for International Operations provides a helpful supplement to U.S. case law and a useful tool in predicting where U.S. enforcement action may be taken. Local antitrust law must also be examined.

Joint venture agreements sometimes contain restrictions on the joint venture partners from entering each others' domestic market. In general, such market division arrangements between competitors or potential competitors are per se illegal under U.S. antitrust law. While the restrictions on the part of the U.S. shareholder not to enter the foreign market may not have an adverse "effect" on U.S. commerce, the prohibition on U.S. sales by the foreign partner denies U.S. consumers of its product.

If the foreign partner is a direct competitor of the U.S. partner, this arrangement would probably be objectionable. Even if not yet a direct competitor, however, the arrangement could be a violation of U.S. antitrust law if it continues for such a term so as to permanently prohibit the foreign partner from entering the U.S. market. The strength of the foreign joint venture partner in the market as well as the difficulty in developing a competitive product would be analyzed to determine how long such prohibition could be justified. If the joint venture partners are not currently competitors, a restriction which is not longer than the period of time which would be required for the parties to develop and commence marketing a competing product would not violate U.S. antitrust law.

A similar market division issue is often presented as a result of restrictions on the joint venture itself from exporting or entering

[7] Generally Bradley, "Joint Ventures and Antitrust Policy," 95 Harv L Rev 1521 (1982).

[8] See §§11:04 and 17:03.

into certain markets. The Antitrust Guide, following some U.S. case law, suggests that a permanent prohibition on the joint venture from selling in the United States would be objectionable. Restrictions on export may also run afoul of foreign antitrust law. The EEC and Japanese law may render such restrictions unenforceable or subject to penalties.[9]

Another common antitrust issue presented by joint ventures is a tying arrangement. The joint venture frequently obtains one of the joint venture partner's technology or trademarks, often under an express or implied condition that it also acquire parts or components from such partner. Alternatively, the joint venture may be required to accept certain lines of products as a condition to its acquiring the rights to sell certain other products. The "effect" of such a tying arrangement may be to foreclose other suppliers from making sales in the foreign market.

As noted previously,[10] a tying arrangement generally constituted a per se violation of U.S. antitrust law. The Guide, however, suggests that tying arrangements may be justifiable in international commerce where the undesired product or technology is necessary to insure proper production or maintenance of the desired product. The Department of Justice currently objects to tying arrangements in foreign commerce where they facilitate horizontal collusion between two parties which can thereby dominate a market. The potential objections to a tying arrangement can generally be eliminated by revising the agreement to allow the joint venture to purchase parts or components from U.S. suppliers approved by the U.S. shareholder as competent to supply merchandise of comparable technology and quality.

Market division, tying and other antitrust issues are also frequently present by clauses contained in the distribution and license agreements between the joint venture and its shareholders. Accordingly, these agreements should be carefully scrutinized with respect to distribution agreements[11] and license agreements.[12]

---

[9] See §11:04.
[10] See §17:03.
[11] See §12:02.
[12] See §18:02.

CHAPTER 25

JOINT VENTURE AGREEMENT

§ 25:01.   General Approach to Documentation.

As the foregoing discussion suggests, an international joint venture is typically structured as a distinct legal entity in which the participants' interests are represented by stock ownership. The fundamental task of the joint venture agreement, therefore, is to set forth the understanding between the joint venture partners who will become the shareholders of the company. The joint venture agreement thus addresses such issues as the name and purposes of the joint venture company, the capital and other contributions to be made by the participants, both initially and in response to future needs, the respective stock ownership of each participant and any special provisions governing shareholder rights and restrictions on the transfer of shares, the management and administration of the joint venture, the financial supervision of the entity, the distribution of profits, and the liquidation and dissolution of the company.

In some instances, certain of these issues will be governed by specific provisions of the company law of the jurisdiction in which the entity will be organized. More frequently, however, the company law will stipulate a certain legal treatment but allow a different approach as long as the articles or bylaws of the entity expressly provide otherwise. It is therefore common to incorporate the parties' understanding on each of these issues into the articles and bylaws of the joint venture company. For this reason, the agreed form of the articles and bylaws of the prospective company are commonly attached as an appendix to the joint venture agreement. The agreement then provides that the articles and bylaws of the joint venture company shall correspond to the appendix with such modifications thereto (which may be required by the notary or other official responsible for reviewing the proposed articles) as the parties may agree upon. When the articles and bylaws are properly incorporated into a joint venture agreement which expressly survives the incorporation of the joint venture, the provisions contained therein may also bind the parties to the extent that they may be contained in a shareholders' agreement.

In most cases, a party to the joint venture agreement will act not only as a shareholder but also as a supplier of technology, trademarks or components, as a manufacturer or distributor of the joint venture's products or in some other capacity. In certain cases it may perform more than one of these roles. A U.S. partner in a German manufacturing joint venture, for example, may provide technology and component parts to the joint venture and act as its exclusive distributor in the United States and selected other markets. The German joint venture partner may lease a manufacturing facility to the joint venture and act as its exclusive distributor in Europe. The contractual relationship in each such case is between the joint venture company and the shareholder. Since the other shareholder has an obvious interest in such contractual undertakings, however, these agreements must normally be agreed to as part of the overall structure of the joint venture.

Because of the interest of the joint venture partners in agreeing on each of the contracts even before the joint venture is organized, it is common to attach the agreed form of each of these contracts to the joint venture agreement. Once again, a clause will be included in the joint venture agreement providing for a closing (which is normally scheduled to occur as soon as practical after the organization of the joint venture company and the receipt of all necessary governmental approvals) at which such company and the appropriate joint venture partners will enter into the license, distribution, supply, lease, manufacturing and other agreements in accordance with the attached forms. The obligations of the parties under the joint venture agreement should also be conditioned upon the execution of such side agreements at the closing.

This appendix approach to the documentation of the joint venture reduces considerably the length of the joint venture agreement itself. It also eliminates potential disputes between parties which often occur when the articles, bylaws and side agreements must be prepared subsequently based on general terms contained in the joint venture agreement itself. This appendix approach also allows the parties to submit a selected document, say a license agreement, to a governmental authority as may be required under local law without having to disclose other aspects of the joint venture.

It should be noted that while these side agreements are fundamental to the operation of the joint venture itself, their legal terms are, for the most part, unaffected by the fact that the other party is a joint venture rather than an independent third party. The discussion of international distribution and license agreements which is contained in Parts III and IV thus addresses these agreements adequately.

§ 25:02. Organization and Purpose.

A common form of joint venture agreement often begins by calling for the formation of a specified type of entity with a given name and having a given domicile as soon as possible after the execution of the joint venture agreement. As noted above, the joint venture agreement will typically provide that the articles and bylaws (or their equivalent under local law) will be in substantially the form annexed to the agreement. In most cases, both joint venture partners, through their local counsel, will cooperate in forming the legal entity. At times, however, the organization of the company may be expedited by having the local joint venture partner form a wholly-owned subsidiary by itself, and subsequently transfer the agreed percentage of its shares to the foreign joint venture partner. The company laws in many jurisdictions require that a portion of the proposed entity's capital stock be subscribed and paid in before such entity may be organized. The joint venture agreement should require the shareholders to make any such required subscription and payment within a specified period but allow for the liquidation of the joint venture and return of any such capital contributions if subsequent specified conditions are not satisfied within a given period.

One important issue in connection with the preparation of the joint venture's articles and bylaws is the definition of its purpose. Corporate law in the United States has all but eliminated the concept of defined corporate purposes, allowing a company to be formed to pursue any legal business authorized for corporations generally. In many countries, however, the purposes of the entity must be set forth in great detail, including references to the products it will be authorized to manufacture or sell, the types of contracts it will be authorized to enter into, etc. In such countries, the corporation's business activities will be strictly limited to these authorized business purposes. In many cases, these clauses will be carefully scrutinized by notaries and governmental authorities having jurisdiction over foreign investment.

Both in these jurisdictions and in those which do not require detailed business purposes, it is common for the parties to include more specific language on the purposes of the joint venture in the joint venture agreement and in the articles and bylaws of the entity. The objective of such provisions is to limit the activities of the joint venture so that it does not compete with one or both of the joint venture partners and does not enter into other activities without the prior consent of both joint venture partners. Thus, the purpose clause for a manufacturing joint venture may provide that the purpose of the company is to manufacture specified products at a particular location and to sell such products only within a certain country or geographical area. The purpose clause may also provide that any expansion of the joint venture's activities will require the approval of a majority (or supermajority) of the Board or the shareholders.

§ 25:03. Participant Contributions.

Another issue that often requires considerable thought and negotiation is the quantity and form of the participant contributions. In most instances, the joint venture will require some initial capital contribution which will be made by the joint venture partners in exchange for stock or other equity interest. The joint venture agreement will normally specify the initial authorized capital of the company, the number of shares and the par or nominal value per share, and the number and percentage of shares to be issued to each party. The agreement must also specify whether the initial capital contribution will be made in cash or in kind, and if in kind, the nature and amount thereof.

In-kind capital contributions are reasonably commmon in the case of international joint ventures. In some cases, the U.S. joint venture partner will agree to accept stock in the joint venture in lieu of a front-end royalty it would otherwise receive on technology or trademarks which it licenses to the joint venture. The U.S. joint venture partner may also contribute machinery and equipment to the joint venture. The local joint venture partner may contribute a building or other facility. In some jurisdictions, the company law may require an independent appraisal of in-kind capital contributions. In many cases, the parties will agree to conduct such an appraisal, with an understanding that any differences in the value of the contribution be made up in cash.

243

Often, the joint venture agreement will provide that the source and amount of any additional capital contributions required by the company be determined by the Board or the shareholders, thus requiring a joint decision of the joint venture participants. If it is anticipated, however, that additional capital contributions from the shareholders will be required, or that the shareholders will need to make or guaranty loans to the joint venture, the joint venture agreement should set forth the obligations of the shareholders with respect to such additional funding, as well as the rights of a participant who may be required to make up for any shortfall by the other participant. The agreement should normally provide that loans made or guaranteed by the shareholders be in accordance with their respective equity holdings and on identical terms and conditions. A mechanism should also be included to insure equitable treatment of the shareholders in the event of a default on such loans. The currency or exchange rate for future shareholder funding should also be established to avoid inequitable treatment resulting from currency fluctuations.

§ 25:04. Control and Minority Protection.

One of the most important issues presented by a joint venture relates to its control by the participants. This encompasses questions as to the division of shares (50-50, 49-51, etc.), the composition of the board of directors or similar administrative body, and questions as to shareholder action. In the case of joint ventures in which the shareholders do not participate on a 50-50 basis, the control issue also presents questions as to minority shareholder protection.

Perhaps the easiest means of dealing with the control issue is to structure the joint venture on a 50-50 basis with each shareholder entitled to nominate half of the members of the board of directors. Under this arrangement, each shareholder normally agrees to vote its shares in favor of the other's nominees to the board of directors and reserves the right to select its own nominees. If the quorum for board and shareholder action is then set at a majority of the members or outstanding shares, each shareholder will have an effective veto over the joint venture's activities. The parties will also typically specify the officers to be nominated by each party, occasionally electing two president/managing directors or requiring the nominee to be acceptable to the other party.

If the parties intend to share control in this way, careful consideration must be given to local corporate law and to the drafting of the entity's articles and bylaws. Of particular concern are corporate provisions which allow the board or shareholders to take action with less than a majority of the entire board or less than a majority of the entire outstanding stock. At times it is necessary to provide that selected issues be approved by a unanimous or supermajority vote in order to deal with such provisions. Because of the greater risk of a deadlock in a 50-50 joint venture, the consequences and means of dealing with a deadlock under local law should be examined and modified, if desirable, in the articles and bylaws. Finally, in order to insure the 50-50 split, preemptive rights should be provided for.

In many cases, the distribution of equity of the joint venture will be other than 50-50. This may be the result of unequal contributions to the joint venture by the participants, of legal requirements which limit a foreign investor's control, or otherwise. While the assumption of a minority interest in a joint venture obviously reduces one's control over the affairs of the entity, the minority shareholder's interest can usually be adequately protected through the inclusion of various measures in the joint venture agreement and the articles and bylaws of the joint venture. Among the most common of these mechanisms is the delineation of certain important matters that cannot be taken without the consent of the minority shareholder. These issues frequently include increases in the capital of the company; declarations of dividends and reinvestment of earnings; borrowing in excess of a specified amount or approved annual budget, the entering into leases, contracts or mortgages; the making of loans or extension of guaranties; the sale or transfer of any fixed assets; the appointment or discharge of the company's independent auditors; the authorization of transactions between the joint venture and any of its shareholders or their officers, directors of other affiliates; the amendment of the articles or bylaws of the joint venture; any change in its business plan; the entering into new markets or addition of new products; the approval of any annual financial plan, policy or budget; or any other transaction which is not in the ordinary course of the joint venture's business. This is commonly accomplished by providing that any action on these items must be approved by the unanimous or supermajority vote of the board of directors or shareholders, as appropriate. Again, there must be careful attention to local corporate law and to the drafting of the underlying documents in order to insure that this mechanism is permissible and that all loopholes are closed.

In addition to the minority veto on selected matters, it is common to provide for cumulative voting or some other mechanism which insures that the minority will be represented on the joint venture's board of directors. In some countries, this is accomplished by creating two classes of stock, with each class permitted to elect a specified number of directors. The use of two classes of stock can also be used to accomplish the minority veto mechanism by requiring the affirmative vote of both classes for action on specified matters. By providing for two classes of stock, the joint venture can also easily allow for certain other minority shareholder protections, such as the minority's right to nominate specified officers as well as its own statutory auditor (a position created under many company laws).

§ 25:05. Transfer of Interests.

Another important issue which the joint venture agreement and the articles and bylaws of the entity must address is the procedure governing the transfer of a participant's stock or other interest in the joint venture. As in the case of a closely-held corporation, the shareholders of a joint venture are keenly interested in most cases in insuring that they do not suddenly find themselves with a new partner in the enterprise by virtue of the other shareholder's sale of all or a portion of its shares. Moreover, because of the license, distributor and other contractual relationships that the shareholders frequently maintain with the joint venture, as well as the continuing role of the shareholders in the management and support of the joint venture, both joint venture partners usually favor broad restrictions on the transfer of interests which reflect a long-term commitment to work together.

While the prospect of a transfer of one of the joint venture partner's interest in the enterprise is thus somewhat antithetical to the purpose and structure of a joint venture, there are circumstances in which such a transfer may be appropriate. Some of these circumstances may indeed be contemplated from the inception of the joint venture. In certain instances, for example, a joint venture may be organized with the local government or developmental bank with the understanding that such government or bank will subsequently sell its interest, often to the public. It is also not uncommon for the original joint venture shareholders to subsequently transfer their interest to an affiliated corporation whose ownership of such interest may be desirable from tax or regulatory purposes or may simply fit better into the shareholder's overall corporate structure. The joint venture agreement should obviously allow such transfers without requiring the consent of the other joint venture shareholder or any other action.

In most other cases, however, a joint venture participant's desire to transfer its interest in the enterprise, at least in the short term, will be motivated by some unanticipated event. Perhaps the joint venture has simply failed to be successful in terms of profitability, return on investment, or some other measure. Perhaps the parties have been unable to agree on its direction or it has fallen under the control of the majority shareholder. Perhaps the shareholder itself is no longer able or willing to pursue the joint venture because of its own financial constraints or because of more attractive opportunities. For these and many other reasons, a joint venture agreement usually provides for a mechanism which allows the unhappy shareholder to get out of the arrangement, or alternatively, to require its dissolution. A complete prohibition on the transfer of shares may also be contrary to local law, thus requiring the parties to provide for some acceptable transfer procedure.

In most cases, the joint venture agreement will create a broad restriction on the transfer or disposition of shares, as well as on their pledge or hypothecation. The joint venture agreement may thereafter define certain permitted transfers, such as among affiliated companies or upon the written consent of all other shareholders, but require all other transfers to proceed in accordance with specified procedures. One simple procedure is to grant a first right of refusal in favor of the other shareholder to acquire the shares proposed to be transferred at the lower of the proposed transfer price or a price specified in, or calculated in accordance with a formula provided under, the joint venture agreement. The agreement may go on to provide that the non-transferring shareholder then has the option to consent to the proposed sale to a third party (subject to such party's assumption of the transferring shareholder's obligations), to name another party to purchase the shares at such price and on such terms, to purchase the shares itself, to have the joint venture redeem the shares, or to dissolve the joint venture and liquidate its assets.

While the terms under which the nontransferring shareholder may buy out the other shareholder can be structured so as to limit the financial burden which such buy-out would create, a compulsory buyout may be undesirable from both parties' perspectives. The decision on the part of the transferring shareholder to sell its shares may be motivated by its own desire to pursue other opportunities or limit its continued commitment. In this case, it may be unfair to require the surviving shareholder or the joint venture to purchase the shares to prevent their sale to an undesirable buyer. On the other hand, where the decision to get out is motivated by factors beyond the control of the transferring shareholder, such as the enactment of tax or other laws which limit the economic benefits it may obtain, by the failure of the joint venture to generate an acceptable return on investment, or by the failure of the other joint venture partner to respect its rights, then it may be unfair for the transferring shareholder to sell out under terms which favor the surviving partner. For these reasons, a joint venture agreement may attempt to define certain of those circumstances which "trigger" the right of a shareholder to transfer its shares or require its dissolution. The triggering events would include those circumstances mentioned above as well as certain others, which are beyond the control of the transferring shareholder. The agreement may provide that except in the case of such a triggering event, a shareholder shall have no right to transfer its shares or require the dissolution of the joint venture. Assuming that the shareholder could not force the dissolution of the joint venture through other means (such as the creation of a deadlock under local corporate law), this approach would require the shareholder to negotiate acceptable buy out terms in the absence of a triggering event in its favor.

Finally, it should be noted that any restriction on the transfer of an equity interest in a joint venture should be carefully scrutinized to determine its validity under the governing corporate law. The general disfavor and strict construction of contractual restrictions on the alienability of stock which still prevails in some U.S. jurisdictions is also common in many foreign countries. Consideration must also be given to whether the share transfer restrictions must be incorporated into the articles or bylaws of the joint venture entity as well as in the joint venture agreement.

§ 25:06.   Financial Supervision and Accounting Matters.

The joint venture agreement, and in many cases the articles and bylaws of the enterprise, should also address certain issues concerning financial supervision and accounting. While the joint venture partners are mutually interested in the profitability of the venture, their roles as suppliers, distributors, licensors, lessors, managers or manufacturers of the joint venture also create numerous opportunities to maximize their own revenues from the joint venture which they need not share with their joint venture partner. This conflict of interest requires the shareholders to assume a much more active role in the financial supervision of the joint venture.

It is essential that both joint venture partners have the right to veto any contract, arrangement or other transaction between the joint venture and one of its shareholders or its affiliates. Significant agreements, such as licenses, leases and supply and distribution arrangements, should be submitted to the shareholders and require a supermajority approval in a non 50-50 joint venture. Management salaries, as well as the purchase or sale of assets, securing of credits and payment of any fees which involve a shareholder or affiliate should be approved at the board level.

In addition to these measures, however, appropriate financial supervision of the joint venture often requires the board to meet regularly to review the financial condition and activities of the enterprise. Management should be required to submit an annual budget for approval by the board and to seek board authorization for any material expenditure not contemplated by the budget. Management should also be required to prepare and provide the board with detailed annual and quarterly financial statements. The joint venture agreement and articles and bylaws should also provide that each shareholder, as well as its representatives, should have full access to the books and records of the company.

Under many company laws, the financial supervision of a corporation is entrusted to a statutory auditor which is obligated to prepare certain financial reports for examination by the board. In most cases, the statutory auditor is an independent accountant who is appointed each year by the board. As noted above, it is common in the case of joint ventures for each partner to have the right to appoint its own statutory auditor.

Frequently, however, neither the financial statements prepared by the joint venture's management nor the reports prepared by a statutory auditor will provide the type of financial information which a U.S. joint venture partner will need. Neither the financial statement nor the auditor's report will be prepared in accordance with generally accepted accounting principles (GAAP) and often no assurances can be made about the qualification of those who prepare them. For these reasons, it is common for the U.S. partner to insist that in addition to any other financial statements prepared in accordance with local tax or accounting practices, the company will also maintain a set of accounting statements prepared in accordance with GAAP. The joint venture agreement may also provide that the books of the joint venture shall be audited annually by an internationally recognized accounting firm to be appointed by the board. While the costs of such GAAP financial statements and independent audit may have to be borne by the U.S. partner, it is often the only adequate means of assuring the appropriate level of financial supervision. In some cases, it may also be required for purposes of the U.S. shareholder's own audit.

There are two more financial and accounting issues that should be addressed by the joint venture agreement. The first relates to the joint venture's policy regarding the distribution of profits. While this issue should also be presented to the board where either party will have a veto, the manner in which the policy is structured will determine whether a veto means that such profits must be distributed (after the satisfaction of legal resources) or retained. In general, it is desirable to establish a policy of full distribution in the absence of a decision by the board to retain profits for use for a specific purpose. The second issue relates to the fiscal year of the joint venture. In some cases, it may facilitate the U.S. shareholder's accounting treatment of the joint venture to have it utilize a fiscal year which is coterminous with that of the U.S. shareholder. Where the joint venture is acquiring parts or components from the U.S. partner or making other payments to it, it may be desirable for U.S. tax purposes to have it use a fixed year which ends one month after that of the U.S. partner in order to defer taxes.

§ 25:07. Termination of Joint Venture.

Finally, the joint venture agreemnt and the articles and bylaws of the entity should set forth the circumstances and procedures under which the joint venture will be terminated and the entity dissolved and liquidated. Local company law may establish certain circumstances under which either shareholder may petition for the dissolution and liquidation of the joint venture company. The joint venture documents may add to these circumstances, granting a right to either party to petition for dissolution in the event of a defined deadlock or the failure of the other shareholder to purchase or provide for the purchase of such party's shares after a triggering event. The dissolution and liquidation of an equity joint venture will normally take place under local company law, modified if necessary by the articles and bylaws of the entity. The termination of a nonequity joint venture which has joint assets must be provided for in greater detail.

PART VII—SUGGESTIONS FOR FURTHER READING

Books

J Dobkin, J., International Joint Ventures (1986).

Goldsweig, D. (ed.), Joint Ventures Abroad: A Case Study (1985).

Ravine, H. (ed.), The Multinational Joint Venture: Planning & Negotiating (1981).

Articles

Cherin & Combs (eds.), "Foreign Joint Ventures: Basic Issues, Drafting, and Negotiation," 38 Bus Law 1033 (1983).

Swindler, "The New Legal Framework for Joint Venture in China: Guidelines for Investors," 16 Law & Pol'y Int'l Bus 1005 (1984).

Travaglini, "Foreign Licensing and Joint Venture Arrangements," in Foreign Business Practices (1981).

PART VIII

FOREIGN INVESTMENT IN THE UNITED STATES

CHAPTER 26

LIMITATIONS ON
FOREIGN INVESTMENT

---

§ 26:01. In General.

Foreign investment in the United States has grown tremendously in the last two decades. In 1970, the book value of foreign direct[1] investment in U.S. assets was estimated at $13.3 billion. That figure expanded to $27.7 billion in 1975 and $83 billion in 1980.[2] The most significant growth, however, has occurred in the last few years. As of the end of 1985, foreign direct investment was estimated at $183 billion.[3] The preliminary figure for 1986 was $209.3 billion.[4] Barring a dramatic shift in the world economic

---

[1] See §2:04 for the distinction between direct and portfolio investment.

[2] Department of Commerce, Statistical Abstract of the United States (1987) at 780.

[3] Id.

[4] BNA International Inc., Investment USA (July 1987) at 11.

conditions or in the U.S. attitude toward foreign investment, this trend is expected to continue.[5]

The investment of foreign funds in the United States is not limited to any particular industry or geographical area. Manufacturing, high-technology, financial services, publishing, petroleum, and other industrial sectors have experienced the effects of foreign investment, whether through the establishment of new U.S. corporations or the acquisition of existing companies. While some states, such as Tennessee and Kentucky, have added hundreds of jobs as a result of foreign investment, foreign firms have also moved broadly into the coastal states, the south and the midwest.

All of this foreign investment has resulted in a significant amount of work for U.S. lawyers. It has also opened up a new area of the practice which, though not yet a specialty in itself, presents a number of unique issues for attorneys. In general, these issues fall into two broad categories: (i) those relating to the right of a foreign investor to acquire an interest in a particular investment, and the disclosure and reporting requirements applicable thereto, and (ii) those relating to the federal and state tax implications of the investment to the investor.

The principal focus of this discussion is to familiarize the attorney with the various federal and state laws which limit foreign investment in the United States and which impose important disclosure and reporting requirements on the investor (or, in some cases, its attorney). The most important of these laws, the International Investment Survey Act[6] and the Agricultural Foreign Investment Disclosure Act [7] may be completely new to many attorneys, and are therefore discussed in some detail. Certain other disclosure and reporting requirements, such as those imposed under the federal securities laws, apply both to foreign and U.S. investors and are presumed to be more familiar. Accordingly, their treatment

[5] See U.S. Department of Commerce, International Direct Investment: Global Trends and the U.S. Role (1984).

[6] 22 USC §3101 et seq.

[7] USC §3501 et seq.

herein is more limited. Important state laws regulating foreign investment are also discussed.

Foreign investment in the United States also presents a number of important tax issues. Wholly apart from the taxes imposed on the U.S. business itself, the Internal Revenue Code (the "Code") contains a number of special provisions which tax the foreign owner of such a U.S. business. The states have also been active in structuring their income tax systems to encourage foreign investment while obtaining what is perceived to be their fair share of tax revenues from foreign-owned companies doing business within their borders.

§ 26:02.   General Policy.

Before embarking on a discussion of the laws imposing special requirements on foreign investment, it is important to understand this country's policy toward foreign investment. In general, the United States has maintained an "open-door" approach toward foreign investment. Under most of its approximately 40 bilateral Treaties of Friendship, Commerce and Navigation, the United States has confirmed the right of foreign nationals of the other contracting state to enter, trade, invest, establish, and operate businesses in the United States. Most of these treaties provide that citizens and companies of the other contracting state shall be accorded "national treatment" with respect to their engaging in all types of commercial, industrial, financial, and other business activities within the territorial limits of such other contracting state.[8] The concept of "national treatment" implies that the foreign party will be accorded treatment which is no less favorable than the treatment accorded nationals in like situations. These treaties expressly authorize such citizens and companies (i) to establish and maintain branches, agencies, offices, factories and other establishments, (ii) to organize companies and to acquire interests

[8] See, e.g., Treaty of Friendship, Commerce and Navigation, April 2, 1953, United States-Japan, 4 UST 2063, TIAS 2863, 206 UNTS 143.

in other companies, and (iii) to control and manage enterprises which they have established.[9]

The policy expressed in the bilateral treaties is also contained in the Code of Liberalization of Capital Movements of the Organization for Economic Co-operation and Development (OECD). The OECD Code requires members (including the United States) to allow direct foreign investment by means of creating or acquiring full ownership of an enterprise, participation in new and existing enterprises, and providing long term loans. The OECD's Declaration on International Investment and Multinational Enterprises, to which the United States is a signatory, requires members to accord national treatment to enterprises operating within territories owned or controlled by nationals of another member country.[10]

The general openness toward foreign investment and the confidence that foreign investors have in this policy are important factors in the growth of foreign investment in the United States. This will be of little help, however, if the foreign stock of the parent company or other evidence of ownership or the right to control the U.S. investment are seized abroad. Moreover, under the Trading with the Enemy Act[11] and the International Emergency Economic Powers Act,[12] it is at least possible that a foreign investor's assets could be seized by the U.S. government in the event of hostilities between the United States and the home country of the investor. This risk has led some investors to utilize various trust devices, often combined with trusts or corporations in third countries, designed to isolate the U.S. investment in the event of an attempted expropriation.[13] Such an arrangement should be considered whenever circumstances suggest some risk of any of these governmental actions.

Finally, it should be noted that increasing concern about the level of foreign investment in the United States occasionally results

[9] Id.

[10] 15 ILM 967 (1967).

[11] 50 USC App §1 et seq.

[12] 50 USC §1701 et seq.

[13] See e.g., Knight, "Failsafe Legal Structures to Protect U.S. Assets of Foreign Investors," 9 Int'l Bus Law 109 (1981).

in legislative proposals which would impose broader limitations on foreign investments. A number of the provisions in the House version (HR-3) of the 1987 omnibus trade bill—The Trade and International Economic Policy Reform Act of 1987—would dramatically affect foreign investment in the United States.[14] While the Senate version (S-490) of the legislation has few of the investment provisions contained in HR-3, some compromises may be made in conference.

§ 26:03. Limitations.

An important exception to the general policy established under the Treaties on Friendship, Commerce and Navigation allows the United States to establish special rules for public utilities, shipbuilding, air and water transportation, banking, and the exploitation of land or other natural resources. These sectors are traditionally regarded as important to the national interest, and therefore subject to a higher level of regulation. A series of federal and state laws limit or impose other restrictions on foreign investment in these and certain other areas.[15]

(i) *Energy.* The Federal Power Act allows the Federal Energy Regulatory Commission to issue licenses for the development, transmittal and utilization of power on land and water subject to U.S. government control only to U.S. citizens and domestic corporations.[16] Similarly, the Atomic Energy Act of 1954 prohibits the Nuclear Regulatory Commission from issuing a license for nuclear facilities to a corporation which it believes to be owned, controlled or dominated by an alien, foreign corporation or foreign government.[17] While not prohibiting foreign investment, language in the

[14] See BNA International Inc., Investment USA (May, 1987) at 2.

[15] See generally Goodman & Sanders, Federal Regulations of Certain Foreign Investments in the United States, 13 Int'l Bus Law 7 (1985).

[16] 16 USC §797(e).

[17] 42 USC §2133(d).

Natural Gas Act has been relied on by the Federal Power Commission to solicit information on the citizenship of officers, directors and shareholders of corporations seeking licenses to import or export natural gas into or out of the United States.[18]

(ii) *Lands and Mining.* While various federal laws restrict the acquisition of public lands, desert lands and U.S. territories[19] by noncitizens, these are all of limited applicability to most foreign investors. Of potentially more significance are provisions of a law enacted in 1900 which prohibit aliens from acquiring a certificate of occupation, right of purchase lease, cash freehold agreement or special homestead agreement in public lands in Hawaii unless he has declared his intentions to become a U.S. citizen.[20] Similar provisions affect the right of aliens to own land in U.S. territories generally.[21] The Taylor Grazing Act prohibits the Secretary of the Interior from leasing or issuing permits to allow grazing on public lands to U.S. citizens, persons who have declared their intentions to become U.S. citizens, and associations comprised of corporations controlled by such persons.[22]

Federal laws also regulate the right of aliens in the mining and petroleum industries. The Mining Act of 1872 and the Mineral Lands Leasing Act of 1920 limit the exploration and development of mineral deposits on public lands to U.S. citizens, persons intending to become U.S. citizens, and domestic corporations.[23] Citizens of another country can acquire an interest in such corporations, however, if their country allows similar privileges to U.S. citizens on a reciprocal basis.[24] Regulations under the Outer Continental Shelf Lands Act of 1953 allow the Secretary of the Interior

[18] 15 USC §717(b).

[19] See Homestead Act of 1862, 12 Stat 392 (1862); Desert Lands Act, 43 USC §321 et seq.; Natural Resources Act of 1887, 48 USC §1501.

[20] 48 USC §§1509-152.

[21] 48 USC §1501 et seq.

[22] 43 USC §315b; 43 CFR §4121.1-1.

[23] 30 USC §§22, 181.

[24] Id.

to grant mineral and petroleum loans only to U.S. citizens, resident aliens, and domestic corporations.[25] The provisions of the Geothermal Steam Act of 1970 contain similar restrictions with respect to leases for the development and utilization of geothermal steam and associated resources.[26]

A significant number of states also impose special restrictions on the ownership and use of land (including mineral, timber and other rights) on aliens. These laws vary greatly with respect to the type (agriculture, forest, etc.) and size of land to which they apply, the status of alien (nonresident, nondeclarant, citizen of a reciprocal country, enemy) to which they extend and the remedy for noncompliance (escheat or mandatory disposition within a specified time). Some of these laws do not impose absolute prohibitions on foreign ownership, but only on reporting or prior license requirements.[27]

(iii) *Transportation and Communication.* Federal transportation laws impose special restrictions on alien ownership. Under the Intercoastal Shipping Act of 1933 coastwise trade (including moving freight or passengers between different U.S. ports) is limited to vessels owned by U.S. citizens or domestic corporations controlled by U.S. citizens.[28] Certain benefits available under the Ship Mortgage Act of 1920,[29] The Merchant Marine Act of 1936,[30] the Merchant Ship Sales Act of 1946,[31] and the Shipping Act of 1946[32] are also available only to U.S. citizens and citizen-controlled domestic corporations.[33] Similarly, in the air transpor-

---

[25] 43 CFR §3300.1.

[26] 30 USC §1001 et seq., 30 USC §1015.

[27] See §27:09.

[28] 48 USC §§883, 888.

[29] 46 USC §911 et seq., 46 USC §922(a)(5).

[30] 46 USC §1101 et seq., 46 USC §1151.

[31] 50 USC §1735 et seq., 50 USC §173(b).

[32] 46 USC §801 et seq., 46 USC §80.

[33] The fishing industry in the United States is also affected by laws which favor U.S. controlled enterprises. See e.g., 16 USC §1801 et seq.

tation industry, non U.S. citizens (including corporations not controlled by U.S. citizens) are prohibited from obtaining U.S. registry of their aircraft. This effectively precludes them from engaging in interstate and intrastate flights, except with prior authorization of the Department of Transportation (formerly, the Civil Aeronautics Board).[34]

The Communications Act of 1934 limits the issuance of a broadcasting license to U.S. citizens and domestic corporations at least 80% of whose shareholders and all of whose officers and directors are U.S. citizens.[35] The Act also authorizes the Federal Communications Commission to deny a license to a corporation controlled by another corporation in which an officer or more than 25% of the directors are aliens or in which 25% of the capital stock is beneficially owned by aliens.[36]

(iv) *Banking*. The regulation of banking and related activities by foreign nationals occurs at both the federal and state level. The regulations are further complicated by the ability to engage in such activities in the United States through a branch or U.S. subsidiary, and the variety of financial corporations, including bank holding companies, Edge Act corporations and multistate banks.

With the adoption of the International Banking Act of 1978,[37] foreign banks now have the option of operating in the United States as federal branches as well as state branches. A state branch would be governed by applicable state law. A federal branch must be established in one state which serves as its home state for purposes of the International Banking Act and the Bank Holding Company Act.[38] A foreign bank holding company is considered to have as its home state the state in which its U.S. bank subsidiary is located. Since the Bank Holding Company Act allows banks to expand into other states only if permitted under the law of the bank's home

[34] 49 USC §1301 et seq., 49 USC §1401.

[35] 47 USC §151 et seq., 47 USC §310.

[36] 47 USC §310(b)(4).

[37] Pub L No. 95-369, 92 Stat 607 (codified in various sections of 12 USC).

[38] 12 USC §1841 et seq.

262

state, the choice of where a foreign bank locates its branch or subsidiary is extremely important.

The International Banking Act allows foreign banks some flexibility in the areas of multistate banking. Previously existing multistate organizations were grandfathered, and the foreign bank was authorized to establish branches or agencies outside the home state, subject to certain limitations. Foreign branch banks may also form Edge Act corporations and are not subject to the Glass-Steagall prohibition on carrying on both depositary and investment banking. The Bank Holding Company Act also has special exemptions applicable to foreign banks regulated under the International Banking Act. At the same time, foreign banks who become subject to the Bank Holding Company Act face certain additional restrictions. An investor seeking to create a U.S. banking subsidiary must elect to organize the bank under Federal or state law. A requirement under the National Banking Act that at least a majority of the interests of a national bank be U.S. citizens has discouraged organization of national banks. State laws may also impose special requirements on the management and control of state banks. The acquisition of existing banks by foreign investors is also regulated by both state and federal law.[39]

(v) *Government Contracting.* Finally foreign investors should be apprised of the laws which favor U.S. controlled companies in any of several industries which provide products or services to the U.S. or state governments. A variety of federal laws create substantial preferences for U.S. contractors, particularly in the defense industry.[40] While the GATT Agreement on Government Procurement and the Trade Agreements Act of 1979[41] have caused some relaxation of these preferences, significant advantages for

---

[39] See generally Sheehan, "Foreign Acquisitions of U.S. Banking Institutions: The Current Climate," 4 Wis Int'l L J 20 (1985).

[40] See e.g., Buy American Act, 41 USC §10a-d; Balance of Payments Program, DAR §6-800 et seq., published in 32 CFR Parts 1-31.

[41] 19 USC §2501 et seq.

U.S. contractors remain.[42] A number of states have also enacted laws which can discriminate against foreign-controlled contractors.[43]

[42] See Swennen, "Federal Restrictions on Participation by Foreign Investors in Defense and Other Government Contracts," in J. Marans et al (eds.), Manual of Foreign Investment in the United States (1984) at 164.

[43] See Brossi & Swennen, "State Restrictions on Public Procurement," in J. Marans et al (eds.), Manual of Foreign Investment in the United States (1984) at 194.

CHAPTER 27

DISCLOSURE AND REPORTING REQUIREMENTS

§ 27:01. In General.

As the foregoing discussion illustrates, restrictions on foreign investment in the United States exist only in a relatively limited number of areas. Concern about the growth of foreign investment in the United States has resulted in recent years mostly in the enactment of federal laws designed to allow the U.S. government to monitor the amount of foreign investment. Two important laws are the International Investment Survey Act and the Agricultural Foreign Investment Disclosure Act.

A number of other federal laws impose disclosure or reporting requirements which may be applicable to a proposed foreign investment in the United States or to the activities of their U.S. lawyers and other representitives.

§ 27:02.   International Investment Survey Act.

The International Investment Survey Act[1] requires certain reports to be filed whenever a foreign person creates, acquires or disposes of a 10% or greater interest in a U.S. business enterprise or an equivalent interest in an incorporated U.S. business enterprise, including a branch. In order to secure the necessary jurisdictional nexus, the actual reporting obligation is imposed on the U.S. affiliate (10% or more owned) of the foreign person, or persons, such as law firms, investment bankers and business brokers, who assist or intervene in the acquisition of a U.S. business enterprise by, or enter into a joint venture with, a foreign person. "Foreign person" is defined broadly to include any nonresident alien, foreign government or agency thereof or entity located abroad or subject to the jurisdiction of another country.[2] A U.S. business enterprise includes virtually any enterprise which exists for profit purposes and any ownership of real estate.[3]

While the application of the Act is extremely broad, several exemptions and exclusions are available.[4] Residential real estate held exclusively for personal use or for the personal use of the

[1] 22 USC §3101 et seq.; 15 CFR Part 806. Special rules applicable to investments in U.S. banks are not included in this discussion. The International Investment Survey Act also requires certain reporting of portfolio investment (31 CFR Part 129) and trade in services between U.S. and foreign persons (31 CFR Part 801).

[2] 22 USC §3102(5).

[3] 22 USC §3102(6).

[4] 15 CFR §805.15(j)(3).

owner's shareholders need not be reported. A primary residence may also be leased while the owner is abroad without becoming subject to the reporting requirements. The formation of a new enterprise whose capitalization (including loans) is less than $1 million, and the acquisition of an existing enterprise whose total assets are valued under $1 million, are not required to be reported, provided that in each case such enterprises, in the aggregate, own less than 200 acres of U.S. land. It should be noted, however, that a claim must be filed to perfect these exemptions. An existing U.S. affiliate may also avoid reporting acquisitions through merger where the consideration is $1 million or less, the purchase does not involve the acquisition of 200 or more acres, and the acquired enterprise is merged into the operating affiliate.

Where an exemption is not available, the U.S. affiliate of the foreign person must report the transaction to the Bureau of Economic Analysis of the U.S. Department of Commerce within 45 days following the date of the investment. The U.S. affiliate reports the transaction on Form BE-13.[5] The Form BE-13 requires information as to (i) the type of transaction and the date of completion, (ii) the identity and ownership structure of the new U.S. affiliate, (iii) the identity of the U.S. business enterprise that has been acquired by or merged into an existing U.S. affiliate, (iv) certain financial and operational information, (v) any investment incentives or services provided by state or local governments, and (vi) the cost of the investment. The ownership information includes the identity of the foreign person who owns or controls the U.S. affiliate as well as the identity of the "ultimate beneficial owner" of such foreign person (i.e., the person at the end of the chain of ownership which is not owned more than 50% by another person). The completed Form BE-13 must be accompanied by a Form BE-607, Industry Classification Questionnaire.[6] All information on the report is to be used only by the Federal government and shall remain confidential.[7]

---

[5] Id.
[6] 15 CFR §806.15(j)(1).
[7] 22 USC §3104(c).

A U.S. person who assists or intervenes in a transaction reportable on Form BE-13, such as a law firm, real estate broker, business broker and brokerage house, as well as a U.S. person who enters into a joint venture with a foreign person, is required to complete and file a Form BE-14.[8] Under certain revisions made in 1982, however, the Form BE-14 is not required with respect to the acquisition of a U.S. business enterprise which was duly reported on a Form BE-13 by the U.S. affiliate.

In addition to the reports on Form BE-13 and BE-14, certain periodic reports must be filed. An Annual Report on Form BE-15 must be filed by May 31 of each year to report certain information as of the end of the U.S. affiliate's fiscal year which ended in the previous calendar year.[9] United States affiliates are exempt from the annual reporting requirements if their total assets, annual sales or gross profits (excluding sales taxes) and net income (after taxes) are each less than $10 million on a consolidated basis. Quarterly reports on Form BE-605 must also be filed by U.S. affiliates sold exceeding this $10 million exemption.[10] Once again, the U.S. affiliate must file a claim to validate the exemption for the annual and quarterly reporting requirements. Finally, a benchmark survey is conducted every five years, requiring the filing of an additional report on Form BE-12.[11] A benchmark survey is scheduled for 1988.

The Act provides various sanctions for noncompliance.[12] A penalty not to exceed $10,000 may be imposed for failure to file any of the required transactional or periodic reports under the Act, or to comply with any rule, regulation, order or instruction. Willful violations by corporate entities are subject to fines of up to $10,000, while individual violators can be fined, imprisoned or both. The Act also authorizes the courts to issue injunctive relief to mandate compliance with the Act.

[8] 15 CFR §806.15(j)(4).
[9] 15 CFR §806.15(i).
[10] 15 CFR §806.15(h)(1).
[11] 15 CFR §1303(b); 15 CFR §806.15(j)(2).
[12] 15 USC §3105.

§ 27:03. Agricultural Foreign Investment Disclosure Act.

The Agricultural Foreign Investment Disclosure Act[13] was enacted in 1978 to monitor the effect of foreign persons acquiring, transferring and holding agricultural land, particularly on family farms and rural communities. Under the Act, any foreign person who acquires or transfers an interest in agricultural land must file a report on Form ASCS-153 with the Office of the Agricultural Stabilization and Conservation Service having jurisdiction over such land within 90 days following such transaction. A foreign person, for purposes of the Act, generally includes (i) an individual who is not a U.S. citizen or permanent resident, (ii) a foreign government, and (iii) a corporation or other entity which is organized or has its principal place of business abroad or which is owned 10% or more by such an individual, government corporation or entity.[14] An interest in agricultural land includes any proprietary interest under contracts of sale or options to purchase, noncontingent future interests, leaseholds of ten years or more, and interests in mineral and surface rights, but not security interests or easements, profits and rights of way for purposes other than agricultural production.[15] Agricultural land includes land currently used (or if idle, then within the previous five years, most recently used) for farming, ranching, forestry, or timber production but does not include landholdings not exceeding 10 acres in the aggregate with respect to which the gross sales from natural products therefrom do not exceed $1,000.[16]

The information required to be reported under the Act includes (i) the legal description and acreage of the subject land, (ii) the date of transfer and the fair market value of the land at the time of transfer, (iii) the price or other consideration paid or to be paid, (iv) the legal interest transferred and the use contemplated by the transferee, (v) the identity of the transferor and the transferee and

---

[13] 7 USC §3501 et seq.; 7 CFR Part 781.

[14] 7 USC §3508(2)(4); 7 CFR §781.2(g).

[15] 7 CFR §781.2(c).

[16] 7 CFR §781.2(b).

the economic relationship between them, (vi) information concerning the representative of the reporting person completing the forms, and (vii) the identity of each foreign person owning a 10% or greater interest in the reporting entity. Foreign persons with a 10% interest in the reporting person must, in turn, file their own additional reports.[17] Unlike the information supplied under the International Investment Survey Act, the information disclosed under the Agricultural Foreign Investment Disclosure Act is available for public inspection.[18]

The Act imposes strict penalties not only for noncompliance but also for late filings. For incomplete, false or misleading reports, or failure to update reportable information, fines of up to 25% of the fair market value of the interest can be imposed.[19] Late filings are subject to fines of $1/10$ of 1% of the fair market value of the subject interest for each week that the violation remains uncorrected, up to a maximum of 25% of the value of the interest.[20]

§ 27:04.   Other Federal Disclosure and Reporting Requirements—Antitrust Improvements Act.

The Hart-Scott-Rodino Antitrust Improvements Act of 1976[21] requires prenotification to the Federal Trade Commission and the Antitrust Division of the U.S. Department of Justice of certain business combinations, whether by merger or purchase of stock or assets. The Act applies generally to transactions by which (i) one party has consolidated assets or annual sales (including all entities under common control) of $100 million or more and the other party has consolidated assets or annual sales of $10 million or more, and (ii) as a result of the acquisition, the acquiring person

[17] 7 CFR §781.3(f).

[18] 22 USC §3506. The information is available at the Department of Agriculture in Washington, D.C. within ten days of its receipt.

[19] 7 CFR §781.4(b)(2).

[20] 7 CFR §781.4(b)(1).

[21] Pub L No. 94-435, 90 Stat 1383 (codified in various sections of 15 USC).

would have aggregate voting securities or assets of the acquired person in excess of $15 million or at least 15% of the voting securities or assets of the acquired person.[22]

§ 27:05.　—United States Securities Laws.

The Domestic and Foreign Investment Improved Disclosure Law of 1977[23] amended the Securities Exchange Act of 1934 to require additional disclosure by a foreign person of a 5% interest in the voting securities of a U.S. corporation subject to Section 12 of the 1934 Act.[24] The information is required to be reported to the Securities and Exchange Commission on Schedule 13D. The provisions of the 1934 Act which regulate the acquisition of Section 12 companies by means of a tender offer for shares would also apply to tender offers by foreign investors.[25]

§ 27:06.　—Currency and Foreign Transactions Reporting Act.

The Currency and Foreign Transactions Reporting Act,[26] as amended, requires any person who physically transports, mails or ships currency or other "monetary instruments" in an aggregate amount in excess of $10,000 on any occasion into or out of the United States to file Customs Form 4790 with the Customs Service.[27] The term "monetary instruments" includes investment securities in bearer form or in registered form if endorsed in blank, as well as promissory notes and other negotiable instruments

---

[22] 15 USC §18a; see generally S. Axinn, B. Fogg & N. Stoll, Acquisitions Under the Hart-Scott-Rodino Antitrust Improvements Act (1984).

[23] Pub L No. 95-213, 91 Stat 1498.

[24] 15 USC §78m(d).

[25] 15 USC §78n(d).

[26] Pub L No. 91-508, 84 Stat 1118.

[27] 31 USC §5316.

payable to bearer or endorsed so that title passes upon delivery.[28] Transfer of funds by bank check, bank draft or wire transfer are exempt.

§ 27:07. —Foreign Investment in Real Property Tax Act.

The Foreign Investment in Real Property Tax Act of 1980 (FIRPTA)[29] created a number of reporting requirements designed to illicit information about the tax liability of nonresident aliens upon the sale or disposition of real estate located in the United States as well as interests in corporations and other entities whose assets included U.S. real property interests. Because of the controversies surrounding the regulations under FIRPTA's reporting requirements, however, the reporting requirements were never implemented. Finally, under the Tax Reform Act of 1984, Congress decided to enforce payment of the tax by means of withholding rather than reporting.[30] While the Internal Revenue Service still has authority to require reporting,[31] the implementation of the reporting system would require the adoption of regulations.

§ 27:08. —Foreign Agents Registration Act.

The Foreign Agents Registration Act of 1938,[32] as amended, requires a representative of a foreign principal who engages within the United States, directly or indirectly, in political activities, public relations or political consultation for, or dispenses or collects money, loans or other valuables on behalf of, a foreign principal or represents its interests before any U.S. agency or

[28] 31 USC §5312(a)(3).

[29] Pub L No. 96-499, 94 Stat 2682.

[30] IRC §1445.

[31] IRC §6039C.

[32] 22 USC §611 et seq.

official to register with the U.S. Attorney General.[33] A foreign principal is defined under the Act to include a foreign investment or political party, any person outside the United States, and any corporation, partnership or other entity organized or having its principal place of business outside the United States.[34] While the Act exempts persons who are engaged solely in private and non-political activities on behalf of their foreign principals, the Act may require registration of attorneys and other representatives of foreign investors in many cases.[35]

§ 27:09. State Law Requirements.

In many areas, state law imposes an additional level of regulations with which foreign investors must comply. These laws deal generally with the organization of local corporations and qualifications of foreign corporations; securities, banking, insurance and related activities; and taxation of local activities. In general, however, these laws usually treat foreign individuals and corporations in the same manner as residents and corporations of other U.S. states.

With respect to the acquisition of interests in local real estate, however, many states impose special restrictions and reporting requirements that apply to foreign investors. The reporting requirements are normally independent from and in addition to the reporting obligations imposed under federal law. In certain cases, however, the state laws merely require the filing of the federal forms with the relevant state agencies, thus obviating the need to prepare additional reports.

Because these laws vary significantly in terms of the sole persons required to whom they apply, the types of real property interests concerned, the nature of the obligations and the exemp-

---

[33] 22 USC §611(c).

[34] 22 USC §611(b).

[35] See generally Pattison & Taylor (eds.), The Regulation of Foreign Agents in the United States: A Practical and Legal Guide (1981).

tions available, generalizations are difficult to make. Certain publications have assembled summaries of the various state laws.[36] Investment USA, a monthly, also publishes current information on state laws affecting foreign investment. It is, of course, incumbent on the attorney advising foreign investors to identify and ensure compliance with any of the special state laws with respect to the acquisition of real estate property interests in a state.

[36] See, e.g., Goodman, "Federal and State Disclosure Requirement and Restrictions in Connection with U.S. Acquisitions by Foreign Purchasers," 21 Real Prop, Prob & Tr J 623, 635 (1986); J. Marans et al. (eds.), Manual of Foreign Investment in the United States (1984) at 194.

CHAPTER 28

TAX TREATMENT OF FOREIGN INVESTMENT IN THE UNITED STATES

§ 28:01. Basic Principles.

Foreign investors, whether individuals or corporations, are generally subject to U.S. income tax on their investment activities in the United States in one of two ways: (i) at the graduated rates applicable to U.S. citizens and Corporations, or (ii) at a gross rate of 30% (or less if reduced by an applicable tax treaty). The actual tax applicable in a given case depends on a number of variables, including the extent of the taxpayer's activities in the United States and the source and nature of the income.

Resident aliens are generally subject to U.S. taxation on their world-wide income at the graduated rates applicable to U.S. citizens. Nonresident aliens and foreign corporations not deemed to be engaged in a U.S. trade or business are generally subject to tax at the 30% (or lower treaty rate) on their passive ("fixed or determinable annual or periodical") income from U.S. sources only. Nonresident aliens and foreign corporations which are deemed to be engaged in a U.S. trade or business are taxed at the graduated rates applicable to U.S. citizens and resident aliens with respect to income which is effectively connected with the U.S. trade or business and certain other nonpassive income. The passive income of such taxpayers is generally subject to the gross withholding tax.

These general principles imply a number of issues. First, what is the distinction between a resident alien and a nonresident alien? Second, what is U.S. source income and effectively connected income? Third, how is the tax computed? These and certain other issues are discussed in this chapter.

§ 28:02. Resident versus Nonresident Aliens.

The Tax Reform Act of 1984 greatly reduced prior confusion in determining the residence of an alien for U.S. tax purposes by creating a statutory definition of a "resident alien." Under §7701(b) of the Code, an alien (i.e., a non U.S. citizen) is deemed a resident alien of the United States if he or she satisfies either (i) the lawful permanent residence test, or (ii) the substantial presence test.

(i) *Lawful Permanent Residence Test*. Section 7701(b)(1)(A)(i) of the Code provides that an alien individual will be treated as a resident alien of the United States for a calendar year if at any time during the calendar year such individual is a "lawful permanent resident" of the United States. The Code goes on to provide that an alien qualifies as a "lawful permanent resident" if at any time (i) such individual has the status of a permanent resident under U.S. immigration law, and (ii) such status has not been revoked or judicially or administratively determined to have been abandoned.[1] The lawful permanent residence test is also known as the "green card" test, referring to the document issued to an immigrant lawfully admitted for permanent residence under the immigration laws.

(ii) *Substantial Presence Test.* An alien who is not a lawful permanent resident under the immigration laws may nevertheless be deemed a resident alien for U.S. income tax purposes if he or she meets the substantial presence test.[2] The substantial presence test is based on the number of days an alien is present in the United States either in the current year or over the past three years. Under §7701(b)(3), an alien is deemed a resident alien of the United States if (i) such alien is physically present in the United States for 183 days or more during a calendar year, or (i) the sum of the days the alien is physically present in the United States during the current calendar year, plus one-third of the number of days the alien is physically present in the United States during the immediately preceding year, plus one-sixth of the number of days the alien is physically present in the United States during the second preceding calendar year, equals or exceeds 183 days. In certain cases a special election is available to be treated as a resident alien even though the mechanical test is not met.[3]

An individual is treated as present in the United States for any day during which the alien is in the country.[4] Thus, the day the alien arrives and leaves would be included in the day count. Days during which an alien is present in the United States as an "exempt individual," however, are not taken into account for purposes of the substantial presence test.[5] For such purpose, an "exempt individual," includes (i) foreign diplomats and employees of certain international organizations (generally, A and G-4 visa holders), and their immediate family; (ii) certain teachers and trainees present in the United States under a J visa for a limited time, and who are in compliance with the terms and conditions thereof; and (iii)

---

[1] IRC §7701(b)(6).

[2] IRC §7701(b)(1)(A)(ii).

[3] IRC §7701(b)(1)(a)(iii).

[4] IRC §7701(b)(7)(A).

[5] IRC §7701(b)(5).

certain students present in the United States for a limited time under F or J visas and who are in compliance with the terms and conditions thereof.[6] Days in which an alien is unable to leave the country due to medical conditions as well as periods of less than 24 hours in which an alien may be in the United States in transit between two foreign ports are also disregarded.[7] Days in which commuters from Canada and Mexico are present are also not counted for purposes of the physical presence test.[8] The physical presence test thus requires the alien to keep careful records of his or her visits to the United States in order to avoid or to qualify for resident alien status.

There are two other important exceptions to the physical presence test. Under the so-called "31-day exception," an alien who otherwise meets the physical presence test will not be deemed a resident alien for a calendar year in which he was present in the United States for fewer than 31 days.[9] For example, an alien who is in the United States for only 30 days in the current tax year but who spent 310 days in the country in each of the previous calendar years would be deemed a resident under the substantial presence test ($30 + 310/3 + 310/6 = 185$). Under the 31-day exception, however, the alien would not be deemed a resident for the current year since he was present in the country for fewer than 31 days of such year. A second exception provides that an alien who is not present in the United States for at least 183 days in the current calendar year but who otherwise meets the physical presence test will nevertheless be treated as a nonresident for such year if (i) such alien establishes that his "tax home" for such year was in a foreign country and he had a "closer connection" to such country than with the United States, and (ii) such alien neither had an application pending for adjustment of status nor took any other steps to apply for permanent residency at any time during such calendar year.[10] The "tax home" issue is governed by §162(a)(2)

[6] Id.
[7] IRC §7701(b)(7)(C).
[8] IRC §7701(b)(7)(B).
[9] IRC §7701(b)(3)(A)(ii).
[10] IRC §§7701(b)(3)(B), 911(d)(3).

278

of the Code (relating to deductions, travel expenses while away from home) and the location of the taxpayer's "abode." While there is not complete agreement on the tax home issue, the term is usually defined in terms of the taxpayer's residence and principal place of business. The closer connection issue requires an analysis of various factors evidencing the alien's contacts with the foreign country versus the United States, such employment, business, investment, family and social ties, all of which must be examined and weighed as under prior law. Finally, the tax home/closer connection test also requires that the alien himself neither file for adjustment of status nor take any other steps to obtain permanent residency under U.S. immigration laws. Steps taken by the alien's relative or U.S. employer to obtain permanent residency for such alien are curiously ignored for purposes of this test.

(iii) *Impact of Tax Treaties*. It is important to note that the new definition of a resident under §7701(b) is not intended to override the determination of residency under international tax treaties between the United States and a foreign country.[11] These tax treaties often contain provisions designed to prevent both contracting states from treating the same individual as a resident for tax purposes. The so-called "tie-breaker" provisions contained in the current U.S. model tax treaty accomplish this by reference to the individual's permanent home, economic relations, abode, nationality and other factors. An alien who is deemed to be a resident of a foreign country under a relevant tax treaty will not be taxed as a U.S. resident regardless of whether he meets the lawful permanent residence test or substantial presence test. Aliens would also be subject to tax as U.S. residents if they meet either of these tests.

§ 28:03. Classes of Income.

As noted above, resident aliens are subject to U.S. taxation on their world-wide income in the same manner as U.S. citizens. Nonresident aliens and foreign corporations, on the other hand, are

[11] HR Rep No. 861, 98th Cong 2nd Sess, p 967 (1984) (Conf Rep).

generally subject to U.S. income taxation only on their income from sources within the United States. The tax treatment accorded such U.S. source income differs depending on whether or not it is deemed to be effectively connected with the conduct of a trade or business wtihin the United States. Income which is effectively connected with a U.S. trade or business is taxed, after allowable deductions, at the graduated rates to which U.S. citizens and resident aliens are subject. Income that is not connected with a trade or business in the United States (i.e., passive type income) is taxed at a flat 30% (or lower treaty) rate, without any deductions.

The purpose of the two types of tax treatment is largely practical. A flat tax on passive type income is easier to administer and collection is assured through withholding at the source. Effectively connected income can be more easily reached and as business-type income, it is more appropriate to tax it on a net income basis similar to U.S. resident taxpayers engaged in the same business.

(i) *U.S. Source Income*. The initial question is thus to determine the extent of one's U.S. source income. Sections 861-864 of the Code contain a series of rules for determining the source of various types of income. The most important of these are interest, dividends, personal services income, rents and royalties, and income from the sale of property. The source of each of these types of income are summarized below.

Interest. In general, all interest income on bonds, notes or other interest-bearing obligations of U.S. borrowers, whether corporate or otherwise, is deemed U.S. source income, subject to certain exceptions.[12] Interest earned on deposits or withdraw-able accounts with banks, credit unions, savings and loan associations and insurance companies is now treated as a U.S. source income, but is exempt from U.S. tax.[13] Interest received from domestic corporations who derive not more than 20% of their gross income from sources within the United States and interest

[12] IRC §861(a)(1).
[13] IRC §§871(i), 881(d).

on deposits with a foreign banking branch of a U.S. corporation or partnership is not deemed U.S. source income.[14]

Dividends. Dividend income is considered to be U.S. source if received from a U.S. corporation. A portion of the dividends received from a foreign corporation would also be considered U.S. source income if 25% or more of its gross income is effectively connected with a U.S. trade or business.

Personal Services Income. Salary, wages, professional fees and other compensation received for labor or other services is deemed U.S. source income if such services are performed within the United States.[15] The Code creates an exception to this rule, however, where the following three conditions are met: (i) the alien was in the United States for not more than 90 days during the tax year, (ii) the services were performed as an employee of or under contract with a nonresident alien individual, foreign partnership or foreign corporation not engaged in a U.S. trade or business, or for a foreign office or place of business of a U.S. citizen or resident or a U.S. corporation or partnership, and (iii) the amount received does not exceed $3,000.[16] A number of other exceptions exist under tax treaties for limited amounts of income received by visitors, and for income received by teachers, professors and employees of foreign governments.

Rents and Royalties. Rental and royalty income is deemed to be derived from sources within the United States to the extent that it is received from patents, trademarks, copyrights, know-how and similar property located or used within the United States.[17]

Sales Income. Finally, income derived from the disposition of U.S. real property interests is considered U.S. source.[18] U.S. real property interests normally include any interest in real

---

[14] IRC §861(a)(1)(B) and (C).

[15] IRC §861(a)(3).

[16] Id.

[17] IRC §861(a)(4).

[18] IRC §861(a)(5).

property located within the United States.[19] Income derived from inventory property purchased outside the United States and sold or exchanged within the United States is also considered U.S. source.[20] Special source rules apply to income from the sale or exchange of noninventory personal property.[21]

(ii) *Effectively Connected Income.* As noted above, U.S. source income of a nonresident alien or foreign corporation is subject to taxation at the graduated rates to the extent that it is effectively connected with the conduct of a trade or business in the United States, while other U.S. source income is subject to a flat withholding tax. The Code contains a narrow definition of a U.S. trade or business that applies only to the performance of personnel services in the United States.[22] Under §864(c)(3), however, except for certain investment income discussed below, all U.S. source income received by a nonresident alien or foreign corporation is treated as effectively connected with the conduct of U.S. trade or business, regardless of whether such taxpayer is engaged in any activities which fall within the definition of a U.S. trade or business.[23] In certain limited circumstances, a nonresident alien may also elect to treat income received on the sale of real property as effectively connected with a U.S. trade or business, thus being subject to net tax at the graduated rates rather than the gross withholding tax.[24]

The U.S. source income which is not deemed to be effectively connected with the nonresident alien or foreign corporation's trade or business includes "fixed and determinable annual and periodical" income (interest, dividends, rents, salaries, wages, premiums, annuities, etc.) and certain other gains, provided that such income meets one of two tests.[25] Under the "asset use" test, the

[19] IRC §897(c).
[20] IRC §861(a)(6).
[21] IRC §865.
[22] IRC §864(b).
[23] IRC §864(c)(3).
[24] IRC §§871(d), 882(d).
[25] IRC §§871(a)1, 881(a).

above-mentioned types of income are deemed to be effectively connected with a U.S. trade or business if such income is derived from assets used in or held for use in the conduct of such trade or business.[26] Under the "business activities" test, the specified categories of investment income will be deemed to be effectively connected with a U.S. trade or business if the activities of such trade or business were a "material factor" in the realization of such income.[27] The "asset use" test is usually important in the context of a sales or manufacturing business which receives interest, dividends or other income on notes, evidences of indebtedness, deposits, stock certificates, real property or other assets owned by it. The "business activities" test is applicable in the case of dividends or interest received by securities dealers, royalties received by licensors, service fees received by servicing businesses and similar situations. The fact that the income was accounted for through the books of the trade or business should be given considerable weight.[28]

It should be noted that various categories of foreign source income are treated as effectively connected with a U.S. trade or business if received by a nonresident alien or foreign corporation who maintains an office or fixed place of business wtihin the United States to which such income is attributable.[29]

§ 28:04. Computing Applicable Tax.

In computing their U.S. tax, nonresident aliens and foreign corporations must divide their income which is subject to U.S. taxation between that which is effectively connected with a trade or business in the United States and that which is not. Certain exemptions apply in the case of "portfolio interest" from certain

[26] IRC §864(c)(2)(A).

[27] IRC §864(c)(2)(B).

[28] IRC §864(c)(2).

[29] IRC §864(c)(4).

debt instruments[30] and certain other interest and dividends.[31] Special rules also apply in the case of capital gains of nonresident aliens who are present in the United States for more than 183 days in a taxable year.[32] While certain exclusions may be available under applicable tax treaties or otherwise from both categories of taxable income, the tax treatment of each category is otherwise quite distinct.

Income received by nonresidents and foreign corporations which is effectively connected with the conduct of a U.S. trade or business is taxed at the same graduated rates that apply to U.S. citizens and resident aliens.[33] Unlike the 30% gross tax applicable to income which is not effectively connected with a U.S. trade or business, the graduated rates of tax applicable to effectively connected income are assessed on a net basis after certain deductions and credits. Nonresident alien individuals are allowed deductions with respect to their U.S. source effectively connected income, while foreign corporations are allowed deductions on all their effectively connected income.[34]

The tax on income which is not effectively connected with a U.S. trade or business is calculated separately. The tax on such income is assessed at a flat 30% rate and is required to be withheld at the source. As noted above, however, such rate may be reduced for specified types of income in the case of residents of certain countries with whom the United States has a tax treaty. For example, under the tax treaty between the U.S. and Canada, the tax rate on interest is reduced to 15%, on dividends to 10% or 15%, on royalties to 10%, and on pensions to 15%. Accordingly, reference must always be made to any applicable tax treaty in order to determine the applicable rate of tax.[35]

[30] IRC §871(b).

[31] IRC §871(i), 88(d).

[32] IRC §871(a)(2).

[33] IRC §§871(b), 882(a).

[34] IRC §§873(a), 882(c).

[35] For a list of countries with which the United States has tax treaties, see CCH, Standard Federal Tax Reporter, §350.

§ 28:05.   Branch Profits Tax.

As discussed above, the Code imposes a withholding tax on most dividends and interest paid by a U.S. person to a foreign person. Because withholding is applied only to dividends and similar payments abroad, however, this tax could be avoided by operating in the United States as a branch of a foreign corporation which could repatriate funds other than by means of such payments. In order to prevent such tax avoidance, the Code imposed a "second-tier" withholding tax on dividends and interest paid by a foreign corporation to foreign persons where 50% or more of the corporation's gross income for the prior three years was connected with a U.S. trade or business.[36]

Because the second-tier withholding tax was difficult to enforce and frequently avoided, operation in the United States through a branch of a foreign company presented certain tax advantages over operating through a U.S. subsidiary. The branch profits tax, which is contained in §884 of the Code and was added by the Tax Reform Act of 1986, was designed to eliminate these advantages. In fact, it may have tipped the scales in favor of investing in U.S. real property and other assets by means of a U.S. subsidiary rather than a U.S. branch of a foreign corporation.[37]

Under new §884, which is effective for tax years beginning in 1987, a foreign corporation with a U.S. branch is subject to a 30% tax on the annual earnings and profits of the branch that are not reinvested in assets connected with the branch's U.S. trade or business.[38] In addition, a 30% branch profits tax is generally imposed on all interest paid by the branch to foreign lenders, as well as on certain interest deemed to be paid by the branch to the home office under a fictional loan arrangement.[39]

[36] IRC §§871(a), 881(a), 1441, 1442. The second-tier withholding tax was often eliminated by tax treaties or the use of multi-country branches.

[37] See Hudson, "Planning for Foreign Investment in U.S. Real Estate After the Tax Reform Act of 1986," 16 Tax Mgt Int'l J 3 (1987).

[38] IRC §884(a)–(d).

[39] IRC §884(f).

It is important to note that the branch profits tax for a taxable year cannot be offset by losses incurred by the branch in prior years, or by any foreign tax credits.[40] Moreover, the branch tax is imposed on earnings and profits rather than on taxable income. Thus, a foreign corporation which invests in U.S. real estate or other assets which are depreciated on an accelerated basis could face branch tax liability even if it has no positive taxable income. There is also a risk that the IRS could apply the tax to large cash balances which it deems to be in excess of the branch's needs.

Where the branch profits tax is prohibited by treaty, the second-tier withholding tax will continue to apply to the foreign corporation's payment of dividends, except that the threshold for second-tier withholding is reduced from 50% to 25%.[41] In all other cases the branch tax will replace the second-tier withholding tax.[42] In general, however, the provisions of §884 establishing the branch tax on profits and interest and second-tier withholding on dividends are not intended to override any existing treaties that would prohibit or reduce these taxes unless "treaty shopping" is deemed to be present.[43]

§ 28:06.   State Taxation.

State taxation must also be considered in planning foreign investments in the United States. These include not only income taxes, but also sales, personal and real property, use, franchise, capital, and other taxes. While these taxes are usually lower than the federal income tax, the aggregate tax burden in a given state may be quite onerous. Moreover, because foreign investors frequently have some flexibility in the location of the assets in which they invest and the office or other location in the United States, if any, from which they will manage the investment, there can often

[40] Reg §1.312–6(d); HR Rep No. 841, 99th Cong, 2d Sess II–647.

[41] IRC §884(e)(2)(B), (3)(A).

[42] IRC §885(b)(3)(A).

[43] IRC §884(e)(4)(A)(i).

be more opportunity for tax planning with respect to state taxes than federal taxes.

While even a brief discussion of state tax laws affecting foreign investors is beyond the scope of this work, the jurisdictional basis upon which states attempt to obtain their fair share of tax revenues from foreign-owned enterprises doing business within their borders warrants mention. In the past, many states adhered to a worldwide unitary method of accounting for income tax purposes. Under the unitary method, a state calculates the total income earned by a multinational and its subsidiaries, and then imposes state tax on a portion of the total determined in accordance with the multinational's payroll, sales and property within the state compared to those outside the state. This approach is often disadvantageous for the multinational since it does not necessarily reflect the company's actual income in the state and taxes profits from foreign operations.

Most states have now adopted a "waters edge" approach to tax apportionment under which activities of foreign corporations that are carried on outside the United States are not considered in determining the apportionable income base for state tax purposes. Federal legislation designed to prohibit states from utilizing the worldwide unitary tax method in determining state tax liability has been introduced in each of the last several sessions of Congress, but has not been enacted. Approximately seven states still utilize the unitary tax method, though some states, such as California, allow taxpayers to elect to have their taxes determined in accordance with the waters edge approach.[44]

[44] See generally J. Hellerstein, State Taxation (1983 and 1986 Supp).

PART VIII—SUGGESTIONS FOR FURTHER READING

Books

Committee to Study Foreign Investment in the United States of the Section of Corporation, Banking and Business Law of the American Bar Association, A Guide to Foreign Investment Under the United States Law (1979).

Forry, J., A Practical Guide to Foreign Investment in the United States (2d ed. 1982).

Marcus, J., *et al* (eds) Manual of Foreign Investment in the United States (1984).

Rhoades, R., & Langer, M., Income Taxation of Foreign Related Transactions (1987).

Articles

Goodman, "Federal and State Disclosure Requirements and Restrictions in Connection with U.S. Acquisitions by Foreign Purchasers," 21 Real Prop, Prob & Tr J 623 (1986).

Gudgeon, "United States Bilateral Investment Treaties: Comments on their Origin, Purposes and General Treatment Standards," 4 Int'l Tax & Bus Law 105 (1981).

Kavass, "Foreign Investment in the United States: A Survey of Current Literature," 18 Vand J Trans L 375 (1985).

Shepro, "Foreign Direct Investment in the United States: A Legal Analysis," 4 Wis Int'l L J 46 (1986).

INTERNATIONAL DISPUTE RESOLUTION

CHAPTER 29

CHOICE OF LAW AND FORUM IN INTERNATIONAL DISPUTES

§ 29:01. In General.

Despite the goodwill of the parties to an international business transaction, and the concerted efforts of their lawyers to cover every contingency, disputes do arise. The risk of disagreements over contractual responsibilities are, in fact, even greater in international transactions where communication is often more difficult and local customs and practices, which are often implicitly incorporated within agreements, differ considerably between the parties. If the misunderstanding is fundamental, it may jeopardize the entire relationship between the parties. Even an apparently minor dispute, however, can result in considerable loss of time and money while the parties work out a resolution.

The best means of dealing with an international commercial

dispute is to avoid it in the first place. This is perhaps best accomplished by insuring that the other side is happy with the contractual relationship, and understands that its interest is better served by promptly and completely performing its contractual undertakings. United States companies, or their legal advisers, who use a superior bargaining position to force a foreign firm to accept unreasonable terms frequently find themselves with a legal claim rather than a contract. Another means of helping avoid disputes is through careful drafting of the underlying agreements. This, however, is by no means failsafe. Individuals in many countries do not feel the same obligation to comply strictly with their contractual responsibilities and their local courts may sympathize with their position.

While the focus of the negotiations and agreements should thus be on the avoidance of disputes, consideration must also be given to the proper management of disputes which do arise. Proper management means that the international dispute be concluded as inexpensively and expeditiously as possible and in a manner which maximizes one's gain, or at least, minimizes one's loss. Two important questions in the proper management of international commercial disputes are the choice of law and the choice of forum which will give the dispute.

§ 29:02. Choice of Law.

Even the most complete commercial contracts do not cover every contingency or regulate the parties' conduct in respect of every matter. A standard sales representative agreement would not, for example, specify all the remedies available to the principal in the event of the representatives' taking action beyond the scope of his agency. International loan agreements, despite their length and complexity, do not typically set forth all the procedures for enforcing payment upon the borrower's default. Efforts by a draftsman to expand an agreement beyond the scope of reasonably possible eventualities or to define procedures that are regulated by law often create confusion on the fundamental points of the agreement and meet with resistance on the part of the parties themselves.

It is thus essential, both because of the need for predictability in contractual undertakings and for the prompt resolution of disputes, to set forth a legal structure under which these issues will be handled. By choosing the law applicable to the agreement, the parties agree to be governed by a much broader scheme of rules and procedures for all matters not expressly covered in the agreement itself.

An express choice of law is particularly important in international agreements. In an agreement between a Los Angeles lender and a San Francisco borrower, both parties could perhaps fairly assume that any dispute arising out of the loan agreement or related documents would be governed by California law. Where the same lender advances funds to a Korean borrower, however, the absence of an express choice of law clause leaves the issue of applicable law in doubt. Under existing U.S. principles of conflicts of laws, a U.S. court would normally seek to apply the law of the jurisdiction which has the most significant relationship to the matter by identifying the "contacts" each jurisdiction has with the case. These contacts include the place the contract was negotiated, entered into and performed, the location of the subject matter of the contract, and the domicile and nationality of the parties.[1] A Korean tribunal may use quite different criteria to determine the applicable law. Often the most likely result, however, is that both courts would favor resorting to their own law, so that the party who is first able to file an action and obtain jurisdiction over the other may be able to determine the applicable law.

An express choice of law is also more important in international agreements since the manner in which the dispute is resolved can differ radically due to the great differences among foreign bodies of law. If, in our example above, the Los Angeles lender was dealing with a Washington borrower, the absence of a choice of law in the loan documents would not present a significant problem in most cases since the law of both jurisdiction is quite similar. The

---

[1] Restatement (Second) of Conflict of Laws, §§186, 188 (1971).

same omission from the loan agreement with the Korean borrower, on the other hand, could dramatically prejudice the lenders' interests.

While inclusion of a choice of law clause in any international agreement is thus essential, the limits of such a clause should also be understood. A U.S. lawyer who succeeds in conveying his foreign counterpart to accept a clause which provides that the agreement will be governed by U.S. law may be surprised when such a clause is ignored by a foreign court. Many foreign courts, particularly in developing countries, long ago learned that a particular choice of law may be more the result of one party's bargaining position, than an agreement among the parties. A foreign court may resort to a more traditional basis for determining the applicable law, such as lex fori, in order to circumvent the choice of foreign law. In some cases, local law protects local parties by expressly providing that such law will apply regardless of a contrary choice of law provision in an agreement. Even U.S. courts still generally require the jurisdiction whose law is chosen to have a "reasonable relationship" to the transaction in question and will not apply a legal principle which violates fundamental public policy.[2]

The choice of law decision in an international commercial agreement depends on a number of factors. As a general principle, each party should obviously argue for the law which it believes will best serve its interests. In practice, however, other factors often play a larger role. Many U.S. lawyers will insist that an agreement be governed by U.S. law either because they feel it is more developed (and therefore affords greater predictability) or because they simply are unaware, and unwilling to determine, how their interests would be served under some other body of law. More experienced lawyers understand the importance of analyzing the effect of the various choices of law on the proposed transaction and advocating a choice of law which they believe will be most favorable to their clients under the circumstances in which a dispute is likely to arise. In some cases, this will mean a dual choice

---

[2] Restatement (Second) of Conflict of Laws §187(2) (1971); UCC §1–105 (1978).

of law clause, such as those contained in most loan agreements covering the rescheduling of Mexico's foreign debt. These agreements typically provide for the applicability of New York law if an enforcement action is brought in the United States, and Mexican law (which accords important summary proceedings) in the case of an enforcement action brought in Mexico.

The precise wording of the choice of law clause has become quite standard. An example follows:

> This Agreement shall be governed by and construed in accordance with the laws of the State of New York, U.S.A. as in effect from time to time without regard to principles of conflicts of laws.

The reference to conflicts of law is obviously designed to prevent a court, applying New York law, from determining that the governing law should be something other than New York law. This is also sometimes accomplished by referring to the "internal" laws of a given jurisdiction. The reference to the laws as they are in effect clarifies that the parties intend to subject themselves to future changes in such laws. In certain instances, the parties may want to freeze the applicable law by submitting themselves to the laws in effect as of the date of the agreement. In some cases, the clause also provides that disputes arising out of the agreement will be governed by the specified law. This is perhaps redundant where the chosen forum corresponds to the chosen law, but important if it does not. Finally, to the extent that the parties agree to apply dual governing laws or an international body of law such as lex mercatoriam or the U.N. convention on Contracts for the International Sale of Goods, the same should be clearly set forth, even if, as in the case of the CISG, such law will apply by operation of local law.

§ 29:03. Choice of Forum.

Some of the same factors that motivate parties to choose a given body of law are also the reason why they often designate a forum in which disputes arising out of the agreement will be settled. Many international loan agreements, for example, expressly provide that disputes be adjudicated by a New York court to add certainty to the agreement and to insure that the dispute will be heard by a judge who is likely to have considerable experience with international lending transactions. The other chief motivation for a choice of law clause—the perception that it will favor one side in a dispute—is obviously another important reason for advocating a given forum.

At the same time, choice of forum clauses are important for other reasons. Perhaps chief among these is the desire of each party to avoid excessive costs in resolving disputes. In an equipment sales agreement between a Chicago seller and a Sao Paulo buyer, the buyer will incur significantly greater costs in litigating a dispute over the acceptability of the equipment brought in an Illinois court. In addition to hiring high-priced U.S. lawyers, the Brazilian will have to incur substantial communication and travel costs, pay for translation of any non-English documents, and possibly engage a Brazilian lawyer to assist in the suit. Choice of forum clauses are also important where the parties fail to provide for a choice of law; in many cases, the local court will find some basis for resorting to local law to avoid considering the dispute under unfamiliar legal principles.

In most cases, these factors cause each party to favor its own local tribunals. For this reason, the choice of forum is seldom a mutual choice but rather a decision imposed by the party with superior bargaining power. Where the parties are of equal bargaining strength, or are otherwise unable to resolve the issue, they may agree that a third neutral court will be the only body having jurisdiction over disputes. Another alternative is to make the choice of forum dependent upon the party bringing the action. Usually this is stated in a way which discourages rather than encourages judicial dispute resolution. In the example above, for instance, an action by the Brazilian buyer would have to be brought in Illinois, while an action by the Illinois seller would have to be brought in the State of Sao Paulo. It is also possible to horse trade on the choice of law and choice of forum clauses—one party selecting the law and the other the forum—though a dispute in an

Illinois court applying Brazilian law probably serves the best interests of neither party.

One of the most important factors in selecting a forum for judicial disputes is whether the chosen forum will respect the parties' choice. This is a function of both subject matter jurisdiction and personal jurisdiction. If the law of the chosen jurisdiction does not grant a local court subject matter jurisdiction over the dispute, the parties' attempt to extend such jurisdiction by mutual agreement will be without effect. At the same time, the selected court must be able to obtain personal jurisdiction over the parties in order to adjudicate a dispute between them. In the United States, a court which is otherwise competent is normally entitled to assume personal jurisdiction on the basis of consent, provided the consenting party has notice of the action.[3] Thus, the parties' selection of a particular court will normally be sufficient to confer personal jurisdiction on such court if such parties are properly served. For this reason, choice of forum clauses often include a provision appointing a local agent for service of process.[4]

Even if the chosen court is willing to assume jurisdiction over a particular dispute, the foreign courts which would otherwise have jurisdiction may be unwilling to surrender it. This issue is raised for example, where a New York court entertains an action brought by a New York agent against its West German supplier in disregard of a clause in the agency agreement referring disputes to a Frankfurt court. In the United States, such choice of forum clauses had traditionally been construed to confer jurisdiction on the selected court but not to deny jurisdiction from an otherwise competent court.[5] However, the Supreme Court held that a forum selection

---

[3] See, e.g., National Equip. Rental v. Szukhent, 375 US 311 (1964).

[4] See Grunson, Forum Selection Clauses in International and Interstate Commercial Agreements, [1982] U Ill L Rev 133. It should be noted that even a court with subject matter and personal jurisdiction may nevertheless refuse to hear a dispute on the basis of forum nonconveniens.

[5] Restatement (Second) of Conflict of Laws §80 (1971) ("The parties agreement as to the place of the action cannot oust the state of jurisdiction, but such an agreement will be given effect unless it is unfair or unreasonable."); See Grunson, Supra, at 138–42.

clause is prima facie valid and should be enforced unless unreasonable under the circumstances.[6] Under Brennen and its progeny, a forum selection clause is unreasonable and therefore nonbinding if the agreement was procured by fraud or unconscionable conduct, if the chosen forum is seriously inconvenient or if the enforcement of the clause will be otherwise unjust or violate public policy. While this approach is generally consistent with the approach followed in certain other countries, the applicable law in each foreign jurisdiction must be examined to determine whether the choice of the forum clause will prevent actions in other courts.

The foregoing discussion has important implications for the manner in which a choice of forum clause should be drafted. If the chosen forum is intended to be exclusive, a clause which merely provides that "the parties submit to the jurisdiction of" a particular country or state, or "consent to the jurisdiction of" the courts of a particular jurisdiction is insufficient. Rather, the clause should specifically provide that the designated court will have exclusive jurisdiction over the dispute. Moreover, if it is desired that the dispute be brought before federal rather than state courts, such desire must be clearly set forth. Finally, it is important that the choice of forum clause be sufficiently broad to cover all potential claims, including claims under subsequent contract and tort as well as contract claims.[7]

[6] Brennen v. Zapata Off-Shore Co., 407 US 1, 10 (1972); see generally Reese, "The Supreme Court Supports Choice of Forum Clauses," 7 Int'l Law 530 (1973).

[7] See Appendix 17 for an example of a choice of forum clause which incorporates these concepts.

CHAPTER 30

INTERNATIONAL ARBITRATION AND LITIGATION

---

§ 30:01.   Arbitration versus Litigation.

The advantages of arbitration or some other form of alternative dispute resolution (including conciliation, mediation and mini-trials) over traditional litigation have been discussed extensively.[1] Arbitration is usually faster and less costly than litigation. Arbitration also allows the parties to take advantage of the special compe-

---

[1] See, e.g., Hoellering, "International Commercial Arbitration: A Peaceful Method of Dispute Resolution," 40 Arb J 19 (1985); Perlman-Nelson, "New Approaches to the Resolution of Commercial Disputes," 17 Int'l Law 215 (1983); Ribicoff, "Alternatives to Litigation: Their Application to International Business Disputes," 38 Arb J 3 (1983).

tence of the arbitrators, a factor which can be of particular importance in disputes involving complex technical or financial issues. Arbitration is also important where both parties seek to keep the proceedings confidential in order to limit adverse publicity in the industry or disclosure of proprietary information.

In the international context, arbitration has certain additional advantages. In many cases, both state and federal courts have little experience with the special problems presented by international disputes. This often leads to long delays and unpredictable results. There is also the perception, if not the reality, of a national bias by many judicial tribunals. Arbitral proceedings can be structured to eliminate even the appearance of national bias by locating the proceedings in a third country and using arbitrators with diverse nationalities. In this way, arbitration is often more politically acceptable to the parties to an international transaction, particularly when one of the parties is a sovereign government or agency thereof. An international arbitration panel is also typically better equipped to handle the problems presented by different substantive and procedural law as well as language barriers.

Nevertheless, arbitration is not always preferable to traditional litigation, even in the international context. Certain disputes involving international contracts, such as a lender's right to assert specified remedies upon default by a buyer, a foreign agent's liability for funds owed to the principal, or the right of a licensee to disclose proprietary information, are occasionally best reserved for judicial proceedings. The broad availability of interlocutory juducial appeals under applicable law in certain countries may prolong arbitration beyond what might be experienced in a purely judicial proceeding. The lack of acceptable interim security measures under some arbitral systems may render arbitration unsatisfactory. Finally, the inability to compel arbitration or uncertainty about the procedures to be followed or the enforceability of the final award may make arbitration inappropriate.

Thus, while the broad acceptance of arbitration and other forms of alternative dispute resolution may have resulted in a presumption of its appropriateness in most international commercial agreements, the attorney must always confirm that such forms of dispute resolution will best serve the clients' interests in a particular case.

§ 30:02. Arbitration Rules and Forums.

The parties to an international agreement have several options with respect to the rules and procedures governing the arbitration of disputes. In many cases, arbitration is submitted to one of the major arbitration institutions, such as the International Chamber of Commerce, the American Arbitration Association or the London Court of International Arbitration. These institutions provide facilities for the arbitral proceedings, assist in the selection of arbitrators, collect fees, set dates and times of hearings, and generally facilitate the actual holding of the arbitration. Each of these institutions also has its own rules governing the arbitral proceedings. They also allow parties to use the services of the institution but under some other rules. While these institutions are each based in specific locations, the parties may provide that the arbitration be submitted to the institution but be held in another specified location. The alternative to institutionalized arbitration is ad hoc arbitration in which the parties may designate the rules under which the proceedings will be governed but do not submit the dispute to an arbitration agency.

(i) *International Chamber of Commerce.* The International Chamber of Commerce (ICC) is based in Paris, France and has more than sixty regional offices throughout the world. As with other arbitration institutions, however, the ICC can administer arbitration proceedings anywhere in the world. One of the most experienced of the arbitration institutions, the ICC has handled thousands of international disputes, and currently receives approximately 350 requests for arbitration each year. The ICC is well known for its International Centre for Technical Expertise from which it can supply a wide variety of technical experts as arbitrators.

ICC arbitrators are governed by the Rules of Conciliation and Arbitration of the International Chamber of Commerce.[2] The ICC procedural rules are somewhat vague, requiring resort to applicable law and allowing arbitrators more discretion. The rules also permit the arbitrators to take into account customs within the trade in reaching a decision. The rules do not assure or deny the right of the parties to cross-examine witnesses; rather, the introduction of such evidence is within the discretion of the arbitrators.

One disadvantage of the ICC rules is that decisions need not be issued until six months after the close of hearings. Not only does this contrast with the American Arbitration Association strict 30-day rules, but in practice extensions of the six-month rule are frequently granted. A second disadvantage is that a claimant may have to pay or guarantee payment of the respondent's share of the arbitration fees before the proceeding can commence. On the other hand, the ICC rules do permit a party to apply to a court for interim or conservatory measures such as injunctions. This may be critical in certain types of transactions.

The ICC's fees for administering a dispute are determined in accordance with a fixed schedule ranging from 4% of the first $50,000 to .01% for amounts in excess of $100 million. These fees are generally higher than those of the American Arbitration Association or the London Court of International Arbitration. ICC arbitrators are also compensated based on a percentage of the amount of dispute. Total ICC fees for a $1 million dispute would be $14,500 for the administrative charge and from $7,500 to $30,000 for the arbitrators.

(ii) *The London Court of International Arbitration.* Prior to the passage of the 1979 Arbitration Act, London was not a favored site of international arbitration. British law permitted review of the arbitration award and continuing judicial review of the arbitration process itself. Since the 1979 Act and the 1985 revision of its rules, however, the London Court of International Arbitration (LCIA) has become an important new institution to which international disputes may be referred. This is largely due to the fact that

---

[2] ICC Publication 291 (1982).

the 1979 Act allows the parties to a nondomestic arbitration agreement to elect out the judicial review procedures prior to the commencement of the arbitral proceedings. Some commentators now favor the LCIA over the ICC and AAA, arguing that its rules more specifically delineate the arbitration process and grant the arbitrators more extensive powers. This is particularly true in the discovery stage, where LCIA arbitrators are authorized to demand the production of documents and the answering of interrogatories and to compel third parties to testify. The LCIA rules, on the other hand, do not specify a time limit in which the arbitrator(s) must issue the award.

The LCIA charges for its services on an hourly basis rather than as a percentage of the amount in dispute. In most cases, this will be considerably less expensive than the ICC or AAA. Similarly, arbitrators fees are set on an hourly or other business-oriented basis designed to correspond to what the arbitrators are paid in this normal profession.

(iii) *The American Arbitration Association.* The American Arbitration Association (AAA), based in New York, will also act as an administration agency for commercial disputes. The AAA acts as an appointing authority for arbitrators, drawing on a list of some 60,000 experienced arbitrators around the world. Normally, arbitrators are selected from a country other than the country of either party to the dispute. The AAA will also arrange for a facility, transmit communications between or among the parties and arbitrators, set dates and times for hearings, arrange for reporters and interpreters and generally facilitate the arbitration process. Administrative fees range from 3% of the first $20,000 in dispute to .25% for amounts in excess of $160,000. Arbitration fees are arranged separately and there is no fixed schedule.

AAA arbitration is governed by its American Arbitration Association Commercial Arbitration Rules. The AAA has also published its Supplementary Procedures for International Commercial Arbitration. The AAA provides for a single arbitrator unless the arbitration agreement provides otherwise. Examination and cross-examination of witnesses are expressly permitted. An important advantage of the AAA rules is that the arbitrator(s) must make a decision within 30 days after the close of hearings. No extensions are permitted. The parties may rely on common-law procedures in the presentation of evidence and have the right to present witnesses.

(iv) *UNCITRAL Rules.* In 1966, the United Nations established the United Nations Commission on International Trade Law (UNCITRAL) to develop and harmonize international trade laws. One of the most important contributions of the UNICTRAL was the promulgation in 1976 of a special code of arbitration rules designed for all international commercial arbitral proceedings.

Unlike the ICC, LCIA, and AAA, UNCITRAL is not an arbitral institution; its rules are intended for use either in ad hoc arbitration or in arbitral proceedings administered by other arbitration associations. At the same time, the UNCITRAL rules have been broadly accepted as an efficient system of international arbitration. Accordingly, it is now common for arbitration clauses to refer disputes to the ICC, LCIA or AAA as the arbitration institution but to expressly provide that such arbitration will be conducted in accordance with the UNCITRAL rules. Unless the parties provide for an appointing authority in the arbitration clause, the arbitrator will be selected by the Secretary General of the Permanent Court of Arbitration at the Hague.

Some commentators have concluded that arbitration utilizing the UNCITRAL rules is the most cost effective. One reason for this is that the UNCITRAL rules provide that the administrative costs of the arbitration is the actual cost incurred, not a percentage of the amount of dispute as is the case with the AAA and ICC. Like the AAA rules, UNCITRAL provides that the fees paid to the arbitrators must be reasonable. Another important aspect of the UNCITRAL rules is that all costs of the arbitration are to be born by the unsuccessful party, unless the arbitrators determine that a portion is equitable. Under the ICC, LCIA and AAA rules, allocation of cost is within the sole discretion of the arbitrator(s).

UNCITRAL arbitrators also have considerable discretion in conducting the arbitration. They may determine if expert witnesses will testify, and may appoint one. The rules also provide that the parties may cross-examine the expert and present their own expert witnesses at a later hearing if they so desire. One potential disadvantage of the UNCITRAL rules is that they provide no time limit after the close of hearings within which the arbitrator must make their award. This is similar to the LCIA and is in contrast to the AAA's strict 30-day time limit.

(v) *International Center for the Settlement of Investment Disputes (ICSID).* Disputes between foreign investors and host country governments often present special problems. While governments increasingly offer special incentives and other commitments to entice foreign investments, they also are required to protect the national interest. As policies or even governments change, the foreign investor may find that these commitments are not respected. If a dispute results, the government may not wish to subject its policies to the scrutiny of foreign courts or traditional commercial arbitral tribunals. At the same time, the investor cannot rely upon local courts to protect its interests in such circumstances.

For these reasons, the World Bank proposed the adoption of the Convention on a Settlement of Investment Disputes between States and Nationals of other States. The convention, which has now been accepted by more than ninety-five countries, provides for the establishment of the International Centre for the Settlement of Investment Disputes (ICSID). The ICSID, like the ICC, LCIA and AAA, is an institution whose purpose is to facilitate the settlement of disputes. The ICSID is located in Washington, D.C. at the headquarters of the World Bank, from which it receives administrative and financial support. The principal task of the ICSID is to maintain a panel of conciliators and arbitrators from which members are drawn for actual investment disputes which are referred to the ICSID.

The procedures and rules applicable to an ICSID arbitration are contained in its rules and regulations. These rules allow considerable flexibility, deferring to the agreement of the parties in nearly all cases. The rules prescribe procedures, however, for circumstances where the parties are unable to agree on such matters as the number or manner of appointment of the arbitrators, the law governing the proceeding (the law of the state which is party to the dispute), and the place of the arbitral proceedings (Washington, D.C.). Moreover, the rules specifically provide that consent of the parties to arbitration under the Convention shall, unless otherwise stated, be deemed to consent to such arbitration to the exclusion of any other remedy. In this way, the Convention is intended to create a system of dispute settlement which cannot be controlled by the domestic courts of the state which is a party to the dispute. The award must be handed down within 30 days after the closure of the proceedings, except that such period may be extended for an additional 30 days if necessary. The Convention provides that the award is final and binding upon both parties and is to be recognized as a final judgment of a court in the applicable state.[3] These enforcement provisions are arguably stronger than those of the 1958 New York Convention on the Recognition and Enforcement of International Arbitral Awards. It is no defense against enforcement, for example, that the award is contrary to local public policy.

(vi) *Ad Hoc Arbitration.* The alternative to the use of an arbitration agency is known as "ad hoc" arbitration.[4] Ad hoc arbitration is often faster and less expensive than arbitration using the major arbitration institutions. It also allows the parties more flexibility. Ad hoc arbitration may be governed by an established set of rules or, as is increasingly common, by a set of arbitration rules or procedures developed by the parties themselves and supplemented by an established set of rules. While some have questioned the safety of an arbitral award granted in ad hoc arbitration, in most cases its enforceability is no less certain than an award granted by a major arbitration agency. The major disadvantage of ad hoc arbitration is that the parties will not provide for all the possible contingencies, leaving the procedures in doubt and potentially causing considerable delays.

[3] But see Note, "Annulment of Arbitral Award for Failure to Apply Law Applicable under ICSID Convention and Failure to State Sufficiently Pertinent Reasons," 81 Am J Int'l L 222 (1987).

[4] See generally, Arkin "Internatinal Ad Hoc Arbitration: A Practical Alternative," 15 Int'l Bus Law 5(8)(1987).

§ 30:03.   Arbitration Clauses.

Each of the major arbitration institutions have suggested a form of arbitration clause that may be included in a commercial agreement.[5] All of these suggested clauses, however, leave considerable issues to the discretion of the arbitrators. Accordingly, it is often desirable for the parties to construct their own arbitration clause which covers certain other issues which may be important in the particular case.[6]

Certain items should be included in almost all arbitration clauses. First, the substitive law applicable to the dispute itself as well as the procedural law applicable to the arbitral proceedings should be identified.[7] These could also be contained in the governing law clause of the agreement. Second, the place of arbitration should be identified, together with an alternative site. The location of the arbitration will have an obvious affect on the cost of the proceedings to the parties. The location will also affect the nature of the proceedings themselves. Arbitration in the United States, for example, will normally result in a lesser degree of interference from U.S. courts than arbitration in France might have from French courts. Designation of a forum country which is a party to the New York Convention may also expedite the enforcement of the award abroad.

The delineation of certain practical aspects of the arbitration proceeding may also assist in facilitating the arbitration. The language of the proceedings as well as the need to translate any documents submitted thereto should be specified. The number and qualifications of the arbitrators (usually one or three) should be set forth. In some cases it is useful to identify the means by which the neutral arbitrator is to be selected. The arbitration clause should also indicate that arbitration is the sole and exclusive remedy for disputes arising from the agreement and provide that the award may be enforced abroad by any competent court.

[5] See Appendix 18 for these model arbitration clauses.

[6] See generally Ulmer, "Drafting the International Arbitration Clause," 20 Int'l Law 1335 (1986).

[7] See Brunson & Wallace, "Choosing the Substantive Law to Apply in International Commercial Arbitration," 27 Va J Int'l L 39 (1986).

Various additional items may be appropriate for the arbitration clause in certain circumstances. At times it is useful to define the scope of the arbitration so that certain issues are subject to arbitration while others are not. The possible use of conciliation in which high-level officers on each side agree to work on a resolution for a specified period before resorting to arbitration should be considered. If the selected arbitration rules fail to provide for a time limit in which the arbitrators must render an award or omit any other important procedural matter, they should be supplemented by the arbitration clause or a separate arbitration agreement. The parties may also consider special arrangements for the allocation of costs and fees of arbitration as well as a statute of limitations for filing requests for arbitration. Finally, in certain cases, consent to interim security measures and provision for prejudgment interest may be provided in the arbitration agreement.

§ 30:04. Enforcement of Arbitral Awards.

(i) *General.* Unlike a judicial court, an arbitration panel normally has no means available to if for the enforcement of its award. An important exception to this general principle is in the case of a previous agreement by the parties which establishes security or other enforcement arrangements or which expressly authorizes the arbitrators to take certain action to enforce their award. It should also be noted that in perhaps a majority of international arbitrations, the losing party voluntarily complies with the award, thus obviating the need to seek judicial enforcement. Where the arbitral award is not carried out in one of these ways, however, the prevailing party must look to the courts to enforce its award.

The law applicable to the enforcement of an arbitral award is usually the law of the country in which enforcement is sought. Since international arbitrators frequently take place in a neutral country, this often requires a court in a country in which the award is to be enforced to recognize and give effect to an award issued elsewhere. Thus, the local court must often deal not only with the issue concerning the enforceability of arbitral awards generally, but also with the recognition of a foreign award.

Many countries have enacted special laws governing arbitration and the enforcement of domestic arbitral awards. The U.S. Arbitration Act,[8] for example, provides that if the parties to a commercial contract have agreed that a judgment of the court shall be entered upon the arbitration award, then the prevailing party may apply to the agreed court or other court having jurisdiction for an order enforcing such judgment, and such court must grant such order unless certain narrow defenses exist.[9] While the U.S. Arbitration Act did establish the principles of recognizing and enforcing arbitral awards, it did not originally address the special issues presented by foreign awards.

(ii) *The New York Convention.* The United Nations Convention on the Enforcement of Arbitral Awards,[10] also known as the "New York Convention," was designed to reduce the legal obstacles surrounding the enforcement of foreign arbitral awards. Originally concluded in 1958, the Convention was finally ratified by the Senate in 1970. The U.S. Arbitration Act was subsequently amended to provide for its enforcement.[11] Approximately 70 countries, including most of the United States' major trading partners other than certain Latin American countries, are currently signatories to the New York Convention.

Article I(1) provides that the Convention is applicable to the recognition and enforcement of any arbitral awards made outside the territory of the contracting state in which such recognition and enforcement are sought. Most of the signatory countries including the United States, however, have declared reservations to Article I(1) which (i) limit its applicability to disputes arising out of commercial agreements, and (ii) restrict recognition to awards issued in another contracting state. Thus, parties seeking to invoke the Convention should insure that the arbitral proceedings take place within the jurisdiction of a contracting state. Article I(1) also provides that the Convention will not apply to awards which are

[8] USC §1 et seq.
[9] 9 USC §9.
[10] June 10, 1958, 21 UST 2517, TIAS No. 6997, 330 UNTS 3.
[11] 9 USC §§201–208.

considered domestic under the applicable law of the state in which recognition and enforcement are sought.[12]

Article II of the Convention requires the courts of a contracting state to recognize and enforce a written arbitration agreement, including an arbitration clause in a commercial agreement. It also requires such courts to refer such disputes to arbitration upon the request of a party to such agreement, unless the courts find such arbitration agreement void, inoperative or incapable of being performed.

Article III requires each contracting state to recognize arbitral awards as binding and to enforce them in accordance with the rules of procedure of such state and the conditions of the Convention. The Article goes on to provide that such states may not impose substantially more onerous conditions or higher fees on the recognition or enforcement of such awards under the Convention as are applicable to purely domestic awards. Thus, the Convention attempts to secure the same treatment for foreign awards as is applicable to domestic awards. This obviously makes it incumbent on the attorney planning for arbitration to satisfy himself or herself that the site in which enforcement is sought does not present unduly onerous obstacles to the enforcement of domestic arbitral awards.

The party seeking to enforce a foreign award must follow the same procedure as is applicable locally to the enforcement of domestic awards. This normally involves filing an application with a court of competent jurisdiction. Under Article IV of the Convention, the application must include a duly authenticated original award or certified copy thereof as well as the original agreement under which the parties agreed to submit the dispute to arbitration. Certified translations are required if the award or agreement are not in the official language of the country in which recognition and enforcement are sought.

Article IV of the Convention stipulates the grounds upon which the party against whom the award is invoked can successfully

---

[12] See Bergensen v. Joseph Muller Corp., 710 F2d 928 (CA2, 1983); see also 9 USC §202; see generally van den Berg, "When is an Arbitral Award Nondomestic Under the New York Convention of 1958?," 6 Pace L Rev 25 (1985).

challenge the recognition and enforcement of the foreign arbitral award. First, enforcement can be denied for reasons of incapacity of the parties to the arbitration agreement (using the law applicable to such parties) or the invalidity of such agreement under the law to which the parties subjected it or the law of the country in which enforcement is sought. Second, enforcement can be refused if the party against whom the award was invoked was not given proper notice of the appointment of the arbitrator or the proceedings, or was otherwise unable to present his case. A third defense to enforcement is that the award deals with matters beyond the scope of the submission to arbitration. In such cases, however, the Convention provides that if the award includes matters which are within the scope of the submission and such matters can be separated from the others, then the court should enforce the same. A fourth defense to enforcement is that the composition of the arbitral authority or the arbitral procedure was not in accordance with the arbitration agreement or, in the absence of such agreement, the law of the country where the arbitration took place. A fifth grounds for denying enforcement of an award under the Convention is that the award has not yet become binding on the parties, or has been set aside or suspended by a competent authority of, or under the law of, the country in which the award was made.

Under Paragraph 2 of Article V, a court itself may refuse to recognize and enforce an award where it finds that the subject matter of the dispute is not capable of settlement by arbitration under the laws of the state in which enforcement is sought, or if recognition or enforcement of the award would be contrary to the public policy of that state. While the public policy grounds for refusing to enforce an award under the Convention could be construed broadly to undercut many enforcement actions in which the local court may be sympathetic to the position of the party against whom the award is sought to be enforced, U.S. courts have thus far resisted this broad construction.[13]

---

[13] See, e.g., Fotochrome, Inc. v. Copel Co., Ltd. 517 Fd2 512 (CA2, 1975); La Societe Nationale Pour La Recherche, etc. v. Shaheen Natural Resources Co., 585 F Supp 57 (SDNY 1983).

(iii) *Enforcement Outside the New York Convention.* A foreign arbitral award which is not entitled to recognition or enforcement under the New York Convention because it was rendered in a country which is not a signatory to the Convention may nevertheless be enforceable under some other authority. The United States and many other countries have bilateral treaties which include provisions similar to the New York Convention for the enforcement of foreign arbitral awards. Though the Inter-American Convention on International Arbitration[14] has not been ratified by the United States, it may be invoked to obtain recognition of an award issued in one contracting state in another contracting state. The European Convention on International Commercial Arbitration[15] may be useful for enforcing certain European awards in other European countries. Finally, even in the absence of an applicable treaty, most countries allow for the recognizing and enforcement of foreign arbitral awards in compliance with local law.

§ 30:05. Transnational Litigation.

Over the years, litigation in the United States has moved away from straight commercial practice. While Americans do not refer to barristers and solicitors, even law students frequently feel compelled to decide whether they will be "litigators" or transaction-oriented lawyers. And while it is these arbitration lawyers who will obviously be more involved in the issues presented herein, it is the litigator who most likely will assume responsibility for the resolution of international commercial disputes when they move to the courts.

While litigation itself is a speciality, transnational litigation raises a host of unique problems to which even most litigators are unaccustomed. These include questions regarding obtaining jurisdiction over the foreign party, serving process abroad, taking

---

[14] January 30, 1975, PAUTS 42, OAS/Sec A/20 (SEPF), reprinted in 14 ILM 336 (1975).

[15] April 21, 1961, 523 UNTS 364.

evidence abroad, proving foreign law, enforcing foreign judgments in the United States and enforcing U.S. judgments abroad. At the same time, the international legal community, the Congress, and certain states have developed a number of useful tools in order to deal with some of these unique problems. These include the Hague Convention on the Service Abroad of Judicial and Extrajudicial Documents in Civil or Commercial Matters,[16] the Hague Convention on the Taking of Evidence Abroad in Civil and Commercial Matters,[17] the Foreign Sovereign Immunities Act,[18] the Alien Venue Act,[19] and the Uniform Foreign Money-Judgments Recognition Act.[20]

Because of the special nature of the transactional litigation, it is beyond the scope of this work. A number of books and articles explore the special issues presented by transactional litigation in considerable detail.

[16] November 15, 1965, TIAS No. 6638, 20 UST 361, 658 UNTS 163.

[17] March 18, 1970, TIAS 7444, 23 UST 2555, 847 UNTS 231.

[18] 28 USC §1602 et seq.

[19] 28 USC §1391(d).

[20] 13 ULA §261 (1962).

PART IX—SUGGESTIONS FOR FURTHER READING

Books

American Arbitration Association, Arbitration and the Law (1984).

Carbonneau, T. (ed.), Resolving Transnational Disputes Through International Arbitration (1984).

Myrick, R. (ed.), World Litigation Law & Practice (1986).

Nanda & Pansius, Litigation of International Disputes in U.S. Courts (1986).

Redfern, A. & Hunter, M., Law and Practice of International Commercial Arbitration (1986).

Sanders, P. (ed.), International Handbook on Commercial Arbitration (1984).

Articles

"Choosing a Forum for International Commercial Arbitration: A Panel," 76 Am Soc'y Int'l Proc 166 (1982).

Higgins, Brown & Roach, "Pitfalls in International Commercial Arbitration," 35 Bus Law 1035 (1980).

McLaughlin & Genevio, "Enforcement of Arbitral Awards under the New York Convention-Practice in U.S. Courts," 3 Int'l Tax & Bus Law 249 (1986).

Nattier, "International Commercial Arbitration in Latin America: Enforcement of Arbitral Agreements and Awards," 21 Tex Int'l LJ 397 (1986).

Seki, "Effective Dispute Resolution in United States-Japan Commercial Transactions," 6 NW J Int'l L & Bus 979 (1984).

"Symposium on Transnational Litigation," 18 Int'l Law 522 (1984).

Von Mehren, "Transnational Litigation in American Courts: An Overview of Problems and Issues," Private Investors Abroad (1984).

PART X

UNITED STATES IMMIGRATION LAW AFFECTING BUSINESS PERSONNEL

CHAPTER 31

NONIMMIGRANT VISAS

§ 31:01.   In General.

Prior to the 1970's, the practice of immigration law in the United States was largely confined to nonbusiness personnel. Much of an immigration lawyer's practice involved the securing of immigrant visas for foreign individuals who sought to come to the United States to join family members or simply to start a new life. He or she may have also been involved in cases involving refugees and political asylees. From time to time, the immigration lawyer may have assisted in obtaining temporary or nonimmigrant visas for visitors, students or investors. Only occasionally, however, were immigration attorneys called upon to secure visas to allow foreign managers or technical personnel to visit the United States for training or other purposes, or to arrange their permanent residency in the United States.

317

All this has changed dramatically over the last several years. A growing number of U.S.-based multinational corporations have found it necessary or desirable to bring their foreign business personnel to the United States on a temporary basis to familiarize them with the company's management techniques, products or technology. The growth in international trade and investment has brought a corresponding nered for foreign personnel to spend time in the United States. Advances in technology abroad and the success of foreign management strategies have gradually increased the need for U.S. companies to import foreign expertise.

As a result of these developments, it has become increasingly important for the lawyer involved in international business transactions to have at least a basic familiarity with U.S. immigration law and practices as they affect foreign business personnel. In certain cases, such as an acquisition of a U.S. business by a foreign individual or company, the transaction itself may be conditioned on the securing of appropriate visas that will allow foreign personnel to be present in the United States. Occasionally, even the structure of the transaction will be affected by immigration considerations. Thus, while immigration issues were once largely ignored in the planning of an international business transaction and relegated to small specialty firms, they are now being increasingly considered in the planning phases and handled or at least managed by the lawyers who have responsibility for the international transaction as a whole.

For these reasons, a discussion of U.S. immigration law affecting foreign business personnel has been included in this text. As the title of the Part suggests, however, it is limited to a discussion of those visas which are particularly important in the business context. Moreover, this discussion is intended only to provide a basic summary of the visas which are available under U.S. law and the procedures to be followed in securing the same. For more complete information on U.S. immigration law generally, the reader is referred to Gordon & Rosenfeld's Immigration Law and Procedure, Frangomen, Del Rey & Bernsen's Immigration Law and Business, or Frangomen, Del Rey & Bell's 1987 Immigration Procedures Handbook.

The principal source of immigration law in the United States is the Immigration and Nationality Act of 1952, as amended (INA). The INA classifies all aliens seeking to enter into the United States as either immigrants or nonimmigrants. An immigrant includes any person desiring to remain in the United States permanently or for an indefinite period of time. Aliens seeking to enter the country for a temporary period and for a specific purpose are classified as nonimmigrants. The INA creates a presumption that every alien desiring to enter the United States is an immigrant unless such alien can demonstrate that he or she is within a nonimmigrant category.

The INA establishes various categories of nonimmigrants, such as visitors, investors, and intracompany transferees. In order to qualify for a particular type of nonimmigrant visa, the alien must meet the criteria established therefor by the INA as supplemented by the corresponding regulations. While each nonimmigrant visa category has its own specific requirements, all are subject to the general condition that the aliens intend to remain in the United States on a temporary basis. Nonimmigrant visas are issued for a specified period of time, but may be renewed under certain circumstances. In certain instances, it is possible to change from one nonimmigrant category to another or to adjust one's status to that of an immigrant without leaving the United States. There are no numerical limitations or quotas on the number of nonimmigrant visas that may be granted.

An immigrant visa allows the grantee to remain in the United States on a permanent basis. For this reason, an applicant for an immigrant visa is said to seek "permanent residency" in the United States. Unlike nonimmigrant visas, the number of immigrant visas which are granted each year is subject to certain numerical limitations established by law. Because the number of persons seeking permanent residency in the United States greatly exceeds these numerical limitations, the INA establishes a system of preferences which grants certain eligible applicants priority over certain others. These preferences are based either on a close family tie between the alien and a U.S. citizen or permanent resident (first, second, fourth and fifth preference) or on a showing—

by means of a procedure known as alien employment certification—that there are no U.S. workers willing and available to assume the position being offered to the alien (third and sixth preference). Even after an alien has demonstrated, through birth records, employment certification or otherwise, that he or she qualifies for the preference, it is often necessary for such alien to wait until a quota number becomes available.

Many foreigners believe that in order to qualify for a U.S. visa they need only demonstrate a certain degree of financial independence based either on their own resources or on sponsorship of a U.S. citizen or group. Perhaps this belief stems from the requirements for certain visas to prove one's financial resources or to obtain affidavits of support from U.S. citizens or permanent residents. Regardless of the source of this belief, however, it is erroneous. In order to obtain a visa to enter the United States, the alien must meet the particular criteria established for the visa itself. While financial independence is part of the criteria for certain visas, it is never the sole criteria.

The administration of the INA and related immigration laws has been delegated to various federal agencies. The most important of these is the Immigration and Naturalization Service (INS) which handles all visas and related matters which are applied for from within the United States. The INS is headed by a Commissioner based in Washington, D.C. and is organized into regions and districts. Visa applications and underlying documents which are submitted within the United States are usually filed with the District Director or Officer in Charge in the district in which the applicant will reside. As a result of recent changes in INS regulations, many of the applications are required to be forwarded to Regional Service Centers which process application for several districts. Certain determinations made at the district level may be appealed to Regional Commissions, with subsequent appeals to the Board of Immigration Appeals or the federal courts.[1]

The administration of U.S. immigration laws outside of the United States is under the jurisdiction of the Department of State.[2]

[1] 8 CFR Part 3; 8 USC §1105a.
[2] 8 USC §1104.

Visa applications submitted abroad are handled by U.S. consulates. A consulate may refuse to process a visa for an applicant who is not a resident of the country in which the consulate is located. In processing the visa, the consulate has certain authority to make its own determination as to the eligibility of the applicant, even though the applicant may be the beneficiary of a visa petition approved by the INS. Consulates also determine whether the applicant is excludible for several other grounds, including health-related reasons and criminal, illegal or immoral conduct.[3]

Labor certification is the responsibility of the U.S. Department of Labor, which relies upon state labor departments for certain determinations. Their decisions may be appealed to an administrative law judge and thereafter to the federal courts.[4]

The INA creates a total of 13 categories of nonimmigrant visas, some of which have one or more subcategories. Each of these categories is identified by a letter (e.g., visitors—B, students—F or M, etc.) which corresponds to §1(a)(15) of the INA,[5] as well as number which identifies the subcategory. Of these 13 general categories, however, only five are usually available to aliens who may seek to enter the United States for business purposes.

§ 31:02. Business Visitors (B-1).

The first general category which may be available for business personnel desiring to enter the country extends to business visitors (B-1). A visitor for business is a person who is employed abroad or is self-employed and who desires to enter the United States on behalf of an employer or themselves. The holder of a B-1 visa is not permitted to be employed by a U.S. employer. In most cases, this means that the B-1 alien may not receive compensation from any U.S. source. Some instances in which a B-1 visa may be appropriate would include persons entering to solicit sales orders

[3] 8 USC §1182.
[4] 20 CFR Part 656.
[5] 8 USC §1101(a)(15).

or make purchases of goods for foreign employees or principals, persons entering for meetings or conventions and persons entering to negotiate contracts or engage in litigation.

The primary advantage of a B-1 visa is that it is normally fast and easy to obtain. In most cases, the visa can be applied for by a local travel agent upon the submission of an Application for Non-immigrant Visa (Form OF-156) together with a letter from the applicant's company which confirms the employment relationship and verifies the business purpose of the trip. These documents are filed directly with the local U.S. consulate and no prior determination is required by the INS. The disadvantages of the B-1 visa are that it permits the alien to stay in the country for a comparatively short period (up to six months plus a possible six-month renewal) and that the alien may not be employed or be compensated by a U.S. employer.

A B-1 visa may be granted for a specific or indefinite period of time, and may be valid for single or multiple entries. As in the case with other nonimmigrants, a B-1 alien will be subject to inspection by INS personnel at the border who confirm that the purpose of the trip is consistent with the visa and make a determination as to how long the alien may stay. The authorized period of stay, which may be up to six months, is noted on the Temporary Entry Permit (Form I-94) which is generally stapled in the alien's passport upon her arrival and surrendered upon her departure. The failure to leave the country or obtain an extension of the authorized period of stay[6] renders the alien subject to deportation and certain other sanctions.

As with all nonimmigrant visas, a B-1 applicant must demonstrate that the purpose for travelling to the United States is a temporary one. B-1 aliens in particular must prove that they will be entering the country for a limited duration, that they intend to leave the country at the expiration of their visa, and that while they are in the United States, they will maintain a foreign residence which they have no intention of abandoning. Both the foreign consulate and the INS inspector at the border are authorized to

[6] See §31:07.

question the alien's intent to determine if the presumption of immigrant rather than nonimmigrant status has been overcome. B-1 aliens should therefore be prepared to present evidence of their foreign ties and travel purposes both to the consulate in the application for the visa and to the INS inspector upon each entry.

Applicants for B-1 visas must also demonstrate that the activities in which they seek to engage in the United States fall within the scope of the visa. The State Department's internal instructions to consular officers, known as the Foreign Affairs Manual, lists several types of activities it considers appropriate for B-1 visitors. Among these are (i) soliciting orders, negotiating contracts and taking orders from existing customers; (ii) purchasing goods, components and raw materials for use outside the country; (iii) performing service or sales contracts (including installing, servicing, repairing, and providing training with respect to equipment); (iv) conducting certain research and litigation; and (v) attending directors or other meetings and conferences. Aliens who ultimately qualify as treaty investors, professional temporary workers, and intracompany transferees[7] are also entitled to enter the country on a B-1 visa to engage in certain preliminary activities. Aliens should be cautioned, however, against using the B-1 visa to enter the country on an expedited basis and then changing visa status when the original purpose of their visit would have qualified for another visa. This practice could lead to a determination by INS that the alien procured the B-1 visa by fraud, authorizing the INS to deport the perpetrator and to permanently bar entry under any visa.

The spouse and children of a B-1 alien are normally entitled to accompany or follow the alien to the United States under a B-1/B-2 visa which may be obtained simply by demonstrating the family relationship with marriage and birth certificates. In other cases, these family members may obtain a B-2 (visitor for pleasure) visa which is intended for persons coming to the United States for a vacation or holiday. Because B-2 visas are even easier to obtain than B-1 visas, business visitors sometimes apply for B-2 visas

---

[7] See §§31:03, 31:04, and 31:06.

which do not authorize them even to conduct business in the country. This practice should be avoided, however, since, as noted above, the use of inappropriate visas can create significant problems later.

§ 31:03.   Treaty Traders (E-1) and Treaty Investors (E-2).

A second general category of nonimmigrant visas which may be available to business travellers is the treaty or E visas. This category is comprised of two classes, treaty traders (E-1) and treaty investors (E-2). While each of these visas has its own criteria, both require that there be a specific treaty which authorizes the visa between the United States and the treaty trader's or treaty investor's country of nationality. The United States currently has such a treaty with 40 countries for treaty traders and 30 countries for treaty investors. [8]

(i) *Treaty Traders (E-1).* A treaty trader is a person who desires to enter the United States "solely to carry on substantial trade, principally between the United States and the country of which he is a national." [9] "Trade" has been defined with respect to actual transactions between the countries in goods, money or services. While "trade" would obviously include the sale or exchange of manufactured products, it also extends to the insurance, financial and tourism industries. Whether such trade is "substantial" depends not so much on the amount of money involved but on the number of transactions. If the number of transactions is small, even though involving large amounts of money, a treaty trader visa may be denied since the transactions could be handled under a B-1 visa. The treaty investor must also demonstrate that at least 51% of its total trade is between the United States and the country of its nationality in order to satisfy the "principally" test.

In some cases, the alien, as an individual, will be engaged in the

[8] For a list of such countries, see the State Department's Foreign Affairs Manual, §41:40.

[9] 8 USC §1101(a)(15)(E)(i).

requisite trade, thus qualifying for an E-1 visa. In most instances, however, the alien will be an employee of a corporation or other entity which actually conducts such trade. In such cases, the alien employee may qualify for an E-1 visa where it is shown that (i) a majority of the company's stock is owned by nationals of a treaty country; (ii) the alien employee is a national of the same country; and (iii) the alien employee is either employed in an executive or supervisory capacity or possesses "essential skills" which are needed by the employer abroad. The determination of whether an employee occupies an "executive or supervisory" position is a question of fact which includes an analysis of the employee's title, position in the company's overall corporate structure, duties, level of control over the company, number and skill levels of the employees being supervised, and prior executive and supervisory experience. The applicant must be able to demonstrate that his or her primary function is executive or supervisory, with responsibility for the management of a significant portion of the firm's operation. The "essential skills" test has developed into an analysis of whether a U.S. worker is available or could readily be trained to perform the job. Important factors include the alien's proven expertise in the area, the uniqueness of the specific skills, the salary required to be paid, the period of time required to train U.S. workers to perform the job, and the proprietary nature of the technology. In general, persons granted E-1 visas on the basis of essential skills are expected to train U.S. workers, thus obviating the need to replace them after a reasonable period of time.

(ii)   *Treaty Investors (E-2).* A treaty investor is a person coming to the United States "solely to develop and direct the operations of an enterprise in which he has invested or . . . in which he is actively in the process of investing, a substantial amount of capital."[10] Because this visa also allows the holder to remain in the United States on an indefinite basis, aliens who are unable to qualify for permanent residency will often attempt to obtain an E-2 visa on the basis of an investment in the United States. The U.S. State Department believes that there has been a great deal of

[10] 8 USC §1101(a)(15)(E)(ii).

misuse of the E-2 visa, and has issued various guidelines which are employed by the consulates to scrutinize E-2 visa applications.[11] While these guidelines are not dispositive of the law, they are helpful in determining the criteria which are used by U.S. consulates in acting on E-2 applications.

Certain conditions required to be satisfied for an E-2 visa are similar to those of the E-1 visa. First, the investor must have the nationality of a treaty investor country. If the applicant is an employee of the treaty investor, he or she must have the same nationality as the investor and must qualify as a manager or a highly trained and specially qualified employee using criteria similar to that described with respect to an E-1 visa. Like all nonimmigrant visas, the alien must demonstrate an intention to leave the country when the qualifying status terminates, though there is no requirement to maintain a foreign residence as in the case of a B-1 applicant.

There are, however, a number of other conditions that must be met in order to qualify for treaty investor status. First, the applicant must have invested or be in the process of making an investment. The State Department takes the position that an investment means that the funds have been put "at risk" or actually committed to an investment enterprise and are subject to loss if the investment is not successful. An investor is said to be "in the process" of investing only when it is in control of the funds and is about to commence actual business operations, and not merely in the stage of signing contracts or searching for suitable locations or property.[12] Moreover, while cash maintained in a business bank account or expended for office or other facilities, furnishings and equipment may be considered as part of the investment, the State Department disregards indebtedness of the enterprise (unless guaranteed or secured by the investor or its assets) since it views such indebtedness as lacking the element of "risk." Any other assets contributed to or payments made on behalf of the enterprise may also be deemed a qualifying investment provided they are used by or for the benefit of such enterprise.

[11] See Visa Bulletin, No. 20, Vol. V.
[12] Id.

A second condition that must be met in order to qualify for E-2 status is that the investment be made in a commercial or "real operating" enterprise as opposed to a "fictitious paper organization."[13] A "passive, speculative investment" which is held for potential appreciation, such as undeveloped land or a portfolio of stocks, will not qualify as an eligible investment. Rather, the investment must be made in a business venture which produces some service or commodity. The interpretation of this condition is based in part on the language which requires the applicant to be coming to the United States to "develop and direct" the enterprise in which the investment is made. This condition has also been construed to require the investor to have a controlling interest in such enterprise. Control normally requires actual ownership of at least 51% of the enterprise's equity, though a lesser percentage may qualify as control where one's equity ownership constitutes de facto control or where the investor is given certain other rights.

Another condition for E-2 eligibility is that the investment be "substantial." While State Department regulations had once defined "substantial" to mean $40,000, these are now ignored in favor of what it calls a "proportionality" test. The proportionality test involves a weighing of the amount invested against either the total value of the enterprise in question or, in the case of investments which are "in process," the amount normally considered necessary for the enterprise. As always, the burden of proof is on the applicant to prove the satisfaction of this test. In large corporate transactions, the magnitude of the investment itself may obviate the need to utilize the proportionality test. While the State Department is careful not to set a minimum dollar figure in such cases, it has suggested that an investment of $1 million to $2 million "would usually be deemed substantial."[14]

Finally, a qualifying investment may not be deemed "marginal" or made solely to earn a living. The marginality test requires an analysis of the expected return on the investment enterprise and the investor's personal financial resources. The alien must

---

[13] Id.

[14] Id.

demonstrate that the income to be generated by the enterprise will be substantially in excess of what the alien would require for personal use and any dependents or that the alien has other income-producing assets and is therefore not relying on the enterprise to earn a living. There are, however, certain other ways to satisfy the marginality test, such as a showing that the investment will expand job opportunities in the local market or is adequate to insure that the alien's primary function will not be merely as a laborer.[15]

(iii) *Advantages of Treaty Trader and Treaty Investor Visas.* Treaty trader and treaty investor visas present a number of advantages over certain other nonimmigrant visas. First, while the documentation required to be submitted to prove each element of these visas is sometimes difficult or time-consuming to assemble, the actual examination of such documentation and the determination as to the availability of the visas is made by a U.S. consulate rather than the INS. This means that like a B-1 visa, an E-1 or E-2 visa may be secured much faster in most instances than H or L visas which require prior INS determinations. Second, and most important, as long as the applicant continues to qualify as a treaty trader or treaty investor or employee thereof, the E-1 or E-2 visa can be renewed and the holder's authorized stay extended. Except for "essential skills" employees who are expected to ultimately train U.S. workers to assume their positions, E-1 and E-2 aliens can often remain in the United States for many years. E-1 and E-2 visas are thus the closest alternative to permanent residency. Like most other nonimmigrant visas, the spouse and unmarried minor children of a treaty trader and treaty investor are generally eligible for a derivative visa, which allows them to accompany the treaty trader or treaty investor to the United States.

[15] See Matter of Heitland, 14 I&N Dec 563 (1974).

§ 31:04.   Temporary Employees (H-1, H-2, and H-3).

Section 1(a)(15)(H) of the INA creates another category of nonimmigrant visas for persons who may be employed by a U.S. firm for a temporary period. There are three types of temporary employee visas: professionals and persons of distinguished merit and ability (H-1), other temporary employees (H-2), and trainees (H-3). Unlike B and E visas, which are handled solely by a U.S. consulate without any INS determination, H visas require the U.S. employer to file a visa petition (Form I-129B) with the INS in the district where the alien will be located. Only after such petition has been approved and notice of such approval forwarded to the U.S. consulate may the alien apply for the visa. The INS approval of the visa petition should not be confused with the granting of the visa itself, however, since the U.S. consulate may still inquire as to the alien's qualifications for the position approved in the visa petition.

The H-1 visa is reserved for "persons of distinguished merit and ability" coming to work in the United States for a temporary period. This has been deemed to include "members of the professions" and persons who are "preeminent in their fields." In most cases, a member of the professions includes any alien who has obtained the equivalent of a four-year college degree and who is coming to the United States to perform a job that requires that degree. Thus, engineers and certain technical personnel may qualify for an H-1 visa in addition to physicians, teachers, accountants and lawyers. Even persons who have not achieved the equivalent to a four-year college degree can qualify as H-1 professionals if they work in a position normally occupied by a professional and have considerable experience.[16] Significantly, there is no requirement to demonstrate the lack of other U.S. workers for the position in order

---

[16] In August, 1986, the INS proposed new regulations that would define the terms "professional" and "preeminent" and establish certain other guidelines for qualifying for an H-1 visa. 51 Fed Reg 28578 (August 8, 1986). As of July 31, 1987, the regulations have still not been finalized. There is some evidence, however, that the regulations go beyond judicial decisions, especially by requiring a minimum level of formal education to qualify as a professional. See, e.g., Matter of Stratton Industries, 426-442-762 (AAU Dec 4, 1984).

to obtain an H-1 visa. Another advantage of the H-1 visa is that the recognition of the employee as a person of distinguished merit and ability is helpful in obtaining third preference status should the alien subsequently seek an immigrant visa.[17] H-1 visas are now granted for an initial period of up to three years, after which time the underlying visa petition may be renewed and the alien's stay extended. The maximum time an alien can continuously remain in the United States on H-1 status is five years (or six years in certain exceptional cases).[18] The spouse and minor children of the H-1 alien are also entitled to derivative H visas but may not work in the United States unless otherwise authorized.

An H-2 visa is available for an alien who seeks to enter the country on a temporary basis to perform a job which is temporary in nature. An example of where an H-2 visa might be appropriate is in the case of an alien who is employed to train U.S. workers. When the alien leaves the country, the job itself will also cease to exist. While the H-2 visa does not require the alien to have a college degree or meet any other established criteria, the alien and U.S. employer must demonstrate, through a procedure known as temporary employment certification, that there are no U.S. workers able and willing to fill the position.[19] It usually takes several months to complete and considerable time on the part of the U.S. employer. For this reason, H-2 visas are generally sought only where an alternative is unavailable. H-2 aliens are usually granted an initial stay of one year which may be successively renewed for up to a total of three years.[20]

Finally, an alien coming to the United States in order to receive training which is unavailable in his or her country may qualify for an H-3 or trainee visa. The visa petition filed by the U.S. firm must be accompanied by documentation which describes the proposed training program, the benefit of the training both to the proposed trainee and the U.S. firm, and the reasons why such training may

---

[17] See §32:02.

[18] 8 CFR §214:2(h)(6)(ii).

[19] The labor certification process is discussed in §32:04.

[20] 8 CFR §214:2(h)(11)(iii).

not be obtained in the alien's country. The employer must also demonstrate that the alien trainee is not being placed in a position which is in the normal operation of the business and in which U.S. workers are regularly engaged, that the trainee will not be engaged in productive employment (except as may be incidental to the training program), and that the training will benefit the trainee in pursuing a specific job outside the United States to which the trainee will return. Under the proposed rules,[21] the INS will examine the documentation carefully to insure that the training program meets certain other criteria which would suggest that the primary purpose of the transfer is not for training. If it concludes that the proposal fails to meet any of these criteria, it will deny the visa and suggest that a petition be filed for an H-2 visa. H-3 visa petitions are usually granted for the documented training program, though in practice are rarely issued for more than two years. The proposed rules would establish an outer limit of 18 months.

Like all nonimmigrant visas, H-1's, H-2's, and H-3's must all demonstrate that they intend to remain in the United States on a temporary basis only. The H category of visas also requires the alien to maintain a foreign residence while in the United States.

§ 31:05. Exchange Visitors (J-1).

Another class of nonimmigrant visas which may be available to business personnel is referred to as the exchange visitor or J-1 visa. The J-1 is somewhat similar to the H-3. The J-1 visa extends to students, trainees, teachers, researchers, leaders in specialized fields, and similar aliens who come to the United States temporarily as participants in certain government-sponsored programs for the purpose of teaching, studying, observing, conducting research, consulting, demonstrating special skills or receiving training. In the business and industrial context, the J-1 visa is most important for aliens who come to the United States to provide or undergo training.

In order to qualify as an exchange visitor, the alien must be

[21] See §31:04, note 16.

entering the country as a participant in an Exchange Visitor Program designated by the U.S. Information Agency (USIA). Sponsors of such programs include government agencies, educational and other institutions, nonprofit associations as well as businesses and industrial concerns. Sponsors may proceed through a previously existing program, through one of several "umbrella" programs maintained by USIA or through a program established specially for the sponsor. The sponsor of an approved program is authorized by USIA to issue the alien a Certificate of Eligibility (Form IAP-66) which is presented to the consulate to secure the visa.

It should be noted that business and industrial visitors are also generally subject to a foreign residence or "homestay" requirement. This means that they must return to and reside in their foreign residence for a minimum of two years before they are entitled to return to the United States. The homestay requirement extends to aliens whose training and expertise appears on a "skills list," indicating it is in short supply in such country. Under certain circumstances, the INS will waive the homestay requirement if the local government does not object.

While J-1 visas for teachers, scholars, researchers, etc. are valid for stays up to three years, business and industrial trainees are generally authorized to stay not more than a total of 18 months. The alien's spouse and minor unmarried children may accompany or join the alien under derivative visas. In many cases, these aliens are also authorized to work in the country provided their compensation will be used for their own support and not that of the principal alien. J-1 visa holders must maintain a residence abroad at all times while they remain in the United States.

§ 31:06. Intra-company Transferees (L-1).

The rapid growth of multinational corporations has resulted in increased interest in the intra-company transferee (L-1) visas. An intra-company transferee includes an alien who has been employed abroad continuously for one year and who seeks to enter the

United States in order to continue to render services to the same employer or a parent, subsidiary or affiliate thereof in a managerial or executive capacity or in a capacity which involves specialized knowledge.[22] As in the case of the H visas, the prospective U.S. employer of an intra-company transferee is required to file a visa petition with the INS in the United States. Only after the visa petition is approved will the alien be entitled to apply for the visa at a U.S. consulate abroad.

Like other nonimmigrant visas, an L-1 requires the applicant to meet several conditions. The requirement that the alien be coming to the United States to work in a managerial or executive capacity or one that involves specialized knowledge is similar though not identical to the condition described above with respect to treaty trader employees.[23] Recently, however, the INS amended its regulations to include definitions of "managerial capacity," "executive capacity" and "specialized knowledge" for purposes of the intra-company transferee visa.[24] These definitions should be carefully considered in planning an application for an L-1 visa. It should also be noted that unlike E-1 aliens, an L-1 applicant must have worked in such a capacity or possessed such specialized knowledge upon the filing of the petition.

Another condition to L-1 eligibility is that the alien have worked abroad for the employer of a subsidiary or affiliate thereof for at least one year immediately prior to the application. Any continuous proir employment for the employer or its subsidiaries or other affiliates may be aggregated to meet the one-year requirement. Any break in servicesb02, however, will cause prior service to be ignored. Any time during the period immediately preceding the petition in which the alien was in the United States will also be ignored for purposes of computing the one-year prior employment abroad.[25]

Another important issue is whether the foreign company and the proposed U.S. employer are properly related. In general, the

---

[22] 8 USC §1101(a)(15)(L).

[23] See §31:03.

[24] 8 CFR §214.2(1)(1)(ii).

[25] 8 CFR §214.2(i)(7)(ii)(A).

petitioner must be a branch or office of the foreign employer, the parent of the foreign employer, or a subsidiary or affiliate of the foreign employer. New regulations define each of these terms.[26] As between corporations, INS usually looks for a majority equity interest to find effective control, though even a 10% interest in a publicly held company may provide sufficient indicia of control. A 50% interest in a joint venture is deemed to constitute control if the venturer has equal control and veto power. Certified copies of stock certificiates or an affidavit from the secretary or other custodian of the corporate group's records may be required to prove the relationships between prior employers and the petitioner.

Recent regulations also require that the transferring firm be doing business in the United States and abroad for the entire period the alien stays in the United States.[27] For this purpose, "doing business" means regular, systematic and continuous provision of goods or services by the foreign firm in the United States, and not merely the presence of an agent or office.[28] This new requirement is designed to prevent abuse where all of the transferor's operations are moved to the United States in connection with the move by the alien.

Typically, an individual L-1 visa petition (Form I-129B) is submitted by the prospective U.S. employer on behalf of the alien beneficiary. In 1983, however, the INS amended its regulations to authorize the filing of a "blanket" petition in certain cases. A blanket petition may be filed by petitioners who meet certain criteria and who have (i) transferred at least ten L-1 executive, managerial or specialized knowledge beneficiaries to the United States during the previous twelve months, (ii) have U.S. subsidiaries or affiliates with combined annual sales of at least $25 million, or (iii) have a U.S. workforce of at least 1,000 employees.[29] The blanket petition allows the petitioner to simply identify the positions within the corporate group to which L-1

[26] 8 CFR §214.2(1)(1)(ii).
[27] 8 CFR §214.2(1)(1)(ii)(G).
[28] 8 CFR §214.2(1)(1)(ii)(H).
[29] 8 CFR §214.2(1)(4)(i).

beneficiaries may be assigned. In certain cases, the petitioner may simply submit a description of its personnel structure and identify the level above which it may employ foreign managers or executives. The blanket petition is approved for an initial period of three years, and may thereafter be renewed indefinitely.[30] Once the petition is approved, qualified employees who are being transferred to such positions can apply for the visa at a U.S. consulate without being named in the petition. The new blanket petition has reduced considerably the paperwork and time required to secure L-1 visas for managers and executive transferees.

L-1 visa petitions may be approved for up to three years though the L-1 beneficiary may seek an extension of stay for up to two additional years. The entire period of stay may not exceed five years except that an additional year may be granted in extraordinary circumstances. It is important to note that under new rules, an alien who has spent five or six years in the United States on an H-1 or L-1 visa may not be readmitted under those visas without leaving the country for at least one year.[31] The spouse and unmarried minor children accompanying or following to join the beneficiary are entitled to the same visa classification and length of stay. Unless otherwise authorized, however, they may not accept employment in the United States.

§ 31:07.   Certain Procedural Issues.

(i)   *Application.* As noted above, applications for all U.S. visas must be made abroad at a U.S. embassy or consulate. The only exception to this rule is that aliens who are already in the United States may be authorized to "change" their status from one nonimmigrant category to another or "adjust" their status from nonimmigrant to immigrant or vice versa under certain circumstances. Applications for nonimmigrant visas are made on Form OF-156

---

[30] 8 CFR §214.2(1)(7)(i)(B)(2).
[31] 8 CFR §214.2(1)(15).

and must generally be accompanied by photographs, a passport valid for at least six months beyond the expiration date of the initial period of stay and, in most cases, certain other documentation which establishes the applicant's eligibility for the visa. Aliens seeking visas which require the prior approval of a visa petition by the INS will be notified of the consulate's receipt of the approved petition.[32]

In most cases the spouse and unmarried minor (under 21) children who accompany or later join the principal applicant will be granted the same visa as the applicant on a derivative basis, provided an application is filed for each. Generally, however, such dependents are not authorized to accept employment unless they qualify for working visas themselves. Like any other nonimmigrant visa, the derivative visas are automatically revoked when the holder ceases to maintain his or her status, such as in the event of a divorce by the spouse or marriage or reaching one's 21st birthday in the case of the alien's children.

(ii) *Extension of Stay.* While an alien's underlying visa may be valid for a number of years, he or she is authorized to remain in the United States only for the period determined by the INS upon entry. The authorized period of stay is noted on the alien's Temporary Entry Permit (Form I-94) upon entry into the country.

An alien who has not completed the objective for which he or she was authorized to enter the country may apply to the INS for an extension of temporary stay. The application in most cases is made on Form I-539 and must be accompanied by the alien's Form I-94. The applicant's spouse and unmarried minor children may be included on the same application provided that they are in the same visa category. The Form I-539 must be submitted not less than 15 nor more than 60 days before the expiration of the current authorized stay. In the case of E, H or L visas, the application must be

---

[32] In some cases, it is possible to expedite the granting of H and L visas by sending the petitioner's copy of the INS Notice of Approval (Form I-171C) to the alien who would then present it directly to the consulate. There also exists a procedure for having the information on the Notice of Approval cabled by INS to the consulate.

accompanied by certain documentation demonstrating that the alien continues to qualify for such status.

(iii) *Change of Status.* In certain cases, it may be necessary or desirable for an alien to change status from one nonimmigrant category to another. For example, an alien may enter the country with a B-1 (visitor for business) visa, and subsequently decide to change to an E-2 (treaty investor) after having made the required investment. Requiring such aliens to leave the country and to reapply abroad would often result in considerable costs and possible other hardships. For this reason, the regulations under the INA allow certain aliens who are in compliance with their visa status to apply to the INS for a change in nonimmigrant status without leaving the country.[33]

An application for change of nonimmigrant status (Form I-506) must be submitted by the alien to the INS office having jurisdiction over the alien. It must be accompanied by a visa petition and/or other documentation which is required to be submitted in order to establish the alien's eligibility for the nonimmigrant visa to which the change is sought. The alien's spouse and unmarried minor children may be included on the same application. If the application is approved, the change in status will be noted on the applicant's Form I-94 which is submitted with the application. Since the Form I-94 is surrendered upon the alien's departure from the United States, however, an alien who succeeds in changing status must return to a U.S. consulate upon leaving the country in order to have the visa stamped into the passport itself. For this purpose, the alien should take along the original Form I-171C which confirms the alien's approved change of status together with a letter from the employer confirming the continued position when he or she leaves the country.

[33] 8 CFR Part 248.

CHAPTER 32

IMMIGRANT VISAS

---

§ 32:01.   Permanent Residency.

An alien who seeks to become a permanent resident in the United States, or who otherwise plans to remain in the country indefinitely, must seek an immigrant visa. Permanent residency status—which is evidenced by the celebrated green card (it is actually white)—carries with it most of the rights and obligations of a U.S. citizen. Moreover, while under no obligation to do so, a permanent resident may become a U.S. citizen through naturalization after residing continuously in the United States for three years in the case of spouses of U.S. citizens and five years for others.[1] An alien may continue as a permanent resident indefinitely, but may lose such status under certain circumstances described below.

[1] 8 USC §1427.

§ 32:02. Numerical Limitations and the Preference System.

Section 201 of the INA limits the total number of immigrant visas that may be granted each year to 270,000.[2] While legislation is occasionally enacted to allow for the special admission of a class of immigrants in excess of this figure, the 270,000 numerical limitation or quota represents the maximum in most cases. Since the number of applicants for permanent residency greatly exceeds this number, however, many aliens must wait for extended periods for a visa number to become available even after they have established their eligibility for the visa. Although it is impossible to predict how long it may take for an immigrant number to become available, an approximation can sometimes be made based on an understanding of the procedure for the allocation of the numbers and the monthly State Department reports on such allocation.

The allocation of immigrant numbers is made partly on a first-come-first-served basis and partly on a preferential basis under a system established under the INA. Section 203(a) of the INA creates six preference classes plus a nonpreference class for aliens who do not fall within any of the other classes. These preference classes are based either on the applicant's family relationship with an existing U.S. citizen or permanent resident (first, second, fourth and fifth preference) or on the applicant's professional qualifications or specialized skills (third and sixth preference). Above the preference system itself is a class known as immediate relatives (children, spouses and parents)[3] of U.S. citizens who are always eligible to receive an immigrant visa, regardless of the numerical limitations.[4] In general, however, an applicant who fails to qualify as an immediate relative or in one of the six preference groups will not be able to obtain an immigrant visa since visa numbers are not available for nonpreference immigrants.

The preference categories based on family relationships extend

---

[2] 8 USC §1151.

[3] In the case of parents, the petitioner citizen must be at least 21 years of age. 8 USC §1151(b).

[4] Id.

to unmarried sons and daughters of U.S. citizens (first preference), spouses and unmarried sons and daughters of U.S. permanent residents (second preference), married sons and daughters of U.S. citizens (fourth preference) and brothers and sisters of U.S. citizens twenty-one years of age or older (fifth preference). The preference categories based on job offers extend to aliens who are members of the professions or have exceptional ability in the sciences or arts (third preference) and skilled or unskilled workers with offers of permanent employment (sixth preference).

Third and sixth preference are generally more important for business personnel and warrant some elaboration. First, it should be noted that both are based on an offer of permanent full-time employment by a U.S.-based employer who acts as the petitioner for purposes of securing the visa. Second, alien employment certification is required for both third and sixth preference. Such certification was mentioned briefly with respect to H-2 visas; the process and certain exemptions are further discussed.[5] In order to obtain such certification, the alien beneficiary must meet the minimum requirements for the certified job and both the alien and the employment must intend that the alien will undertake such job. Finally, with respect to third preference, the employer must be offering a position that requires a professional or a person of exceptional ability in the science or arts, and the alien must actually be such a person. This condition is similar to the conditions described for H-1 visas.

An alien's position within the six preference categories is established by filing a preference petition with the U.S. consulate or the INS. The documents which must accompany the preference petition depend on the preference being sought. For those preference categories based on family relationships, birth and marriage certificates are normally required. Third and sixth preference petitioners must file the labor certification (or a completed Application For Alien Employment Certification in the case of applicants who believe they are exempt from labor certification). It is important to note that the date on which an alien files a preference petition (or

[5] See §32:03.

application for employment certification as described below) which is subsequently approved is considered the priority date for purposes of the allocation of visa numbers within the alien's preference category.

Under §203(a) of the INA, the immigrant visa numbers are allocated to the preference categories as follows:

First preference: 20% of the overall limitation of 270,000 in any fiscal year;

Second preference: 26% of overall limitation plus any numbers not required for first preference;

Third preference: 10% of overall limitation;

Fourth preference: 10% of overall limitation, plus any numbers not required by the first three preference categories;

Fifth preference: 24% of overall limitation, plus any numbers not required by the first four preference categories;

Sixth preference: 10% of overall limitation;

Nonpreference: numbers not used by the six preference categories:

As noted above, immediate relatives of U.S. citizens are above the preference system and are always eligible for a visa number.

Both the preference category established by the alien and the priority date are relevant to the determination of when an immigrant number will be available. Each month, the Visa Office of the State Department issues a Visa Bulletin setting forth the cut-off dates for each preference category.[6] In some cases, there is an excess of numbers available for a particular preference category, so that the numbers are available on a current basis with no wait required. In most cases, however, the numbers are oversubscribed. The cut-off dates contained in the chart represents the priority date of the first applicant who could not be reached in the oversubscribed preference category. Thus, any alien who qualified for such preference category and has a priority date which is prior to the cut-off date is entitled to a number.

[6] See Appendix 19 for an example of these cut-off dates.

Certain countries are identified in the Visa Bulletin of cut-off dates. This is because the INA sets ceilings on the number of visas that may be issued to natives of any single state. Aliens eligible for third preference must endure a significantly shorter waiting period than aliens relegated to sixth preference. For this reason it is almost always desirable to seek third preference where eligibility is possible.

An application for permanent residency in the United States may be filed only after a visa number is available. For aliens seeking a preference category which is current, the preference petition may be filed together with the application for permanent residency. In such cases, the preference petition will be adjudicated first to determine whether the immigrant falls within a preference category which is current. This one-step filing procedure is particularly important for aliens who are present in the United States under a nonimmigrant visa. Because the filing for a preference petition is arguably inconsistent with the intention to leave the United States which underlies all nonimmigrant visas, the INS might otherwise seek to revoke the nonimmigrant visa. The filing of an application for permanent residency with the preference petition, however, allows the alien to remain in the country at least until the petition and application are adjudicated. If both are approved, the alien may immediately obtain the immigrant visa from a U.S. consulate abroad or, if eligible, adjust status to that of a permanent resident without leaving the country.

§ 32:03.   Alien Employment Certification.

Alien employment or labor certification refers to the procedure in which a U.S. employer who desires to hire an alien for a particular position satifies a statutory requirement to demonstrate that there are no U.S. workers willing or able to assume such position. As has been seen, such a showing is a condition to qualifying for a temporary worker (H-2) nonimmigrant visa as well as for third and sixth preference status to obtain permanent residency. While the procedures for temporary employment certification (for H-2 visas)[7] are slightly different from those for permanent employment certification (for permanent residency)[8] they are both discussed. Except with respect to the so-called "Schedule A" occupations which the Secretary of Labor has determined to be in continual short supply for purposes of application for permanent employment certification, the certification process is rather long and involved, usually taking a minimum of four months to complete. Moreover, since the labor certification is applied for by the employer and not the alien, it requires a considerable commitment on the part of the prospective employer in order to be completed.

The labor certification procedure commences with the careful completion of an Application for Alien Employment Certification (Form ETA-750). Part A of such form must be completed by the prospective employer and applies both for temporary and permanent employment certification. It solicits information about the employer itself, the job for which certification is sought, the minimum requirements (including education, training and experience) needed to perform such job, and the efforts made by the employer to recruit U.S. workers to fill such job. Each of these responses is carefully scrutinized. The employer must be willing to pay the prevailing wage for the position in the relevant locality, and not only a wage that the alien is willing to accept. Moreover, the job requirements must be the minimum necessary for a worker to perform the specified duties on a satisfactory basis. Job requirements which are tailor-made for the alien, especially foreign language capabilities, are carefully scrutinized. If the job requirements include training provided to the alien by the employer itself, the employer must be willing to offer the same type of training to any U.S. workers. All job requirements should be justifiable based on business necessity. Prior recruitment efforts by the employer should be as extensive as possible, and include such activities as recruiting within the company, advertising in newspapers or trade publications, using employment agencies, etc.

Part B of Form ETA-750 is completed by the alien for whom

[7] 20 CFR Part 655. Note that special regulations govern agricultural, mining, and certain other workers.

[8] 20 CFR Part 656.

permanent employment certification is sought. Part B solicits extensive information on the education, training and prior experience of the alien. It is designed to demonstrate that the alien meets the job requirements contained in Part A. Obviously, such job requirements cannot exceed the qualifications of the alien. Any additional education or experience of the alien, however, should be listed and documented with certified copies of degrees as well as letters of reference from former instructors and employers. Part B also requires the alien to state whether he or she will apply for adjustment of status in the United States or obtain the visa at a U.S. consulate abroad.

Except in the case of aliens seeking to qualify for a Schedule A occupation, the completed and executed Form ETA-750 is filed with the state employment services office having jurisdiction over the place in which the position is being offered. Significantly in the case aliens seeking permanent residency, the filing of such application establishes the alien's priority date for purposes of obtaining an immigrant visa number. This can be extremely important since such alien may not file a preference petition (the other way of establishing a priority date) until labor certification is complete some several months after the ETA-750 is filed. After an initial review of the application, the state employment services office will prepare a work-up for the position and commence seeking applicants in accordance with its local procedures. During this time, such office will also make a determination as to whether the proposed compensation meets the prevailing wage. It is important to insure that the employment services office has at least conditionally approved the wage before the employer proceeds to the next step of the procedure. Any objection made to the wage or job requirements can usually be handled by negotiation and modification, if necessary, of the ETA-750 without having the application rejected and losing one's priority date.

The next step is for the employer to post a notice advertising the position within the facility in which the job will be performed. The employer must also advertise the position with a newspaper or trade publication. The requirements for the notice and advertisement are quite detailed, and any failure to satisfy these requirements in strict compliance with the regulations may cause considerable delay or denial of the application. The employer or its counsel should work closely with the state employment services office in order to insure that the notice and advertisement have been properly drafted and posted or published. In certain cases, employers may be required to take certain other steps to recruit U.S. workers for the position.

Following the employer's satisfaction of the notice and advertising requirements, it must wait for a period of 30 days to see if anyone applies for the position. Any persons who apply during this period must be interviewed by the employer to determine whether they meet the job requirements. If, after the interview, an applicant is still interested in the position, the employer must either hire such applicant or be able to demonstrate a lawful, job-related reason for rejection. The primary reason that may be utilized is that the applicant somehow failed to meet the specified job requirements. The fact that the U.S. applicant is not as qualified or, from the employer's perspective, would simply not be as good as the alien is irrelevant, so long as such U.S. worker meets the job requirements. The results of all such interviews must then be carefully described in a report from the employer to the employment services office. Only if such office is satisfied that any applicants for the position were validly rejected, will it forward the application.

Once the state employment services office completes its work, the application is forwarded on to the regional Office of Alien Labor Certification of the U.S. Department of Labor (OALC). If the OALC proposes to deny the application, it must issue a Notice of Findings to the employer setting forth specifically the reasons for the proposed denial and providing the employer with an opportunity to rebut the findings or take corrective action. The employer must respond to the Notice of Findings within 35 days. If no such response is made or if the certifying officer is not satisfied with the response, the application will be denied. Such denial can be appealed to Department of Labor administration law judges who have shown a much greater degree of understanding than OALC personnel for failure to comply with some of the technical procedures provided for under the Department of Labor regulations, provided harmless error can be shown.

Upon the approval of an application for temporary employment certification, the employer may immediately file the H-2 visa petition with the INS. After the INS approves such application, the alien may apply for the H-2 visa at the foreign consulate if abroad or under a change of status application if already in the country. If permanent employment certification was sought, the alien may immediately file such petition but, as noted above, may not file an application for the immigrant visa itself unless or until a visa number becomes available. When the alien is finally able to file for permanent residence, he or she will also have to file a current offer of employment from the employer for the certified position and have a present intention of occupying such position once the visa is granted.

Most of the foregoing may be avoided in cases where permanent employment certification is being sought for one of the occupations which the Secretary of Labor has declared to be in continual short supply. These so-called Schedule A occupations are broken down into four groups. Of particular importance to business immigrants is Group IV which extends to persons who have worked abroad for at least one year for a foreign affiliate of the U.S. employer in an executive or managerial capacity and are being transferred to an executive or managerial position with the U.S. employer. The conditions for qualifying for precertification under Schedule A Group IV are similar to those applications for executive and managerial L-1's. Accordingly, most persons who qualify for L-1 visas (other than persons who qualify solely on the basis of specialized skills) will also qualify for precertification if they subsequently seek permanent residency. Schedule A Group II, which extends to persons with exceptional ability in the arts and sciences, is also important for business personnel. Persons who meet the conditions for H-1 visas or third preference should usually qualify for precertification based on Schedule A Group II. Aliens who will be employed in Schedule A occupations need only complete the Form ETA-750 and file it with the INS as though it had already been certified by the Department of Labor. This process thus avoids the entire recruitment procedures and saves considerable time and expense on the part of the employer.

Finally, it should be noted that the Secretary of Labor has also designated certain occupations which will not qualify for permanent employment certification.[9] These so-called Schedule B occupations include drivers, caretakers, cleaners, cooks, guards and several other unskilled jobs.

§ 32:04.   Certain Procedural Issues.

(i) *Application.* Once the preference petition has been approved and a visa number becomes available, the alien may apply for permanent residency. An application for permanent residency must generally be filed at a U.S. consulate abroad.[10] However, there are circumstances under which an alien legally present in the United States under a nonimmigrant visa may be eligible to adjust status to that of an immigrant without leaving the country.

The application for permanent residency requires the alien to submit numerous documents including passports, biographical information, medical information, birth and marriage records, police certificates, photographs, etc. Moreover, each applicant for permanent residency is interviewed by a consular office (or INS officer in the case of an adjustment of status) before the visa is issued.

(ii) *Adjustment of Status.* In many instances, aliens who decide to seek permanent residency may already be in the United States under a nonimmigrant visa. The alien may have been employed on a temporary basis under an H or L visa, and for example, elect to apply for permanent residency so as to remain on a permanent or at least indefinite basis. The adjustment of status procedure allows an eligible alien to apply for permanent residency

[9] See Department of Labor Technical Assistance Guide, §§656:11–656.23.

[10] The application must normally be filed at the place of residence or last residence of the alien. In certain cases, however, aliens may be eligible for visa processing in Canada or Mexico under the so-called "stateside-criteria."

without having to leave the country. The application for permanent residency in such case is filed with the INS rather than a U.S. consulate abroad.

The decision to seek permanent residency may present certain problems under the alien's nonimmigrant visa, since the same is issued under the condition that the alien intend to leave the country upon the expiration of the visa. In some cases, INS will take the view that the filing of an application for labor certification or a preference petition are evidence of a change in the alien's intentions, thus allowing INS to revoke or not renew the nonimmigrant visa. Unlike the filing of an application for permanent residency, the filing of an application for labor certification or a preference petition does not automatically extend the alien's authorized stay under her nonimmigrant visa. Thus, the revocation of such visa or refusal to grant an extension of stay would require the alien to depart. Such action on the part of the INS could be challenged since the filing for labor certification or preference status are not conclusive of the alien's intentions nor inconsistent with the required intention to leave the country upon the expiration of the nonimmigrant visa. If possible, however, one should attempt to avoid this issue by insuring that the alien will not have to seek an extension of stay under a nonimmigrant visa after labor certification or preference status are applied for.

The significance of the foregoing issue is not so much that the alien may be deported if he or she continues to stay in the country beyond the authorized stay. While deportation would impair the alien's right to an immigrant visa, the alien would almost always leave before a deportation order is issued. The principal significance is that if the alien remains in the United States beyond the authorized stay, he or she would be ineligible for adjustment of status.[11] This is an important sanction, since the costs and loss of time which result from having to leave the country to secure the immigrant visa abroad may be significant. The sanction would

[11] 8 USC §1255. This provision was added by the Immigration Reform Act of 1986. It denies adjustment of status to any alien who has ever been present in the United States out of status, either currently or at any time since entry, except for technical violations of status which occur through no fault of the alien.

also prevent the spouse or minor children of the alien from adjusting their status within the United States.

The filing for labor certification, preference status and permanent residency thus involve important timing considerations. On the one hand, permanent residency (and therefore adjustment of status) cannot be applied for until a visa number is available. On the other hand, one cannot establish a priority date other than by filing an application for labor certification or a preference petition. If the alien is expected to fall within a preference group for which immigrant numbers are currently available, the preference petition and application for permanent residence can be filed together, thus resulting in an automatic extension of stay until adjudicated. In any other case, there will be a risk that the alien will not be authorized to stay under the nonimmigrant visa until a number becomes available, thus eliminating the possibility of adjustment of status.

Finally, it should be noted that an alien's departure from the United States during the processing of an adjustment of status application will constitute a revocation of the application. If travel outside the country is required during this period, the alien must apply for and obtain "advance parole" from the INS in order to leave temporarily without affecting the alien's adjustment of status application.

(iii) *Loss of Permanent Residency Status.* Permanent residency status can be lost under certain circumstances. Permanent residents who are outside the country for more than one year may not reenter on their green cards alone. They must apply for and obtain a "special immigrate" visa at the U.S. consulate abroad by demonstrating that they did not abandon their permanent residency. An alien who anticipates a lengthy absence from the United States may apply for a Reentry Permit from the INS before leaving. A Reentry Permit will normally allow the alien to reenter the United States as a permanent resident for up to two years from the date of the alien's departure. While it is possible to obtain successive Reentry Permits to cover regular, lengthy absences, it should be anticipated that extended absences would normally be viewed as indicia of the immigrant's abandonment of her permanent residency.

PART X—SUGGESTIONS FOR FURTHER READING

Books

Frangomen, A., Del Rey, A., & Bell, S., 1987 Immigration Procedures Handbook (1987).

Frangomen, A., Del Rey, A., Bernsen, Immigration Law & Business (1984).

Gordon & Rosenfeld, Immigration Law and Procedure (1984).

APPENDIXES

APPENDIX 1

EXCERPT FROM TARIFF SCHEDULES OF THE UNITED STATES

TARIFF SCHEDULES OF THE UNITED STATES ANNOTATED (1987)
SCHEDULE 7. - SPECIFIED PRODUCTS; MISCELLANEOUS AND NONENUMERATED PRODUCTS
Part 2. - Optical Goods; Scientific and Professional Instruments; Watches,
Clocks, and Timing Devices; Photographic Goods; Motion Pictures;
Recordings and Recording Media

Page 7-38

7 - 2 - D
711.04 - 711.30

Item	Stat. Suf- fix	Articles	Units of Quantity	Rates of Duty 1	Special	2
		Subpart D. - Measuring, Testing, and Controlling Instruments				
		Subpart D headnotes:				
		1. The provisions of this subpart covered by items 711.04 to 711.88, inclusive, do not apply to electrical measuring, checking, analyzing, or automatically-controlling instruments or apparatus, as defined in headnote 2 below.				
		2. For the purposes of this subpart, the provisions herein (items 712.05 to 712.52, inclusive) for "electrical measuring, checking, analyzing, or automatically-controlling instruments and apparatus" apply only to the following articles: (a) appliances, instruments, apparatus, or machines of kinds described in subpart C of this part or in the provisions of this subpart (subpart D) covered by items 711.04 to 711.88, inclusive, the operation of which depends on an electrical phenomenon which varies according to the factor to be ascertained or automatically controlled; (b) instruments or apparatus for measuring or checking electrical quantities; and (c) instruments or apparatus for measuring or detecting alpha, beta, gamma, X-ray, cosmic, or similar radiations.				
		Balances of a sensitivity of 5 centigrams or better, with or without their weights, and parts thereof; weights suitable for use with such balances and sets of weights containing any such weights:				
711.04	00	Jewelers' balances and parts thereof...............	X......	5.7% ad val.	Free (A,E,I)	45% ad val.
711.08	00	Other...	X......	6.6% ad val.	Free (A,E,I)	40% ad val.
711.25		Machines and appliances for determining the strength of articles of materials under compression, tension, torsion, or shearing stress, and parts thereof..	X......	4.7% ad val.	Free (A,E,I)	40% ad val.
		Hydrometers an similar floating instruments; thermometers, pyrometers, barometers, hygrometers, and psychrometers, whether or not recording instruments; any combination of the foregoing instruments; and articles in which one or more of such instruments are incorporated as significant integral parts and which are ordinarily used in the home or office where they are usually hung on the wall, or placed in mantels, shelves, or furniture:				
711.30		Hydrometers and similar floating instruments, whether or not incorporating thermometers..........	X......	8.4% ad val.	Free (A,E) 3.4% ad val.(I)	85% ad val.

TARIFF SCHEDULES OF THE UNITED STATES ANNOTATED (1987)
SCHEDULE 7. - SPECIFIED PRODUCTS; MISCELLANEOUS AND NONENUMERATED PRODUCTS
Part 2. - Optical Goods; Scientific and Professional Instruments; Watches,
Clocks, and Timing Devices; Photographic Goods; Motion Pictures;
Recording and Recording Media

Page 7-39

7 - 2 - D
711.31 - 711.67

Item	Stat. Suf- fix	Articles	Units of Quantity	Rates of Duty		
				1	Special	2
		Hydrometers and similar floating instruments, etc. (con.): Thermometers, pyrometers, barometers, hygrom- eters, and psychrometers, whether or not recording instruments: Non-recording instruments: Thermometers: Liquid-filled thermometers with the graduations on the tube or on a scale enclosed within an outer shell:				
711.31	00	Clinical......................	No......	19.8% ad val.	17% ad val.(D) Free (A,E) 6.8% ad val.(I)	85% ad val.
711.32	00	Other......................	No......	8.4% ad val.	Free (A,E) 3.4% ad val.(I)	85% ad val.
711.33	00	If certified for use in civil aircraft (see headnote 3, part 6C, schedule 6)...............	No......	Free		85% ad val.
711.38	00	Other......................	X......	4.7% ad val.	Free (A*,E,I)	40% ad val.
711.39	00	If certified for use in civil aircraft (see headnote 3, part 6C, schedule 6)...............	X......	Free		40% ad val.
711.40	00	Pyrometers: Optical pyrometers..................	X......	10% ad val.	Free (A,E) 4% ad val.(I)	50% ad val.
711.42	00	Other......................	X......	4.2% ad val.	Free (A,E,I)	45% ad val.
711.45	00	Barometers: Aneroid: Surveying, with altimeter setting........................	X......	5.6% ad val.	Free (A,E,I)	40% ad val.
711.47	00	Other.........................	X......	2.8% ad val.	Free (A,E,I)	40% ad val.
711.49	00	Other.........................	X......	4.6% ad val.	Free (A,E,I)	45% ad val.
711.55	00	Hygrometers and psychrometers...........	X......	3.9% ad val.	Free (A,E,I)	45% ad val.
711.60	00	Thermographs, barographs, hygrographs, and other recording instruments..................	X......	3% ad val.	Free (A,E,I)	35% ad val.
711.67	00	Other...	X......	4.7% ad val.	Free (A,E,I)	50% ad val.

Appendixes

TARIFF SCHEDULES OF THE UNITED STATES ANNOTATED (1987)
SCHEDULE 7. - SPECIFIED PRODUCTS; MISCELLANEOUS AND NONENUMERATED PRODUCTS
Part 2. - Optical Goods; Scientific and Professional Instruments; Watches,
Clocks, and Timing Devices; Photographic Goods; Motion Pictures;
Recordings and Recording Media

Page 7-40

7 - 2 - D
711.70 - 711.88

Item	Stat. Suf- fix	Articles	Units of Quantity	Rates of Duty 1	Special	2
		Pressure gauges, thermostats, level gauges, flow meters, heat meters, automatic oven-draught regu- lators, and other instruments and apparatus for measuring, checking, or automatically controlling the flow, depth, pressure, or other variables of liquids or gases, or for automatically controlling temperature, all the foregoing and parts thereof not provided for in subpart C of this part:				
		Flow meters, heat meters incorporating liquid supply meters, and anemometers, and parts of the foregoing:				
711.70	00	Instruments and apparatus..................	No......	49c each + 7.6% ad val.	Free (A,E) 19.6c each + 3% ad val.(I)	$4.50 each + 65% ad val.
711.71	00	If certified for use in civil aircraft (see headnote 3, part 6C, schedule 6)....	No......	Free		$4.50 each + 65% ad val.
711.72	00	Parts.......................................	X.......	9% ad val.	Free (A,E) 3.6% ad val.(I)	65% ad val.
711.73	00	If certified for use in civil aircraft (see headnote 3, part 6C, schedule 6)....	X.......	Free		
711.78		Other.....................................	....	4.7% ad val.	Free (A,E,I)	65% ad val.
	20	Instruments and apparatus..................	X			35% ad val.
	40	Parts......................................	X			
711.79	00	If Canadian article and original motor- vehicle equipment (see headnote 2, part 6B, schedule 6).........................	X.......	Free		
711.81	00	If certified for use in civil aircraft (see headnote 3, part 6C, schedule 6)...............	X.......	Free		35% ad val.
		Polarimeters, refractometers, spectrometers, gas analysis apparatus and other instruments or apparatus for physical or chemical analysis; viscometers, porosimeters, expansion meters and other instruments and apparatus for measuring or checking viscosity, porosity, expansion, surface tension, or similar properties; photometers (except photographic light meters), calorimeters, and other instruments or apparatus for measuring or checking quantities of heat, light, or sound; microtomes; all the foregoing, and parts thereof:				
711.86	00	Optical instruments or apparatus, and parts thereof...	X.......	10% ad val.	4% ad val.(I) Free (A,E)	50% ad val.
711.88	00	Other...	X.......	6.2% ad val.	Free (A,E,I)	40% ad val.

357

TARIFF SCHEDULES OF THE UNITED STATES ANNOTATED (1987)
SCHEDULE 7. - SPECIFIED PRODUCTS; MISCELLANEOUS AND NONENUMERATED PRODUCTS
Part 2. - Optical Goods; Scientific and Professional Instruments; Watches,
Clocks, and Timing Devices; Photographic Goods; Motion Pictures;
Recordings and Recording Media

Page 7-41

7 - 2 - D
711.90 - 712.27

Item	Stat. Suf- fix	Articles	Units of Quantity	Rates of Duty		
				1	Special	2
		Revolution counters, production counters, taximeters, odometers, pedometers, counters similar to the foregoing articles, speedometers and tachometers, all the foregoing not provided for in subpart C of this part; parts of the foregoing:				
711.90	00	Taximeters and parts............................	X.......	15% ad val.	Free (A,E) 6% ad val.(I)	85% ad val.
711.91	00	If Canadian article and original motor-vehicle equipment (see headnote 2, part 6B, schedule 6)......................	X.......	Free		
711.93	00	Bicycle speedometers and parts thereof..........	X.......	17% ad val.	Free (E) 6.8% ad val.(I)	110% ad val.
711.98		Other...	....	Free		35% ad val.
	20	Speedometers and tachometers, and parts.......	X			
	40	Other...	X			
711.99	00	If Canadian article and original motor-vehicle equipment (see headnote 2, part 6B, schedule 6)........................	X.......	Free		
712.00	00	Speedometers and tachometers, and parts thereof; all the foregoing if certified for use in civil aircraft (see headnote 3, part 6C, schedule 6).........................	X.......	Free		35% ad val.
		Electrical measuring, checking, analyzing, or automatically-controlling instruments and apparatus, and parts thereof:				
712.05	00	Optical instruments or apparatus, and parts thereof..	X.......	10% ad val.	Free (A,E,I)	50% ad val.
712.06	00	Optical instruments or apparatus, if certified for use in civil aircraft (see headnote 3, part 6C, schedule 6).........	X.......	Free		50% ad val.
		Other: Ships' logs, and depth-sounding instruments and apparatus, and parts thereof:				
712.10	00	Instruments and apparatus.................	No.......	4.8% ad val.	Free (A,E,I)	70% ad val.
712.12	00	Parts.....................................	X.......	10% ad val.	Free (A,E) 4% ad val.(I)	65% ad val.
712.15		Instruments and apparatus for measuring or detecting alpha, beta, gamma, X-ray, cosmic or similar radiations, and parts thereof....................................	....	4.7% ad val.	Free (A,E,I)	40% ad val.
	10	Instruments and apparatus.................	X			
	60	Parts.....................................	X			
712.20	00	Seismographs, and parts thereof..............	X.......	4.9% ad val.	Free (A,E,I)	40% ad val.
712.25	00	Anemometers, and parts thereof: Anemometers...............................	No.......	49c each + 7.6% ad val.	Free (A,E) 19c each + 3% ad val.(I)	$4.50 each + 65% ad val.
712.27	00	Parts.....................................	X.......	9% ad val.	Free (A,E) 3.6% ad val.(I)	65% ad val.

Appendixes

TARIFF SCHEDULES OF THE UNITED STATES ANNOTATED (1987)
SCHEDULE 7. - SPECIFIED PRODUCTS; MISCELLANEOUS AND NONENUMERATED PRODUCTS
Part 2. - Optical Goods; Scientific and Professional Instruments; Watches,
Clocks, and Timing Devices; Photographic Goods; Motion Pictures;
Recordings and Recording Media

Page 7-42

7 - 2 - D
712.47 - 712.49

Item	Stat. Suf- fix	Articles	Units of Quantity	Rates of Duty 1	Special	2
		Electrical measuring, checking, analyzing, or automatically-controlling instruments and apparatus, and parts thereof (con.): Other (con.):				
712.47	00	Automatic flight control instruments and apparatus designed for use in aircraft, and parts thereof...........................	X.......	4.2% ad val.	Free (A,E,I)	40% ad val.
712.48	00	If certified for use in civil aircraft (see headnote 3, part 6C, schedule 6)....	X.......	Free		40% ad val.
712.49		Other...................................	....	4.9% ad val.	Free (A,E,I)	40% ad val.
	10	Surveying (including photogrammetrical surveying), hydrographic, navigational, meteorological, hydrological, and geophysical instruments and parts thereof.................................	X			
	20	Balances of a sensitivity of 5 centigrams or better, with or without their weights, and parts thereof.........	X			
	30	Machines and appliances for determining the strength of articles or materials under compression, tension, torsion, or shearing stress, and parts thereof....	X			
	41	Hydrometers and similar floating instruments; thermometers, pyrometers, barometers, hygrometers, and psychro- meters, whether or not recording instruments; any combination of the foregoing instruments; and parts thereof.................................	X			
		Pressure gauges, thermostats, level gauges, flow meters, heat meters, automatic oven-draught regulators, and other instruments and apparatus for measuring, checking, or automatically controlling the flow, depth, pressure or other variables of liquids or gases, or for automatically controlling temperature, all the foregoing and parts thereof, not specially provided for:				
	50	Instruments and apparatus...........	X			
	55	Parts...............................	X			

TARIFF SCHEDULES OF THE UNITED STATES ANNOTATED (1987)

SCHEDULE 7. - SPECIFIED PRODUCTS; MISCELLANEOUS AND NONENUMERATED PRODUCTS
Part 2. - Optical Goods; Scientific and Professional Instruments; Watches,   Page 7-43
Clocks, and Timing Devices; Photographic Goods; Motion Pictures;
Recordings and Recording Media

7 - 2 - D
712.49 - 713.19

Item	Stat. Suf- fix	Articles	Units of Quantity	Rates of Duty		
				1	Special	2
		Electrical measuring, checking, analyzing, or automatically-controlling instruments and apparatus, and parts thereof (con.): Other (con.): Other (con.):				
712.49 (con.)	60	Polarimeters, refractometers, spectro- meters, gas analysis apparatus and other instruments or apparatus for physical or chemical analysis; visco- meters, porosimeters, expansion meters and other instruments and apparatus for measuring or checking viscosity, porosity, expansion, surface tension, or similar properties; photometers (except photographic light meters), calorimeters, and other instruments or apparatus for measuring or checking quantities of heat, light, or sound; all the foregoing, and parts thereof.................................	X			
	71	Instruments and apparatus to measure or check electrical quantities, and parts thereof.................................	X			
	75	Other.....................................	X			
712.51	00	If Canadian article and original motor- vehicle equipment (see headnote 2, part 6B, schedule 6)......................	X.......	Free		
712.52	00	If certified for use in civil aircraft (see headnote 3, part 6C, schedule 6)....	X.......	Free		40% ad val.
		Gas and liquid supply or production meters; watt- hour meters, ampere-hour meters, and other electricity supply or production meters designed to register the total amount of electricity or electrical energy produced or consumed; standard meters for checking and calibrating any of the foregoing meters; all the foregoing and parts therefor: Meters:				
713.05	00	Valued not over $10 each......................	No......	30c each + 6.4% ad val.	Free (A,E) 12c each + 2.6% ad val.(I)	$3 each + 65% ad val.
		Valued over $10 each: Electricity supply or production meters and standard meters therefor:				
713.07	00	Valued not over $15 each.............	No......	45c each + 6.4% ad val.	Free (A,E,I)	$4.50 each + 65% ad val.
713.09	00	Valued over $15 each.................	No......	45c each + 4.4% ad val.	Free (A,E,I)	$4.50 each + 65% ad val.
713.11	00	Other.....................................	No......	45c each + 7% ad val.	Free (A,E,I)	$4.50 each + 65% ad val.
713.15	00	Parts.....................................	X.......	9% ad val.	Free (A*,E) 3.6% ad val.(I)	65% ad val.
		Stroboscopes of all kinds, and parts thereof:				
713.17	00	Stroboscopes...................................	No......	45c each + 7% ad val.	Free (A,E) 18c each + 2.8% ad val.(I)	$4.50 each + 65% ad val.
713.19	00	Parts.....................................	X.......	9% ad val.	Free (A,E,I)	65% ad val.

APPENDIX 2

COMMERCIAL INVOICE

NIHON LTD.

52-3, KAMIUMA 4-CHOME
SETAGAYA-KU, TOKYO, JAPAN

TLX 462131 NIHON
PHONE 621-3421

No. 78-06

Tokyo. April 27, 19_ _

INVOICE of 25,500 Gas Tube Arresters

shipped per Aircraft   sailing on or around April 26, 19_ _

from Tokyo   Japan to Chicago, Ill., USA   via

consigned to AGA Company, Inc.
231 South LaSalle

Bank Cert. No. RC-AF(26)77-0967   Dated: April 19, 19_ _

Mark and Number	Quantity	Description	Unit Price	Amount

FOB Tokyo in U.S. Currency

Gas Tube Arresters

	6,000 Pcs.	3YZ-400 P24288	US$1.54	$9,240.00
CHICAGO MADE IN JAPAN C/S No.1-5	19,500 "	SR800 P21769	0.304	5,928.00
				$15,168.00

Freight $519.32
Insurance   67.20
CIF Chicago $15,754.52

Your P.O. No.:
    6,000 3YZ-400   495807 & 494877-2
   19,500 SR800   496101

L/C No. 4639421 issued by Continental Illinois
National Bank & Trust Co. of Chicago, U.S.A.

Nihon, LTD.

H. Szu~, Manager
Foreign Trade

APPENDIX 3

PACKING LIST

NIHON LTD.

PACKING LIST

523, KAMIUMA 4-CHOME,
SETAGAYA-KU, TOKYO, JAPAN

CONSIGNED TO	INVOICE NO. 78-06	DATE TOKYO, April 27, 19 _ _
AGA Company, Inc. 231 South LaSalle Rosemont, Ill, 60018, U.S.A.	L/C NO. 628433	DATE Jan. 3, 19
	ISSUED BY Continental Illinois National Bank & Trust Co. of Chicago	

SHIPPED PER Aircraft	ORDER NO.	
FROM Tokyo, TO JAPAN Chicago, Ill., U.S.A.	CONTRACT NO. REF.	

MARK & NOS	QUANTITY	DESCRIPTION	NET WT	GROSS WT	MEASUREMENT

⬦ AGA

CHICAGO
MADE IN JAPAN
C/S No. 1-5

C/S No. 1	2,000	3YZ-400 P21769	29.0 kgs	32.0 kgs
" 2	2,000	-do-	29.0 "	32.0 "
" 3	2,000	-do-	29.0 "	32.0 "
" 4	10,000	SR800 P24288	14.0 "	16.5 "
" 5	9,500	-do-	13.3 "	15.5 "

Five (5) Cartons Only	114.3 kgs	128.0 kgs

Nihon, Ltd.

H. Szuki

H. Szuki, Manager
Foreign Trade

APPENDIX 4

MARINE INSURANCE POLICY

SPECIAL MARINE POLICY

№. C 846667

NATIONAL AMERICAN INSURANCE
PHILADELPHIA
INCORPORATED A D 1794

Open Policy No. 484294
of .. Chicago.. Service Office

ORIGINAL (ORIGINAL AND DUPLICATE ISSUED ONE OF WHICH BEING ACCOMPLISHED, THE OTHER TO BE NULL AND VOID)

$ 1470.00

(PLACE AND DATE) Rosemont, Illinois April 18, 19 _ _

This Company, in consideration of a premium as agreed, and subject to the Terms and Conditions printed or stamped hereon and/or attached hereto does insure, lost or not lost AGA Company, Inc., Rosemont, Illinois
For account of whom it may concern, to be shipped by the vessel John Paul Jones
and connecting conveyances

From Rosemont, Illinois via Baltimore
To Bangkok, Thailand
Interest Aluminum Foil Duct Tape

Number of Packages: 20 Cartons

Insured for ONE THOUSAND FOUR HUNDRED SEVENTY AND 00/100 DOLLARS
Valued at Sum hereby insured
Loss if any payable to Assured or order

MARKS AND NUMBERS
AEC 027/77-KH
LANG KANG INDUSTRY CC.
LTD.
BANGKOK
MADE IN U.S.A.
Case No. 1 and up

TERMS AND CONDITIONS—SEE ALSO BACK HEREOF

Not transferable unless countersigned

Countersigned
AGA Company, Inc.
by:

INSTRUCTIONS TO CLAIMANTS ON REVERSE SIDE
MA 2098a 8/75 Printed in U.S.A.

In Witness Whereof, this Company has caused these presents to be signed by its President and attested by its Secretary in the City of Philadelphia.

JC Peters
Secretary

Michael John
President

Printed with permission of Continental Illinois Bank and Trust Company of Chicago.

365

APPENDIX 5

MARINE INSURANCE CERTIFICATE

Form 1461

ORIGINAL

$ 8,665.00   **CERTIFICATE OF INSURANCE**   No. **F 501438**

NATIONAL AMERICAN INSURANCE
INCORPORATED UNDER THE LAWS OF NEW JERSEY

BIBBS & SON INC., Manager   90 John Street, New York, N. Y. 10038

NEW YORK, N.Y. JUNE 17, 19___

This is to Certify, That this Company has insured under Policy No. **FO-89797**,
for AGA Company, Inc.

the sum of **EIGHT THOUSAND SIX HUNDRED SIXTY-FIVE AND NO/100**U.S.---------Dollars**
on **2 (TWO) CASES ROAD MAKING MACHINERY PARTS**

valued at **SUM INSURED**   shipped on board of   John Paul Jones
at and from **INTERIOR U.S.A. VIA NEW YORK**
to **LONDON, ENGLAND**

It is understood and agreed that in case of loss the same is payable to the order of **THE ASSURED**

on surrender of this certificate, which conveys the right of collecting, any such loss as fully as if the property were covered by a special policy direct to the holder hereof, and free from any liability for unpaid premiums. This certificate is subject to all the terms of the open policy, provided, however, that t e rights of a bona fide holder of this certificate for value shall not be prejudiced by any terms of the open policy which are i conflict with the terms of this certificate.
THIS INSURANCE IS SUBJECT TO THE AMERICAN INSTITUTE CARGO CLAUSE (FEB. 1949).
ALSO SUBJECT TO THE AMENDED F. C. & S. AND S. R. & C. C. WARRANTIES (OCT. 1959) (SEE REVERSE)
SHIPMENTS TO SOUTH AMERICA ARE SUBJECT TO THE SOUTH AMERICAN CLAUSE.

Original and Duplicate issued, one of which being accomplished the other to stand null and void.

SPECIAL CONDITIONS | **Marks and Numbers**

Except while on deck of ocean vessel:—New Contractors Equipment is insured:—
Against all risks of physical loss or damage from any external cause excepting risks excluded by the F. C. & S. (Free of Capture and Seizure) and Strikes, Riots and Civil Commotions warranties appearing elsewhere hereon.

OHAMED BIN
ORGANIZATION

ALL RISKS OF PHYSICAL LOSS OR DAMAGE FROM ANY EXTERNAL ORDER: 2/412/847
CAUSE IRRESPECTIVE OF PERCENTAGE AND ENDORSE TO   SA
INCLUDE STRIKE, RIOT, CIVIL COMMOTION AND WA RISKS   LONDON
FROM WAREHOUSE TO WAREHOUSE.   PKG. #1 & #2

ON DECK—Merchandise and/or goods shipped on deck which must be so specified in this certificate are insured.—Free of particular average unless caused by the vessel being stranded, sunk, burnt, on fire, or in collision, but including jettison and/or washing overboard, irrespective of percentage.

Where the words "including M. E. C." are typed in the space below at the time the certificate is issued, this insurance is subject to the American Institute Marine Extension Clauses (May 1952).

Where the words "including Strike Risks" are typed in the space below at the time the certificate is issued, this insurance is subject to the American Institute S. R. & C. C. Clauses, form 8-A (July, 1961).

Where the words "including War Risk" are typed in the space below at the time the current tificate is issued, this insurance is subject to the American Institute War Risk Clauses.

"Including M.E.C."   "Including Strike Risks"   "Including War Risk"

It is hereby agreed that any loss or claim under this Certificate shall be paid at the office of the Company in New York, or at the offices of the Agents of the Company, Exchange Buildings, Liverpool, or at the Agency of the Company at port or place of destination, or, if the Company is not represented at port or place of destination, at the nearest Agency amongst those specified in the list on back hereof.
Claims to be adjusted according to the usages of Lloyds, but subject to the conditions of the Policy and Contract of Insurance.
NOTICE—To conform with the Revenue Laws of Great Britain, in order to collect a claim under this certificate, it must be stamped within thirty days after its receipt in the United Kingdom, in other countries similar laws may obtain. The attention of holders of Certificates is particularly drawn to this.

Not valid unless countersigned by an authorized representative of the assured.

BIBBS & SON INC., Manager

Countersigned, _____

Jerry Bibbs
Chairman

Printed in U.S.A.   05091

IMPORTANT—In Case of Loss or Damage Please Follow Instructions on the Reverse Side of this Certificate

Printed with permission of Continental Illinois Bank and Trust Company of Chicago.

367

APPENDIX 6

A BILL OF LADING

American Export Lines, Inc. 17 BATTERY PLACE, NEW YORK, NEW YORK 10004 U.S.A.

SHIPPER/EXPORTER (2) (Complete Name and Address)	DOCUMENT NO (5)
AGA Company, Inc. 231 S. LaSalle St. Rosemont, Ill.	**OOAKB-FS216** EXPORT REFERENCES (6)

CONSIGNED TO: (3) (Complete Name and Address) ORDER OF:	FORWARDING AGENT - REFERENCES (7)
To order of the shipper	
	POINT AND COUNTRY OF ORIGIN (8)

NOTIFY PARTY (4) (Complete Name and Address)	DOMESTIC ROUTING/EXPORT INSTRUCTIONS (9)
Nihon LTD 52-3 Kamiuma 4 Chome Tokyo, Japan	

PIER (10)		
Container Freight Corp.	*If Through Bill, indicate here (Type word "Through")* →	*The Scope of the Sea Voyage is Described in Clause 3 Hereof)*

OCEAN VESSEL (11)	Flag	PORT OF LOADING (12)	ONWARD INLAND ROUTING (15)
KASHU MARU	U.S.A.	Oakland	
PORT OF DISCHARGE (13)		FOR TRANSSHIPMENT TO (14)	
KOBE			

CARRIER'S RECEIPT		PARTICULARS FURNISHED BY SHIPPER		
MARKS AND NUMBERS (16)	NO. OF CONT OR OTHER PKGS (17)	DESCRIPTION OF PACKAGES AND GOODS (18)	GROSS WEIGHT (19)	MEASUREMENT (20)
1350 K KOBE SSIU270285	5	Tierces: General Merchandise FREIGHT PREPAID L/C 200/730/002753(0726382)	3250 lbs.	58 cft. I

On Board
Date Oct. 7, 19
Initial

IN CONNECTION WITH FREIGHT SEE CLAUSES 14 AND 16 ON REVERSE SIDE OF THIS BILL OF LADING			FREIGHT TO BE PREPAID AT
	PREPAID	COLLECT	IN ACCEPTING THIS BILL OF LADING, the Shipper, Consignee, Holder hereof, and Owner of the goods, agree to be bound by all of its stipulations, exceptions and conditions, whether written, printed or stamped on the front or back hereof, as well as the provisions of the above Carrier's published Tariff Rules and Regulations, as fully as if they were all signed by such Shipper, Consignee, Holder or Owner, and it is further agreed that Containers are stowed on Deck, as per Clause 4.
FRT 126.00 per M3	206	77	
			IN WITNESS WHEREOF, the Master of the said vessel has affirmed to (Number) 3 bills of lading, all of this tenor and date, ONE of which being accomplished, the others to stand void.
			By: AMERICAN EXPORT LINES, INC. FOR THE MASTER
Ocean Freight Extra Charge for Declared Value of $ per package			
TOTAL	206	77	John Doe Oct. 6, 19 ___ BILL OF LADING NO DATED
TERMS OF BILL OF LADING CONTINUED ON REVERSE SIDE REV '85' N (REV 6 73)			AEL-492

Printed with permission of Continental Illinois Bank and Trust Company of Chicago.

369

APPENDIX 7

A CERTIFICATE OF ORIGIN

CERTIFICATE OF ORIGIN

The undersigned Joy Dawson
(Owner or Agent or &c.)

for AGA Company, Inc., Rosemont, Ill. declares
(Name and Address of Shipper)

that the following mentioned goods shipped on XX AIRFREIGHT
(Name of Ship)

on the date of APRIL 25, 19____ consigned to The Importer's Bank Ltd, London
Notify: Ministry of Posts, Telegraph & Telephone
P.O. Box 432 London, England are the product of the United States of America

MARKS AND NUMBERS	NO. OF PKGS BOXES OR CASES	WEIGHT IN KILOS GROSS	NET	DESCRIPTION
MINISTRY OF POSTS TELEGRAPH AND TELEPHONE, LONDON, CREDIT 00/89029, CUSTOMS TARIFF NO. 85/15, 1 OF 1, MADE IN U.S.A.	1	172.37	148.78	Pallet of Test Load Units for telephone power equipment. 724.9985 L/C No. 00/89029 ADVICE NO. 9683523 "ONE ITEM SPARE PARTS FOR INTS-PMO ACCORDING TO THE PROFORMA INVOICE NO. I-1045 DATED 12/9/75" "FREIGHT PREPAID" FROM U.S.A. TO LONDON

Sworn to before me
this 7 day of April 19___

Dated at Rosemont on the 7 day of April 19___

Joy Dawson

The CHAMBER OF COMMERCE, a recognized Chamber of Commerce under the laws of the State of _____ has examined the manufacturer's invoice or shipper's affidavit concerning the origin of the merchandise and according to the best of its knowledge and belief, finds that the products named originated in the United States of North America

Secretary _____
CHAMBER OF COMMERCE

Form 10-988 and 10-889 (Carbonized) · Printed and Sold by
Unz & Co. A Division of Scott Ptg. Corp. 190 Baldwin Ave. J C. N J. 07306

Printed with permission of Continental Illinois Bank and Trust Company of Chicago.

APPENDIX 8

WEIGHT AND MEASUREMENT CERTIFICATE

WE   *world express, inc.*

REF K15-77-MM-132   April 27, 19___

WEIGHT & MEASUREMENT CERTIFICATE

We herbs certify that the shipments described herein have been passed
the measurement of WE WORLD EXPRESS, INC.
We therefore declare the statement which it is true and correct.

Consignee Name & Address : AGA Company, Inc.

231 South LaSalle , Rosemont, Illinois, 60018, U.S.A.

Air Port of Departure : Tokyo Int'l Airport

Air Port of Destination : Chicago Int'l Airport

Name of Airlines : FT (WE Consolidation)

Date of Departure : April 26, 19___

Description of Goods : Gas Tube Arresters

Case No.	Net Weight	Gross Weight	Measurement	Remarks
C/S No. 1-3	@29.0Kgs	@32.0Kgs	@69X 17x 34	REC
C/S No. 4	@14.0Kgs	16.5Kgs	29X 30X 32	CHICAGO MADE IN JAPAN
C/S No. 5	13.3Kgs	15.5Kgs	" "	C/: No. 1-5
Total : Five (5) Cartons		N/W: 120.0Kgs. G/W: 128.0Kgs.		

**Consignor: Nihon LTD, Tokyo Japan
**HAWB NO. KWE-15156956
**MAWB NO. 023-17949481
**FLT. NO. FT048/26

WE WORLD EXPRESS, INC.
SHIBUYA SALES OFFICE

Tom Paramus

TOM PARAMUS, SALES MANAGER

IATA APPROVED AGENT INTERNATIONAL FREIGHT FORWARDER CUSTOMS BROKER WAREHOUSING
OFFICE TOKYO NARASAKI NAGOYA KYOTO OSAKA KOBE ICHIKAWA SAPPORO FUKUOKA GIFU JAPAN NEW YORK CHICAGO LOS ANGELES SAN FRANCISCO BOSTON DALLAS
HOUSTON DETROIT PHILADELPHIA CLEVELAND MINNEAPOLIS DENVER(U.S.A.) TORONTO(CANADA) ADELAIDE HONG KONG (HONG KONG) SINGAPORE

APPENDIX 9

CERTIFICATE OF INSPECTION

Development Ltd.
P.O. BOX 134-22 LONDON, ENGLAND

INSPECTION CERTIFICATE

April 21, 19_ _

TO WHOM IT MAY CONCERN :

ORDER NO.	:	55053
QUANTITY	:	15,000 pcs.
COMMODITY	:	Sun Visor
AMOUNT	:	US$2800.50
VESSEL	:	By Air Freight
SAILING DATE	:	Airing on Mar. 19, 19_ _ London, England to Chicago.

We, the undersigned hereby certify that the above cargo have been inspected before packing are in good condition.

Development Ltd.

Printed with permission of Continental Illinois Bank and Trust Company of Chicago.

375

APPENDIX 10

SIGHT DRAFT

CHICAGO. ILLINOIS. August 27, 19--

Sight
(INDICATE ABOVE WHETHER PAYABLE ON DEMAND, ARRIVAL, OR OTHER TIME LIMIT)

PAY TO THE ORDER OF CONTINENTAL ILLINOIS NATIONAL BANK AND TRUST COMPANY OF CHICAGO $ 1359.15

One Thousand Three Hundred Fifty-Nine and 15/100 _____ **DOLLARS**

VALUE RECEIVED AND CHARGE TO ACCOUNT OF

TO XYZ Imports
Avenue Foch
Paris, France

A.B.C. Exports
Chicago, Illinois

Treasurer

1-0-27 8-4-46

TIME DRAFT

EXCHANGE FOR $10,000.00   June 15, 19_ _

180   DAYS AFTER SIGHT OF THIS FIRST OF EXCHANGE (SECOND OF

SAME TENOR AND DATE UNPAID)

PAY TO THE ORDER OF Continental Bank

Ten Thousand and 00/000 Dollars ---

Drawn under Continental Bank, London, England Letter of Credit No. 8712121, Continental Bank,
Chicago Advice No. 9237432
VALUE RECEIVED AND CHARGE SAME TO ACCOUNT OF

TO Continental Illinois National Bank and
Trust Company of Chicago
231 South La Salle Street
Chicago, Illinois 60693

NO. 101

AGA Company, Inc.
Rosemont, Illinois

John Doe   Treasurer

Printed with permission of Continental Illinois Bank and Trust Company of Chicago.

377

APPENDIX 11

EXPORT LETTER OF CREDIT

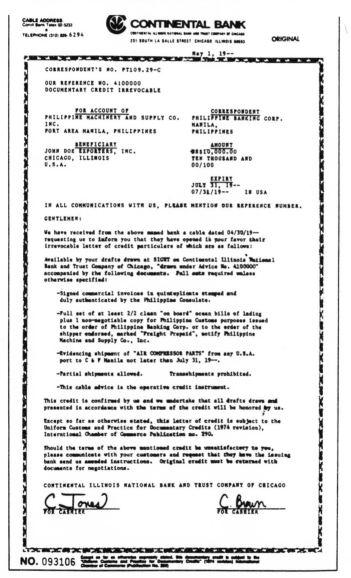

COMMON DISCREPANCIES BETWEEN EXPORT DOCUMENTATION AND DOCUMENTARY CREDITS

—Documents inconsistent with each other.

—Description of goods on invoice differs from that in the credit.

—Weights differ between documents.

—The amounts shown on the invoice and draft differ.

—Marks and numbers differ between documents.

—Credit amount exceeded.

—Credit expired.

—Documents not presented in time.

—Late shipment.

—Short shipment.

—Absence of documents called for in the credit.

—Draft drawn on a wrong party.

—Bills of lading, insurance document or draft not endorsed correctly.

—Absence of signatures, where required, on documents presented.

—Bill of lading does not evidence whether freight is paid or not.

—Insurance risks not specified in credit.

LIFE CYCLE OF A CONFIRMED LETTER OF CREDIT IN AN EXPORT TRANSACTION

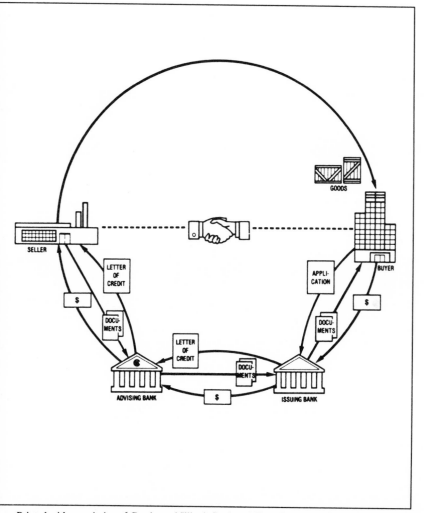

Printed with permission of Continental Illinois Bank and Trust Company of Chicago.

COUNTRY GROUPS UNDER THE EXPORT ADMINISTRATION REGULATIONS

Country Group Q
    Romania
Country Group S
    Libya
Country Group T
  North America
    Northern Area:
      Greenland
      Miquelon and St. Pierre Islands
    Southern Area:
      Mexico (including Cozumel and Revilla Gigedo Islands)
    Central America
      Belize
      Costa Rica
      El Salvador
      Guatemala
      Honduras (including Bahia and Swan Islands)
      Nicaragua
      Panama
      Bermuda and Caribbean Area;
      Bahamas
      Barbados
      Bermuda
      Dominican Republic

French West Indies
Haiti (including Gonave and Tortuga Islands)
Jamaica
Leeward and Windward Islands
Netherlands Antilles
Trinidad and Tobago

South America
Northern Area:
Colombia
French Guiana (including Inini)
Guyana
Surinam
Venezuela
Western Area:
Bolivia
Chile
Ecuador (including the Galapagos Islands)
Peru
Eastern Area:
Argentina
Brazil
Falkland Islands (Islas Malvinas)
Paraguay
Uruguay

Country Group V
All countries not included in any other country group (except Canada).

Country Group W
Hungary
Poland

Country Group Y
Albania
Bulgaria
Czechoslovakia
Estonia
German Democratic Republic (including East Berlin)
Laos
Latvia
Lithuania
Mongolian People's Republic
Union of Soviet Socialist Republics

Appendixes

Country Group Z
    North Korea
    Vietnam
    Cambodia
    Cuba

FOREIGN LAWS REGULATING THE USE OF AGENTS AND DISTRIBUTORS

1. Laws Prohibiting Use of Independent Agents.
   Algeria. Law No. 78-02, of 1978.
   Most Socialist Countries.
2. Laws Restricting Use of Agents for Government Procurement.
   Iraq. Law No. 11 of 1983.
   Israel. Law No. 5757-1976 (December 20, 1976).
   Jordan. Law No. 20 of 1974.
   Saudi Arabia. Royal Decree M/11 of July 23, 1962, as implemented by Ministry of Commerce Order No. 1897 of March 30, 1981.
3. Laws Prohibiting the Use of Foreign Nationals as Agents.
   Abu Dhabi. Law No. 11/1973, Decision No. 25/1979.
   Bahrain. Amiri Decree No. 23 of 1975.
   Egypt. Decree 1906/1974 (*see also* Laws No. 107/1961, No. 93/1974, No. 117/1975 and No. 120/1987, *and* Presidential Decree 14/1976).
   Indonesia. Ministerial Decree No. 314/KP./11/70 and Decree No. 78/KP./111/78.
   Iraq. Law No. 11/1983.
   Jordan. Law No. 20/1974, art. 4 as amended by Provisional Law No. 23/1979.
   Kuwait. Law No. 2 of 1961, Laws No. 36, No. 37 and No. 43 of 1964, and Law No. 32 of 1969 and Law No. 68/1980.
   Qatar. Law No. 12/1964, as amended by Decree No. 25/1966 and Circular 3/93/1973.

Saudi Arabia. Royal Decree M/11 of 1962, as amended by Royal Decree No. 151/1952, art. 2 and Prime Minister Modification No. 14/B 271/15 (February 7, 1980).

U.A.E. Federal Law No. 18/1981, arts. 3, 9 and 10.

Yemen. Laws No. 17/1972 and No. 6/1976.

4. Laws Prohibiting Sales Other Than Through Local Agents.

Burma. Nationalization of Enterprise Laws, 1962.

Saudi Arabia. Royal Decree M/2 of January 20, 1978.

Oman. Royal Decree No. 3/1974, as amended by Royal Decrees No. 2/1975, No. 16/1978 and No. 26/1977.

Yemen. Laws No. 17/1972 and No. 6/1974.

5. Laws Requiring the Registration of Agents.

Argentina. Law No. 20575 of January 2, 1974.

Bahrain. Amiria Decree No. 25/1979.

Bolivia. Commercial Code, Law of March, 2, 1977, art. 1250.

Columbia. Commercial Code, Decree No. 410, art. 1320 (March 27, 1971).

Egypt. Law No. 107 of July, 1961, art. I, as amended by Law No. 93 of 1974, Decree No. 14 of January, 1976; see also Law No. 120/1982 0 and Regn. M. Order No. 342/1982.

France. Decree No. 58-1435 of December 23, 1958, art. 4.

Iraq. Law No. 11 of 1983, art. 9.

Jordan. Law No. 20/1974.

Kuwait. Law No. 36/1974, art. 3.

Netherlands. Handelsregisterwet, art. 1(1,b).

Saudi Arabia. Royal Decree M/2 of January 20, 1978.

South Korea. Antimonopoly and Fair Trade Law, art. 24 (1981).

Switzerland. Code of Obligations, arts. 418a, 418c.

Syria. Law No. 151/1952, art. 19.

This list is intended to be illustrative and not exhaustive.

FOREIGN LAWS REGULATING THE TERMINATION OF AGENTS AND DISTRIBUTORS

1. Distributors Only
    Belgium. Law of July 27, 1961 (Oct. 5, 1961), and Law of April 13, 1971, (April 21, 1971).
2. Agents Only
    Austria. Merchantile Agents Law of 1921, as amended on June 15, 1978.
    Brazil. Law No. 4886 of Dec. 10, 1965.
    Finland. Law No. 389 of May 30, 1975.
    France. Decree No. 58-1345 of Dec. 23, 1958.
    West Germany. Commercial Code, arts. 84-92c.
    Italy. Civil Code, art. 1742, et seq.
    Netherlands. Commercial Code, arts. 75a.75p.
    Spain. Royal Decree 2033/1981, Official State Bulletin No. 209 (Sept. 12, 1981).
    Sweden. Act of April 18, 1914, as amended by Law 219 of May 1974.
    Switzerland. Law of Agency Agreements of February 4, 1949.
3. Agents or Distributors.
    Bahrain. Amiri Decree No. 23 of September, 1975; Amiri Decree No. 28 of November, 1975.

Columbia. Commercial Code, arts. 1317-1331.

Costa Rica. Law No. 6209 of Mar. 9, 1978.

Dominican Republic. Law 173 of April 6, 1966, as amended by Law 263 of Dec. 31, 1971, Law 622 of Dec. 28, 1973 and Law 664 of 1977.

Ecuador. Supreme Decree 1038-A, Official Register No. 245, Dec. 31, 1976.

El Salvador. Commercial Code, arts. 392-399B.

Guatemala. Decree No. 78-71, Official Gazette of Oct. 1, 1971.

Honduras. Decree No. 50, of Oct. 8, 1970, as amended by Decree No. 549, Nov. 24, 1977 and Decree No. 804 of Sept. 10, 1979.

Jordan. Law No. 20-74 of May 1, 1974, as amended by Law No. 23-79, effective May 16, 1979.

Kuwait. Commercial Law, arts. 281-282.

Lebanon. Decree No. 34 of 1967, as amended by Decree No. 9639 of 1975.

Nicaragua. Decree No. 13 of Dec. 22, 1979 (reenacting and modifying Decree No. 287 of Feb. 2, 1972).

Oman. Royal Decree No. 26/77, Omani Official Gazette of Jan. 6, 1977.

Panama. Cabinet Decree No. 344 of Oct. 31, 1969; Executive Decrees No. 9 of Feb. 7, 1970 and No. 48 of April 6, 1971.

Philippines. Presidential Decree No. 1789.

Puerto Rico. Act No. 75 of June 24, 1964, as amended by Act No. 105 of June 23, 1966. P.R. Laws Ann., tit. 10, §§278-278(d) (1975).

Saudi Arabia. Royal Decree M/11 of 1962, as amended by Royal Decrees M/5 of 1969, M/8 of 1973 and M/32 of 1980; Ministerial Decision No. 1897, Official Gazette No. 2865 (April 17, 1981).

Thailand. Civil and Commercial Code, art. 827.

United Arab Emirates. Federal Act No. 18 of 1981, art. 9.

This list is intended to be illustrative and not exhaustive.

SAMPLE CHOICE OF FORUM CLAUSES

Any claim or controversy arising out of or in connection with this Agreement or the breach hereof (including claims in tort, contract or otherwise) shall be heard exclusively in the state or federal courts located in the city of Los Angeles, California.

The parties to this Agreement hereby inevocably submit to the exclusive jurisdiction of any New York State or Federal Court sitting in New York City for any action or proceeding arising out of or relating hereto, hereby waiving, to the fullest extent permitted by law, the defense of an inconvenient forum to the maintenance of such action or proceeding as well as all rights to jurisdiction in any such action or proceeding which either of them may have by reason of its present or future residence, domicile, nationality or otherwise. [Party A and Party B] hereby irrevocably appoint o,0 and, o,0[name and addresses] respectively, as its agent (the "Process Agent"), to receive on its behalf the summons and complaint and any other process which may be served in any such action or proceeding in any such court. Such services of process may be made by mail or delivering a copy of such process to such party in care of its Process Agent at such address, and such party hereby authorizes and directs the Process Agent to accept such process on its behalf. Alternatively, the parties also irrevocably consent to the service of any and all process in any such action or proceeding by the mailing of copies of such process to the address set forth in [the Notice section of the Agreement].

Appendixes

The parties agree that a final judgment in any such action or proceeding shall be conclusive and binding and may be enforced in any other jurisdiction by suit on the judgment or otherwise in accordance with the law of the such jurisdiction.

SAMPLE ARBITRATION CLAUSES

International Chamber of Commerce

"All disputes arising in connection with the present contract shall be finally settled under the Rules of [Conciliation and] Arbitration of the International Chamber of Commerce by one or more arbitrators appointed in accordance with the said Rules."

London Court of International Arbitration

"Any dispute arising out of or in connection with this contract, including any question regarding its existence, validity or termination, shall be referred to and finally resolved by arbitration under the Rules of the London Court of International Arbitration, which Rules are deemed to be incorporated by reference into this clause."

American Arbitration Association

"Any controversy or claim arising out of or relating to this agreement, or the breach thereof, shall be settled by arbitration in accordance with the Commercial Arbitration Rules and supplementary procedures for international commercial arbitrations of the American Arbitrage Association, and judgment upon the award rendered by the Arbitrator(s) may be entered in any court having jurisdiction thereof."

UNCITRAL Arbitration Rules

"Any dispute, controversy or claim arising out of or relating to this contract, or the breach, termination or invalidity thereof, shall be settled by arbitration in accordance with the UNCITRAL Arbitration Rules as at present in force."

International Centre for the Settlement of Investment Disputes

"The parties hereto hereby consent to submit to the International Centre for Settlement of Investment Disputes any dispute relating to or arising out of this Agreement for settlement by arbitration pursuant to the Convention on the Settlement of Investment Disputes between States and Nationals of Other States."

SAMPLE CUT-OFF DATES FOR VISA PREFERENCES

Chargeability	1st	2nd	3rd	4th	5th	6th	Nonpreference
All chargeability areas except those listed below	C	04-01-86	01-01-87	C	01-08-82	01-01-86	U
China-mainland born	C	04-01-86	01-01-87	C	11-08-80	U	U
Dominican Republic	C	05-22-85	01-01-87	C	01-08-82	01-01-86	U
India	C	04-01-86	01-01-87	C	07-08-81	U	U
Korea	C	04-01-86	01-01-87	C	11-01-80	U	U
Mexico	C	11-01-77	01-01-87	11-01-87	12-15-76	06-22-83	U
Philippines	12-01-81	04-22-81	01-08-71	01-01-80	03-15-76	05-22-84	U
Hong Kong	09-19-84	11-09-79	01-26-81	07-01-80	08-05-74	01-08-80	U

INDEX

Index

Index

Index